GLADLY LEARN AND GLADLY TEACH

A Clerk ther was of Oxenford also,
That unto logyk hadde longe ygo. . . .
Sowynge in moral vertu was his speche;
And gladly wolde he lerne, and
  gladly teche.

Chaucer

Martin Meyerson and
Dilys Pegler Winegrad

with the assistance of
Mary Ann Meyers and
Francis James Dallett

Gladly Learn and Gladly Teach

Franklin and His Heirs
at the University of Pennsylvania,
1740-1976

University of Pennsylvania Press

Library of Congress Cataloging in Publication Data

Meyerson, Martin.
  Gladly learn and gladly teach.

  Includes bibliographical references and index.
  1. Pennsylvania. University—History. 2. Franklin, Benjamin, 1706-1790. 3. Educators—Pennsylvania. I. Winegrad, Dilys Pegler, joint author. II. Title.
LD4528.M48   378.748'53   77-82383
ISBN 0-8122-7735-X

Design by Joel Katz

Composition by Deputy Crown, Inc., Camden, NJ

Preface

Shakespeare in *The Tempest* wrote that "past is prologue." When I returned to the University of Pennsylvania in 1970 as its president, I realized once again how much of its past—often a glorious one—had influenced its present and yet was insufficiently appreciated by many of my colleagues and by students and alumni of the University. It was intriguing to observe that this condition was shared by the citizens of Philadelphia, who were often little acquainted with their fascinating community.

Cheyney's *History of the University of Pennsylvania,* published for the University's bicentennial in 1940, like almost all university histories was a diplomatic history of the institution and a splendid one. What seemed to me to be needed was an intellectual and social history—an intellectual history dealing with ideas and scholarship, the transformation of education at a major American university, and a social history relating what was going on at Pennsylvania to the city of which it was a part, to student life and the life of the young in general, and to the cultural currents of this tempestuous new nation and its ties elsewhere in the world.

That aim remains, but it must be left to others, perhaps to some future University historian. Instead, I became more attached to the *dramatis personae*—the cast of characters in the evolution of the University—and to some extent the physical setting in which they performed. My collaborators and I could only choose a few from among many notable contributions. Within this framework, I hope we have also reflected some of the cultural sense of their times. The account which follows is uniquely that of the University of Pennsylvania, but it is something of a microcosm of the development of higher education at major independent institutions as well.

The essays are grouped according to four main periods since the University's foundation. After an introduction to the community of which the University has always been a part, we deal with the eighteenth century collegiate departments. In the nineteenth century, while the University remained small, its early scientific bent was reinforced by the prominent scientists on the faculty. The transition to the recognizably "modern" university with changes in educational philosophy as well as the introduction of new programs is described in association with the leaders who oversaw this period of change.

With expansion in the twentieth century, it becomes problematical to convey a sense of the University as a whole through sketches of individuals. We have nonetheless attempted to do just that by portraying divisions of the University in connection with some of their leading faculty. A final section depicts the physical surroundings in which the University has functioned and is followed by a brief epilogue. A key to a necessarily involved series of events and personalities is provided by chronologies.

Full captions accompany each illustration. Since the illustrations may be pertinent to chapters other than those in which they appear, the descriptive summary intentionally echoes portions of the text.

In *Gladly Learn and Gladly Teach* (a rubric I confess I have used earlier at Harvard and Berkeley, but not for a book), I have had delightful co-workers, three holders of our degrees who combine perspective of the past, affection for the University, and attachment to its future. In particular, I am indebted to my principal collaborator, Dilys Pegler Winegrad.

During the early course of our work, my student assistant, Arnold Eisen, was a valued goad. The manuscript has been read in whole or part and commented upon helpfully by E. Digby Baltzell, Carolyn R. Bargeron, Margaret Boerner Beckman, Paul W. Bruton, Thomas C. Cochran, Hamilton Y. Elliott, Jr., David R. Goddard, D. Bruce Johnstone, Joseph T. Looby, Margy Ellin Meyerson, H. Michael Neiditch, William G. Owen, G. Holmes Perkins, Louis H. Pollak, Peter Shepheard, Eliot Stellar, Harold Taubin, Scott Wilds, and Francis C. Wood. Martha Pamplin Rosso and Sophie Dubil put in long hours typing the manuscript. Joel Katz carried out the graphic design of the book. Robert Erwin, director of the Press provided fruitful counsel.

But mostly the book reflects the devotion of a long and distinguished line of trustees, teachers, and scholars, students and graduates, friends and educational leaders from Franklin to Gaylord P. Harnwell who made the University of Pennsylvania what it is. I first discussed the proposed book with the late William L. Day, our chairman of the trustees. His enthusiasm reinforced the proposal. And, following the bicentennial year of the Republic, a celebration he was anticipating, I dedicate this book to him, to his successor chairmen, Robert G. Dunlop and Donald T. Regan, and the Honorable Thomas S. Gates, who had served as chairman of our Executive Board. I know of no other university which has had such thoughtful lay leadership.

It is my hope that the professors, students and graduates of our University in America's third century will have ever more reason to be proud of the University of Pennsylvania—Franklin's University.

Martin Meyerson
Philadelphia

Contents

Setting the Scene

Proper Philadelphia was . . . the host to the New World's most sophisticated and talented leaders. A class of gentlemen, steeped in the classics as well as the political theory of Locke and Rousseau, reluctantly had taken the lead in rebellion against the British Empire, and subsequently wrote the new nation's constitution after lengthy deliberation on Philadelphia's Independence Square.

E. Digby Baltzell, Class of 1939
Philadelphia Gentlemen

and absolute *Proprietors of the Province of* PENNSYLVANIA *this Perspective View is humbly Dedicated by* Nicholas Scull

1

Philadelphia:
Its College and University

East Prospect of Philadelphia from the Jersey Shore
London, 1754
Historical Society of Pennsylvania
The first pictorial panorama of Philadelphia, engraved from a drawing by George Heap under the direction of Nicholas Scull, surveyor-general of Pennsylvania, was published in London in 1754. In this section of the view, the spire of the Academy building appears second from the left, to the right of the dominant steeple of Christ Church. The "New Building," or "Whitefield's Hall" as it was called, was the largest edifice in the colonial port but stood farther from the waterfront than the other spired buildings.

Philadelphia 1776: by the time the Declaration of Independence was signed there, the city was the metropolis of the American continent, the principal port of the colonies, and, with about 30,000 inhabitants, after London the second center of the English-speaking world. Sharing the spirit of enterprise of the New World, its citizenry attested to the qualities and range of the eighteenth century mind. Practicality and concern with civic and community affairs in no way prejudiced their keen receptivity to the arts and sciences as vocation as well as pastime. Ordinary men and women contributed to the vitality of the thriving commercial city, for these people were in many ways more literate and more politically sophisticated than their Old World counterparts. According to Edmund Burke, almost as many copies of Blackstone's *Commentaries* were sold in the colonies as in England—some indication of the spirit of inquiry which was afoot, if not of the destiny of the United States to become a nation of lawyers.[1] Colonial Philadelphia was at the peak of its political influence, at the heart of the intellectual ferment of the times.

Freed from the constraints of the Old World, and in an atmosphere of toleration unequaled elsewhere in the colonies, talented men were discovering an outlet for an ingenuity and creativity of a uniquely American kind. The most eminent example, Benjamin Franklin, along with his many technological and scientific contributions, was responsible for establishing the intellectual institutions of his adopted city. In large part a result of his ideas and energies, the Library Company of Philadelphia, the American Philosophical Society, and the College of Philadelphia all came into being during the middle of the century. Far from finding itself on the periphery of the intellectual world, Philadelphia was a focus of investigation on the American continent from which knowledge and ideas could be channeled to men of learning in London, Stockholm, or Padua.

The ties between those pursuing knowledge on both sides of the Atlantic were further cultivated through the steady influx of English and Scottish educators who were engaged to teach at the Academy and College of Philadelphia. Franklin played a leading part in establishing the "Academie and Charitable School of the Province of Pennsylvania" after a plan in 1740 for a Charity School typifying the age of benevolence had run into difficulties. He headed the group of citizens who, in 1749, set up the Academy in the Charity School building, obtaining a charter for the College in 1755. During the Revolution, the College was reconstituted as the University of the State of Pennsylvania (1779), the first institution in America to receive the title of university. Ten years later, the colonial College was resurrected, only to be formally combined with the University in 1791. In recognition of its independent status, reference to the state was dropped from its title at that time. Just thirteen months before his death, Benjamin Franklin, the first president of the trustees of the College of Philadelphia, once again presided over the meetings of its reconstituted board.

Following the turn of the century, the ferment of colonial and early federal Philadelphia had abated. After being a hub of Revolutionary activity, the city suffered the indignity of occupation by the enemy, during which time the College of Philadelphia served as a hospital. A few years later, the population of the city was decimated by repeated outbreaks of yellow fever. A disappointment to Philadelphia and its institutions was the decision to move the capital of the new nation to Washington. The mansion constructed to house the presidents of the United States, purchased by the University trustees in 1800, became, instead, the second home of the University of Pennsylvania. In order to satisfy the institution's expanded needs, the stately building on Ninth Street was torn down and replaced in 1829.

Other famous places underwent similar change. Following an act of the Pennsylvania legislature in 1802, the halls of independence which had resonated with noble rhetoric were used to display live and stuffed animals, including Franklin's pet cat, and other natural curiosities.[2] The famous Peale's Museum, founded by the portrait painter Charles Willson Peale and his family, occupied the second floor of the State House, as Independence Hall was then called, and included in its lease the East room, scene of the signing of the Declaration of Independence. Peale's collection of live animals, including bears, monkeys, alligators, and parrots were housed in the State House Yard.[3] In these years, Philadelphia's position as the outlet for the agricultural riches of Lancaster County and the area to the west continued, but the city struggled to compete when the opening of the Erie Canal in 1825 helped to make New York the premier port in the country.

If, in the early nineteenth century, Philadelphia lost some of its luster as *the* metropolis of the English-speaking colonies, unequaled outside of London, the arts and literary life continued to flourish in the city whose classic revival architecture was unsurpassed on the American continent. In the second decade, at a time when New York had seven daily papers and Boston two, Philadelphia had eleven. Forty American magazines were received by the Athenaeum, a subscription library, along with fifty American newspapers, two from France, and three from England. The Philadelphia library had about two-fifths of all the books in public libraries in the nation. In the previous century, the Reverend Jacob Duché, first graduate of the College and its professor of oratory who became chaplain to the Continental Congress, observed that "for one person of distinction and fortune there were twenty tradesmen that frequented the Philadelphia library."[4] The libraries of the American Philosophical Society, the Academy of Natural Sciences, the Mercantile Library, and the Historical Society all had splendid collections. Books and papers were not only received and read in Philadelphia; they were also produced. In 1823 there were four times as many printers as clergymen and almost as many bookbinders as brickmakers.[5] Although Philadelphia was the foremost manufacturing city of the nation, a magnet for European as well as American migrants (including blacks from the South), it had a very high proportion of professionals: more lawyers than bricklayers, more physicians than milliners.

Colonial and federal Philadelphia had produced the first American dramatist, Thomas Godfrey; the first American novelist, Charles Brockden Brown; and the early American composer, Francis Hopkinson, a member of the first graduating class at the College of Philadelphia. Peale's Museum was the first of its kind, and Philadelphia had the oldest continuously used theater as well as the first art school—the Pennsylvania Academy of the Fine Arts, founded in 1805. The Musical Fund Society of 1820 not only had the largest orchestra, with 120 members playing in a hall which could accommodate an audience of 1800; it also taught on a grand scale with 50 noted teachers for 200 students.

Such was the city, important first for its port, then for its industry and its extraordinary technological inventiveness, and always as a center of intellectual life in America. At all times, the College, and later the University, would be influenced by these urban and civic surroundings. "It is certainly more than a coincidence," writes a modern commentator, "that the most comprehensive, and what might be termed encyclopedic, college curriculum of the whole colonial period developed in the city of Philadelphia, then the largest thriving commercial center in English America."[6] The only curriculum of its kind actually to be put into effect was the work of William Smith, the Scot who became the College's first provost. His influence was also felt in the other institutions he helped to found—Washington College and St. John's College, both in Maryland.[7]

The plan of education which he devised differed substantially from the curriculum of the other colonial colleges, which were founded by religious denominations. Bearing in mind the actual conditions in the colonies in a work entitled *Proposals Relating to the Education of Youth in Pensilvania*, Franklin had already put forward a plan of practical study including the

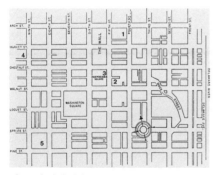

Plan of Philadelphia
Adapted with permission from J. B. Lippincott Company to show sites and years associated with instruction in the early history of the College and University
1. *The College of Philadelphia, built 1740 (1751–1802)*
2. *Surgeons' Hall (1792–1807)*
3. *Philosophical Hall of the American Philosophical Society (1789–1794)*
4. *The University of Pennsylvania (1802–1872)*
5. *Pennsylvania Hospital (1765–   )*

recommendation for English to replace Latin as the most important language taught.[8] In his writings on education, Smith reiterated Franklin's views, and the college curriculum he drew up as provost had a markedly scientific bias. Although neither of these early educational theorists rejected classical European traditions, they made the first serious attempt—and one which would come to be regarded as characteristically American—to graft a utilitarian form of instruction on to the hallowed classical curriculum inherited from the past.

One reason for the marked difference between Franklin's "seminary of learning" in Philadelphia and the colonial college of the type which has been described as "in many ways a blood brother to its English model" was the influence of Scots and the Scottish Enlightenment in the early days of the College.[9] William Smith had studied at King's College, Aberdeen, and the first vice-provost, Francis Alison, although a native of Ireland, had received his education at the University of Edinburgh. James Wilson, who gave the first instruction in law in 1790, was born and raised in Fifeshire and completed his studies at the University of St. Andrews before emigrating. The three original professors in the medical department of the College—John Morgan, William Shippen, and Benjamin Rush—all went to Edinburgh for their medical degree. When John Morgan obtained the trustees' consent to the establishment of America's first medical school in 1765, his plans were inspired by his Scottish alma mater.

Another factor set the College of Philadelphia apart from the other eight pre-Revolutionary colleges: Franklin's alone was intended to be nonsectarian. In fact, "the purpose of training students for the Christian ministry is specified in all colonial college charters with the single exception, again, of the College of Philadelphia."[10] In the medieval world, the preservation of learning had always been linked with training for the ministry. This bond was reaffirmed by the connection between the first colleges in colonial America and various Protestant denominations. The tradition lingered on in the custom of appointing clerics to head the learned institutions founded later in the nineteenth century. Since there was never a divinity school at the University of Pennsylvania, it furnished presidents for the new colleges and universities less often than other institutions.

In its early years, Philadelphia's college might be small in comparison with Harvard, Yale, and the College of New Jersey (Princeton), but it did attract students from the South as well as the North. It was not size, however, which gave the colonial colleges their strength. In fact, "the permanent significance of the colonial achievement in higher education . . . was all out of proportion to the size of student enrollments."[11] And while the other colleges were primarily concerned with "training a special elite for community leadership" and what Cotton Mather described as "the collegiate way of living," "the forming of character" rather than "the fostering of research," the Philadelphia founders looked further ahead to what would later come to be accepted as the main purposes of higher education: contemporary and scientific as well as ancient studies, professional as well as scholarly emphases.[12]

In the early decades of the nineteenth century, the colleges and universities, created with such great hope in colonial times, entered the doldrums. They had lost the respect of the community as a result of a tendency for rowdiness and rebellion which had existed from the earliest days. Up to the Civil War, "constant warfare raged between faculty and students . . . and . . . the most outrageous pranks and disturbances were provoked by undisciplined and incredibly bold young men."[13] According to Francis Wayland, president of Brown, the few professors who had charge of these riotous student bodies received salaries far below those of other professionals and had small chance of increments or opportunities for supplementing their earnings on the side.[14] Needless to say, it was often no easy task to recruit able people to the position of college professor. Nonetheless, throughout our first century as a republic and ever since, no people has prized formal schooling more than Americans.

During this period, there were frequent clashes between students and most faculty. Violence had, of course, occurred from time to time during the first century of the American republic and afterwards. A side effect of the concept of equality and democracy which is rarely, or reluctantly, acknowledged, although it is one to which de Tocqueville alludes, is the way an American dislike of authority and the emphasis on individual rights tend to encourage a certain lawlessness and a kind of license. This came to be reflected in the turmoil on the campuses and the regular baiting of "townies" on the part of students. Such behavior presented some problems at the University of Pennsylvania, although these tended to be resolved in a more pacific manner than was elsewhere the case—as, indeed, occurred again with the unrest of the late 1960s and early 1970s. Yet, despite the American expression "boys will be boys," suggestive of a special license given to youth, such things as changes in curriculum, relaxation of discipline, and the introduction of sports, resulted in a reduction in rowdyism and destructive rebellion in the period after the Civil War.

By that time, there were over 180 permanent colleges and universities in the United States. Many more had been established but later went out of existence.[15] In the years that followed the Civil War, a smaller proportion of those who took their seats in Congress had attended colleges and universities. The degree might still be a credential socially and a necessity for some occupations, but it was one which men such as Andrew Carnegie dismissed as evidence of a familiarity with "the barbarous and petty squabbles of a far-distant past." In Carnegie's opinion, "the future captain of industry" had no need for any such course of study since the enterprising entrepreneur would rather be "hotly engaged in the school of experience."[16] In other words, there were numerous roads to prosperity and

Plan of the West Philadelphia Campus in 1890
Landscape Development Plan, 1977
The first group of University buildings constructed on old pasture land included College Hall and the Furness Library. Townhouses were going up along newly paved roads, and the commercial area along Market Street and the railroad was expanding. The complex of buildings in the southernmost apex belong to the Blockley Almshouse, later Philadelphia General Hospital.

few of them led through the halls of academe. Proposals for reform and innovation had been put forward as early as the 1820s at some institutions, including the University of Pennsylvania, but these were firmly rebuffed at the time because they were perceived as an attempt to "Germanize" the American college. Steeped in tradition, few people had the foresight to realize that, if higher education was to flourish in an age of rapid social change and advancing technology, there would have to be a thorough rethinking of the university's position and goals.

Ironically, in their enfeebled state following on the Civil War, the American colleges became more receptive to change. The early reforms that had been advocated by people such as George Ticknor of Harvard, a graduate of Dartmouth who had gone in 1815 to study at Göttingen, did not gain immediate currency. Later in the century, these reforms received encouragement from a simple expedient: the newly inaugurated steamship services to Europe. It became less and less possible to ignore the qualities of Germany's universities when thousands of Americans were returning home

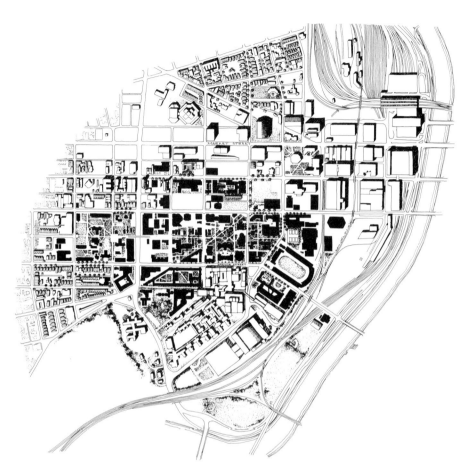

The Campus in 1976
Landscape Development Plan, 1977
*The campus has extended from the
Schuylkill River in the east to Fortieth
Street in the west (school of dental medicine). Various parts of the University
have developed in different quadrants of
the campus; the physical sciences in the
east, the law school to the north, and the
school of medicine and hospital to the
south. The social sciences occupy a
position on either side of the pedestrian
thoroughfare, Locust Walk. Beyond
Thirty eighth Street, high-rise residence
halls in a major open space provide a
focus for the west campus.*

with graduate training. When the faculty of the scientific school at Yale
successfully petitioned for the right to award the degree of Doctor of
Philosophy, they naturally looked to the German universities for their
model. The first earned Ph.D. in the United States was awarded at Yale in
1861.[17] The idea of founding a "national university," as old as the nation,
received a boost when James Smithson of London willed his property to the
United States for "an Establishment for the increase and diffusion of
knowledge among men."[18] The dream of such a university was never
realized, although the Smithsonian Institution came into being as a result of
the bequest. But another project by those who had favored it, under the
leadership of Alexander Dallas Bache—a Philadelphian, descendant of
Franklin, and professor at the University—gained congressional approval.
As a result the National Academy of Sciences was created in 1863.

In this same period, the American tendency to link intellectual with
practical training resulted in a great expansion of higher education when
the mostly new state universities were stimulated by the Morrill Act of

1862. According to this act, federal support was granted to states for colleges that would provide instruction in agriculture and mechanical skills. These were the very areas which both Franklin and Smith had wished to encourage by their writings prior even to the establishment of the College of Philadelphia. Over a century later, the University of Pennsylvania was the only eastern, private institution other than those new institutions, the Massachusetts Institute of Technology and Cornell, to attempt to qualify as a land grant college and to receive "a portion of the public land-scrip." A "collegiate department of agriculture, mines, manufactures, and the mechanic arts" was established, but this bid to change the University's character did not succeed.[19]

As the American university emerged, a break was made with the traditional emphasis on religious exegesis at places of learning. Clerics ceased to predominate on the boards of educational institutions, even though academic robes, reminiscent also of the courts of law, still harked back to the long-lived relation between the schools and the church. In spite of the nonsectarian origins of the University of Pennsylvania, a majority of its provosts had been from the clergy. Provost Smith, depicted in otherwise secular surroundings, was always painted wearing his robe as a divine. In the decades following the Civil War, a succession of energetic lay provosts oversaw the period of transition and expansion which occurred at the University as elsewhere. Charles J. Stillé moved the University to its present site in 1870–1872, and many of his proposals became a reality during the tenure of William Pepper. With his base established in the most reputed medical department in the country, Pepper energetically supported such departures as the development of the first hospital in the United States owned and operated by a university. Unlike those institutions, starting with Harvard, which established a strong presidency, the highest administrator continued to be the provost. Until well into the present century, the University of Pennsylvania was run largely by its trustees.

By the turn of the century, the student body in the colleges and universities of the United States was a quarter of a million—more than that of all of Western Europe combined, and almost as many as the United Kingdom has today. By the end of World War I that figure would more than double. It would double again by 1929, and more than double once more by the end of World War II.[20] In 1900, the Association of American Universities was founded with fourteen original members, including the University of Pennsylvania. Six years later when the Congress of Arts and Sciences convened many of the best minds of the western world at the St. Louis World's Fair, the European contingent still outshone the American. But from that time on, the contributions from the American side steadily gained ground. The influx of refugee scholars from German and other European universities prior to the Second World War reinforced this trend. Then, after the war, tremendous changes came about as federal funds were made available for research. America began to dominate basic research of almost all kinds, a fact attested to in the year of the American Bicentennial when all the recipients of the Nobel Prize came from the United States.

And what of Philadelphia and the University of Pennsylvania two hundred years later? All through its history, the University has been located in the city, its growth and development reflected in the nature of the three principal sites it has occupied since the original Academy building was put up in 1740. The progression of structures which have housed it—including the Reverend George Whitefield's "New Building," and the mansion built for the presidents of the United States, on to the present campus where undergraduate, graduate, and professional schools are all in close proximity to one another—provides material evidence of the evolution of higher education over a period of more than two centuries. During the same period, Philadelphia, having lost its position as first city in the new nation, began to appear as something of the Rip Van Winkle of American cities.

Its inhabitants, however, habitually regard this posture with amused equanimity. For, in Philadelphia, there tends to be a quiet acceptance of things the way they are which comprises every aspect of life in the city—from the superlative to the indifferent. To Henry James, who visited the city in 1904, Philadelphia appeared as "incontestably . . . the American city of the large type, that didn't *bristle*. . . . Philadelphia then wasn't a place but a state of consanguinity."[21] Something of the atmosphere evoked by James carries over to the University. The city and the University share a sense of modesty which can be both admirable and infuriating since Philadelphia is a national center with certain cultural characteristics unequaled in the nation. These are not exclusively the product of a past of which few other eighteenth century cities in the world can boast; they also bear witness to Walt Whitman's dictum that "a great city is that which has the greatest men and women."[22]

There have been periods in its history when the University, with its modesty, seemed to mark time and others when it was exuberant. Yet, during each, the accompanying lack of pressure has been experienced as compatible by able individuals who, unhampered by an overbearing institutional presence, have used their freedom to get on with their work—and to excel. Each of these tendencies survives in the present University, and in particular our inclination to keep our light under a bushel. In the modern world, there is a welcome place for becoming modesty and, certainly, for the ability to goad oneself. These are among the many virtues, gentle and lively, left over from an earlier age, at the University of Pennsylvania in Philadelphia. They have had their part in creating an environment, both accomplished and compatible, for learning, striving—and achievement.

The Colonial College

We may . . . excuse our ancestors, that they established no ACADEMY *or college in this province, wherein their youth might receive a polite and learned education. Agriculture and* mechanic arts, *were of the most immediate importance; the* culture of minds *by the* finer arts *and* sciences, *were necessarily postpon'd.*

Benjamin Franklin
Pennsylvania Gazette
August 24, 1749

2

Benjamin Franklin, Founder

Benjamin Franklin (1706–1790)
by Benjamin Wilson
The White House
Printer, scientist, and statesman, Franklin signed both the Declaration of Independence and the Constitution. He contributed greatly to the cultural advancement of his adopted city, founding the Library Company of Philadelphia and playing an important part in creating the American Philosophical Society and the Academy and College of Philadelphia, which later became the University of Pennsylvania. He served as trustee of both institutions (1749–1790).

In 1740, a group of Philadelphians—pious artisans and merchants who did not adhere to any single religious sect—advertised their intention of erecting "a large Building for a Charity School for the instruction of Poor Children Gratis . . . and also for a House of Publick worship."[1] A deed of trust, promulgated the same year, is the first document associated with the origins of the University of Pennsylvania, where bicentennial celebrations were duly conducted in September 1940. The original "INDENTURE bearing Date the Fourteenth day of November in the year of our Lord One Thousand Seven Hundred and Forty" lists the names of the first trustees.[2] Laying aside "Bigottry and party Zeal," these citizens set about raising funds for the construction of a hall at Fourth and Arch Streets. The "New Building" as it came to be called was the largest structure in colonial Philadelphia. It seems, however, that the subscriptions collected were insufficient to cover the cost of the instruction which had been proposed, and, for a number of years, there were unpaid bills as well as unfulfilled engagements.[3] At this point, Benjamin Franklin stepped in to direct his energies towards the establishment of an institution of learning in his adopted city.

In 1749, twenty-four signatures were affixed to the hand-penned draft of the "Constitutions of the Publick Academy in the City of Philadelphia." Among the orthographic flourishes of prominent Pennsylvanians, including the Reverend Richard Peters, Tench Francis, and Thomas Hopkinson, is that of the self-made man who has been called Philadelphia's first citizen. Benjamin Franklin acted as prime mover in founding a variety of institutions in his city, some of which were unique in the colonies and even the world. His regard for books and the availability of information had led to the establishment of the Library Company of Philadelphia, the first subscription library in the colonies, founded in 1731 and chartered eleven years later. Now the Academy came into being as a direct result of Franklin's active concern with the instruction of the youth of Pennsylvania.

A proposal for a "higher school of Arts and Sciences" had died in council within a year of William Penn's landing. A pamphlet on public schooling appeared in 1685 under the title "Good Order Established in

Pennsilvania & New-Jersey in America," but no further action seems to have been taken.[4] With the Quaker hegemony in the state, there was no urgent call to educate men for the ministry—one of the main purposes of the colleges founded in New England and elsewhere in the colonies. The question of public education administered by members of the Society of Friends, like the question of their holding the reins of government at all, was inherently something of an anomaly. "To govern is absolutely repugnant to the avowed principles of Quakerism," declared a Presbyterian pamphleteer, to which the reply in kind was supplied: "To be governed is absolutely repugnant to the avowed principles of Presbyterianism."[5]

The colonial Friends' failure to organize higher learning as early as the Puritans or as the Presbyterians were later to do was, in part, due to their lack of emphasis on individualistic accomplishments as a road to divine favor.[6] The tradition for a "guarded" education for their children was another way in which sectarian beliefs conflicted with a philosophical concern for the good of all denominations. Although William Penn shared the Quaker conviction that learning was unnecessary for religious leadership and, on occasion, inveighed against the universities, he was nonetheless profoundly interested in the idea of universal education which he considered a right of the people and an obligation for the governor of a province. His guiding principle—that of preserving the civil liberties of the people in a "free colony for all mankind"—led to the foundation of the Friends' Public School, later the William Penn Charter School, which was established in 1683 for the instruction of all, regardless of religion, and at no charge to the poor.

When it came into being, the Academy was a nonsectarian foundation in contrast to the other schools of higher learning in the colonies, although faculty and trustees were required to take an oath upholding the Protestant succession to the throne. With conditions of religious toleration more generous in Pennsylvania than even those of Rhode Island, it is not surprising that the original institution of higher education in Philadelphia should have been founded by the deist Benjamin Franklin, upon the underlying principles of religious freedom espoused by the Quaker founder of the colony.[7]

The spirit of toleration exemplified by the Friends provided a fertile soil for intellectual developments. In the words of the Quaker historian Isaac Sharpless, "free institutions brought free thought, and free thought is the only atmosphere in which science can flourish."[8] By the middle of the eighteenth century, the city was the most cosmopolitan center of culture in the colonies, as well as the busiest port and a hub of commercial activity. The year of the Revolution, a French abbé exclaimed: "Everything here [in Europe] turns into rottenness: religion, law, arts, sciences; and everything hastens to renew itself in America." He went on to advise his correspondent: "Therefore, do not buy your house in the Chaussée d'Antin; buy it in

The Reverend George Whitefield (1714–1770)
by R. Tait McKenzie
Because of the popularity of services led by the most prominent English evangelist to preach in America, George Whitefield, the citizens of Philadelphia erected a building in 1740–1742 to serve for revivalist meetings and also as a Charity School for the instruction of poor children. It became the first home of the Academy and the College in 1751. This statue by the well-known sculptor on the University's staff and faculty was dedicated in 1919 and now stands in the Quadrangle.

Philadelphia."[9] When, in 1749, Benjamin Franklin turned his attention to founding a school with collegiate aspirations, there was a receptive audience ready to support his efforts.

Franklin himself is the link with the deed of trust of 1740. When he became a trustee of the Charity School proposed in that document, he was able to obtain the transfer of the Whitefield Building, as the New Building was also called after the popular English evangelist who had used it, to the purposes of a new Academy. Encumbered by debts, the building was still not fulfilling the educational functions for which subscriptions had been raised. Franklin mentions his lack of any religious affiliation as the reason he found himself in the advantageous position as "Member of both sets of Trustees, that for the Building and that for the Academy," which enabled him to negotiate the purchase of the building. The original contributors had provided for a nonsectarian Protestant establishment, and there was considerable dissension when the sole Moravian on the board of trustees for the Charity School was not replaced at his death, which upset the balance among the various religious persuasions. With his customary irony, Franklin describes how he was instrumental in settling the dilemma: "At length, one mention'd me, with the Observation that I was merely an honest Man, and of no Sect at all; which prevail'd with them to chuse me."[10]

Earlier in that decade, Franklin had given some serious thought to the form that an institution of learning should take. During a period when he had some idea of attracting an able young clergyman, the Reverend Richard Peters, to superintend such an establishment, he had drawn up a proposal for an academy. Then, in a new burst of activity in 1749, he brought his full energies to bear on the enterprise. This point in the University's history is forcefully described in Franklin's autobiography. After a passage on his invention of the Pennsylvania fireplace (later known as the Franklin stove), with a magnanimous comment on the Britishers who subsequently infringed his patent rights, Benjamin Franklin describes the foundation of the Academy, soon to become the College of Philadelphia:

> . . . I turn'd my Thoughts again to the Affair of establishing an Academy. The first Step I took was to associate in the Design a Number of active Friends, of whom the Junto furnished a good Part: the next was to write and publish a Pamphlet intitled, *Proposals relating to the Education of Youth in Pennsylvania.* This I distributed among the principal Inhabitants gratis; and as soon as I could suppose their Minds a little prepared by the Perusal of it, I set on foot a Subscription for Opening and Supporting an Academy; it was to be paid in Quotas yearly for Five Years; by so dividing it I judg'd the Subscription might be larger, and I believe it was so, amounting to no less (if I remember right) than Five thousand Pounds. In the Introduction to these Proposals, I stated their Publication not as an Act of mine,

but of some *publick-spirited Gentlemen*; avoiding as much as I could, according to my usual Rule, the presenting myself to the Publick as the Author of any Scheme for their Benefit.

The Subscribers, to carry the Project into immediate Execution chose out of their Number Twenty-four Trustees, and appointed Mr. Francis, then Attorney General, and myself, to draw up Constitutions for the Government of the Academy, which being done and signed, a House was hired, Masters engag'd and the Schools opened I think in the same Year 1749. The Scholars Encreasing fast, the House was soon found too small, and we were looking out for a Piece of Ground properly situated, with Intention to build, when Providence threw into our way a large House ready built, which with a few Alterations might well serve our purpose, this was the building before mentioned erected by the Hearers of Mr. Whitefield.[11]

The College of Philadelphia (circa 1780) watercolor by nineteenth century artist William L. Breton after the contemporary ink drawing by Pierre Eugène Du Simitière
Historical Society of Pennsylvania
The rectangular brick edifice, built as a Charity School and adapted for use by the Academy and College, stood in Fourth Street south of Arch. Topped by a steeple holding the school bell, it was even larger than the State House (Independence Hall). In a great hall on the upper floor was housed the organ played with a "bold and masterful Hand" at commencements by alumnus Francis Hopkinson. Immediately north of the principal building stood a three-storied dormitory, erected (1762–1763) by the famous Philadelphian architect-builder Robert Smith. The two structures were demolished in 1844 and 1845.

The *Proposals*, to which he refers in this account, are replete with the horticultural images and allusions common to earlier manuals of enlightened education. Franklin gives a brief description of various aspects of the proposed school, including the place he favors for its establishment, "the Situation high and dry, and, if it may be, not far from a River." He details the equipment and provides for a library although, "if in the Town, the Town Libraries may serve"; he notes the moral qualities of the Rector who will be in charge and the accommodations where "boarding Scholars diet together, plainly, temperately, and frugally." There follows the often-quoted statement illustrating the practicality of Franklin's mind: "As to their Studies, it would be well if they could be taught *every Thing* that is useful, and *every Thing* that is ornamental: But Art is long, and their Time is short. It is therefore propos'd that they learn those Things that are likely to be *most useful* and *most ornamental*, Regard being had to the several Professions for which they are intended." His proposed curriculum of academic subjects which follows includes opportunities for learning from practical experience. Indeed, the cultivation which Franklin envisages is not restricted to that of the mind. "While they are reading Natural History," he queries, "might not a little *Gardening, Planting, Grafting, Inoculating*, &c. be taught and practiced?"[12]

Whatever the connection between the *Proposals* of 1749 and his ruminations of six years earlier, the "Paper of *hints*" which Franklin distributed along with his regular newspaper on that occasion already outlined his later views of education as well as reflecting the opinions of his time. The empiricist ideas of John Locke were widely known in the colonies from his *Essay Concerning Human Understanding* and *Some Thoughts Concerning Education* and from works by his disseminators, Isaac Watts and James Burgh. Unlike the partisans of traditional classical education, Franklin inclined to place Bacon, Boyle, Newton, and Locke on a par with the classical authorities. He also favored instruction in good English in opposition to customary emphasis on the languages of antiquity. What he proposed was a form of education which would be best suited to the needs of the colonies. Naturally enough, his ideas were also influenced by his experiments in self-education.

Franklin's personal efforts at improving his own ability to express himself in his mother tongue were responsible for the weight he gives to English in his proposed curriculum. Persuaded that mastery of his own language was a matter of prime importance, he knew from experience the difficulty of achieving the clear, urbane style of the *Spectator* on which he had modeled his early writings. He records the practical advantages of studying the English language in his autobiography, commenting how "prose Writing has been of great Use to me in the Course of my Life, and was a principal Means of my Advancement."[13] One of his methods for improving his style and vocabulary was to distill the thoughts or "Sentiments," sentence by sentence, from essays by Addison and Steele in their influential publication, the *Spectator*. A few days later he would attempt to reconstruct the original in order to discover the shortcomings of his own language. Franklin also devised a method for improving his prose through an exchange of letters on various subjects with "another Bookish Lad" in Boston who "had a ready Plenty of Words."[14] The success of these measures leads him to recommend them in the *Proposals* as methods for teaching English to students: "To form their Stile, they should be put on Writing Letters to each other, making Abstracts of what they read, or writing the same Things in their own Words."[15]

Franklin's argument, taken up a few years later in his *Idea for an English School*, is that of a practical modernist with considerable personal experience of the educational process. Although he may have opposed the

Constitutions of 1749
With this historic document, Benjamin Franklin and twenty-three other "principal Gentlemen of the Province" founded the Academy already suggested by the energetic Philadelphia printer in his Proposals Relating to the Education of Youth in Pensilvania (1749). By their signatures, the trustees pledged their financial support to the new institution. The Academy, merged with the Charity School trust of 1740, was raised to the status of a degree-granting College in 1755.

classical bias of contemporary education, he tempers his reformist beliefs with the sensibility of a cultivated person. His proposals have been criticized as anti-intellectual and narrowly vocational; yet Franklin shows an understanding of the aims of true education when he expresses the hope that, through the formal schooling he receives, the student's appetite will be whetted for further learning. Far from banishing the classics from the curriculum, Franklin nurtures the desire of seeing students motivated to learn "those Languages, which have endured Ages, and will endure while there are Men," for they will have been made aware "that no Translation can do them Justice, or give the Pleasure found in Reading the Originals; that those Languages contain all Science" and "that to understand them is a distinguishing Ornament."[16]

These are not the words of an anti-intellectual iconoclast. Indeed, in later years, Franklin regretted having expressed himself with such moderation in his *Proposals* for, in the face of the forces of tradition, scant attention was paid to his innovative ideas. Franklin was embittered by the spectacle of the gradual attrition of the English school in the Academy with the departure, for want of adequate remuneration, first of David Dove, one of the original masters, and, much later, the resignation from the College of his friend, Ebenezer Kinnersley. In the last year of his life, Franklin spoke out more sharply against the continued dominance of the classical languages in a paper entitled *Observations Relative to the Intentions of the Original Founders of the Academy of Philadelphia,* dated 1789, but which remained unpublished among his papers.

Using the common-sense arguments of all proponents of a vernacular against the ancient languages, Franklin notes in this late document: "The Origin of Latin and Greek Schools among the different Nations of Europe is known to have been this, that until between 3 and 400 Years past there were no Books in any other Language; all the Knowledge contain'd in Books . . . being in those Languages, it was of course necessary to learn them." He goes on to deplore mankind's blind clinging to old ways, the "unaccountable Prejudice in favor of ancient Customs and Habitudes." In a last broadside, he comments on the persistent role of the hat in modern society, noting that headgear was not favored by those paradigms— the Greeks and Romans. With the arrival on the scene of powdered wigs and curls, the hat nevertheless lingered on as an antiquated form of dress worn, not on the head, but under the arm. "The still prevailing custom of having schools for teaching generally our children, in these days, the Latin and Greek languages, I consider therefore, in no other light than as the *Chapeau bras* of modern Literature," he concludes, gracefully knotting together his tirade against the schools and his disquisition on the subject of hats.[17]

If the curriculum of the Academy did not reflect the full intentions of Benjamin Franklin, the establishment of the institution in so relatively short a time and the provision made for its accommodation and financing were almost uniquely the work of the University of Pennsylvania's earliest and most energetic supporter. Franklin's strategy included the use of his printing press. As has been seen, once satisfied of a receptive audience among his friends, he proceeded to circulate the *Proposals* free with a covering statement ascribing this move to people other than himself who "have directed a Number of Copies to be made by the Press and properly distributed."[18] Immediately afterwards, subscriptions were requested and obtained from the citizenry, and the largest donors were invited to serve as trustees. Franklin was elected president of the board in 1749 and was succeeded by the Reverend Richard Peters in 1756, a year before he departed for England. In 1755, a new charter had been obtained, this time for the "College, Academy and Charitable School of Philadelphia." Conscious of having done "what no other could have done," Franklin remained profoundly concerned with the institution he had called into being. In his valedictory remarks in the *Autobiography*, he speaks with pride of what had been accomplished during his lifetime: "Thus was established the University of Pennsylvania. I have been continued one of its Trustees from the Beginning, now near forty Years, and have had the very great Pleasure of seeing a Number of the Youth who have receiv'd their Education in it, distinguish'd by their improv'd Ability, serviceable in public stations and Ornaments to their Country."[19]

After many vicissitudes suffered by both the country and the institution, Franklin was reelected president of the College board in 1789. His fellow trustees honored his great services by meeting, in the last months of his life, at the house of "the venerable Dr. Benjamin Franklin, the Father and one of the first Founders of the Institution."[20]

In the face of countless exploits and aphorisms for which he is customarily acclaimed, Benjamin Franklin has been presented here principally in his role as the University's founder and celebrated for his characteristically far-sighted views on education. Yet he held no degree from the University he founded and which descendants of his frequented.[21] This situation was rectified by the president of the University in ceremonies at the outset of the nation's bicentennial year. A feeling for Franklin's other achievements—for the man and the manifold claims he persists in making on the attention of his compatriots down the years—was expressed in the tribute paid him, on Founder's Day, January 17, 1976, which fell on his 270th birthday. On that day, the president bestowed on Benjamin Franklin the posthumous honorary degree of Doctor of Natural Philosophy with the following citation:

> The Trustees of the University of Pennsylvania, on behalf of all University members, have determined to award their honorary degree to one of their colleagues. The Trustees and the Faculty of the University wish it made known that they do not award

**Thomas Mifflin (1744–1800)
and Sarah Mifflin (ca. 1747–1790)**
by John Singleton Copley
Historical Society of Pennsylvania
*Last president of the Supreme Executive
Council of Pennsylvania and first governor of the state under the constitution of
1790. Born in Philadelphia, A.B. College
of Philadelphia (1760), of which he was
later a trustee and treasurer (1773–1791).
A soldier-politician, he was a member of
the Provincial Assembly and Continental
Congress, chief aide-de-camp to Washington, who appointed him quarter-
master-general and promoted him to the
rank of major-general (1778). He married Sarah Morris in 1767.*

this degree lightly. The individual receiving it must well have proved himself and over a reasonable period of time to be so honored. The Faculty, for example, have generally preferred that the person they recognize have diligently excelled in one field and must have noted, with some reservation, that the man to be honored excelled in several, and in connection with this tendency, was inclined to change jobs and professions rather often. Benjamin Franklin was, for those who may not know his career, a printer, a newspaperowner, an essayist, a politician, an educator, a scientist, an inventor, an experimenter, a diplomat, a statesman, and a philosopher, among other callings. The University has further observed that he encouraged the writer of the so-called "Common Sense," which was seen as no such thing by the established authority of that time, and that he was known to have signed documents—the Declaration of Inde-pendence and the Constitution of the United States—which were at best controversial and at least one of which was basically illegal and even forcibly opposed by large numbers of his countrymen. That, in addition, during his public role as Postmaster General, he even turned the annual postal deficit into a profit, went against not only the established tradition of his day but against that of our own.

The Trustees and the University must also take note of his tendency toward the radical in education—he increasingly ignored the traditional curriculum of classical education of his time in favor of the teaching of English and science, along with broad-based history, geography, and modern languages, in opposition to the expert opinion of his peers. Moreover, the University members have found it necessary to consider his extraordinary behavior of flying a kite in a thunderstorm, which, while scientifically useful, made his neighbors wonder and the man-in-the-street stare. Further, it was brought to their attention that he not only followed eccentric medical practices but, worse, wrote about and proselytized for them as being sensible (the University of Pennsylvania itself had not small expertise in this matter, having established the first medical school in the colonies): at night Benjamin Franklin slept with his windows open to get the benefit of fresh air; he took regular exercise, particularly swimming, until late in life, and not only enjoyed cold air baths early in the morning but bathed, with hot water, regularly, habits that lifted the eyebrows of his contemporaries.

There is yet another matter which the members of the University have found it necessary to respond to, since the incidents were public knowledge and took place before witnesses. Themselves not adverse to a lively face or dancing eyes, the Trustees have been forced, since Franklin literally thrust the matter before them in his writings, to comment on his penchant for the opposite sex. This was marked, for example, even during his years in France as Minister Pleni-potentiary and in his mid-seventies where it is known that, to the dismay of John Adams, he kissed, according to the astonishing French practice, the necks of the admiring women

who crowded about him in the salons of Paris. Too, with regard
to women, he went once more against the accepted ideas of his
day by advocating education for them.

All in all, it is not wondered at that the University of
Pennsylvania did not wish to act rashly, considering that in
spite of his pronouncements on education which firmly set the
University's place in the history of instruction, Benjamin
Franklin had only two years of formal schooling. True, Harvard
rushed in and gave him an honorary Master of Arts degree in
1753 when he was but forty-seven, but the University must put
that to Harvard's pushy desire to be first. If Yale followed suit
only six weeks later in awarding the same degree (Yale was
founded after Harvard), the Trustees frankly could not be
surprised. And if Oxford University gave Franklin in 1762 the
Doctor of Civil Laws, Pennsylvanians could only determine that
Oxford, feeling her age at the six-century or so mark, believed
she must present the degree since her time might be running out.

Nonetheless, after due and careful deliberation, and in the
270th year of his birth, the Trustees on behalf of the University
of Pennsylvania have deemed it proper, even though a charge of
nepotism may be made for so acknowledging one of their
members and their first head, to award their honorary degree to
the founder of the University of Pennsylvania, seeing that in
spite of his own special traits and actions and undertakings,
Benjamin Franklin's reputation seems to have withstood the test
of time and that he has remained very much alive not only at
his University but in the hearts of men and women everywhere.

Thus, won finally by his legacy of wise deeds, lasting words,
brave example, and generous humanity, but most especially by
his leaving them the idea and substance of the educational
institution that has endured and grown beyond even the
measure he gave it, the Trustees of the University of Pennsylvania in this 200th anniversary year of the nation he helped
make sure, name their founder and friend, and the enduring
colleague and teacher of their countrymen and the world, with
affection and pride for their honorary degree, Doctor of Natural
Philosophy.

Franklin has never ceased to be an inspiration for educational policy
as well as for human values. He continues to dazzle his countrymen and the
world, no less than his heirs at the University, with the character and charm
that affected, for so long, his own generation.

3

William Smith
and the College of Philadelphia

William Smith (1727–1803)
by Benjamin West
*First provost (1755–1779) of the College
of Philadelphia. Born in Scotland, educated for the ministry at the University
of Aberdeen, Smith arrived in 1751 in
New York, where he wrote* A General
Idea of the College of Mirania *(1753),
sending copies to two trustees of the
Academy and Charitable School of Philadelphia, Benjamin Franklin and Richard
Peters. In 1779, Smith moved to Maryland
where he founded Washington College.
He served as provost of the restored
College of Philadelphia until it became
the University of Pennsylvania (1789–
1791). He received the honorary D.D.
from Aberdeen, Oxford, and Trinity
College, Dublin.*

Among the men of the Scottish Enlightenment who left their mark on the colonial College, none had a greater influence than its provost, William Smith, whose tenure as the first academic executive lasted, with interruptions, for more than a quarter of a century. Smith had originally come to the attention of Benjamin Franklin as a result of a utopian plan for a college which he published in 1753. Ultimately, the differences in the two men's views on education as well as their divergent political opinions contributed to Franklin's disaffection with the College in its later developments. In 1754, however, after three years in the colonies as a private tutor, William Smith was called to Philadelphia as a direct result of the efforts of Benjamin Franklin, to teach "Logick, Rhetoric, Ethics and Natural Philosophy."

Born in Aberdeenshire in 1727, the year Franklin settled permanently in Philadelphia, Smith was the son of a landholder. He had been educated at King's College, Aberdeen, and, after a year or two in London, had accompanied the family of Colonel Josiah Martin to New York. At that time there was a great deal of discussion on the subject of establishing a college in the province. Smith contributed to this debate with a pamphlet in which he stated that an institution of higher learning was needed and set forth his opinions as to how and where it should be founded, as well as describing methods for raising the necessary funds. With this tract, entitled *Some Thoughts on Education,* Smith entered the lists as an influential spokesman for educational change. In 1753, before returning to London for ordination to the Anglican priesthood, he composed *A General Idea of the College of Mirania* and saw fit to send a copy to Franklin in Philadelphia. Franklin replied, agreeing to forward his comments on the work "per next Post" and adding that he would be "extreamly glad to see and converse with you. . . . For an Acquaintance and Communication with Men of Learning, Virtue and Publick Spirit, is one of my greatest Enjoyments."[1]

In addition to his other writings, Smith also composed verses in the Augustan vein. A visit to the Academy, two months after Franklin's invitation, was the occasion for a poem dedicated to its trustees. In lofty

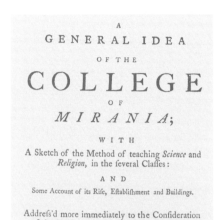

A General Idea of the College of Mirania
by William Smith
New York, 1753, title page
William Smith's book A General Idea of the College of Mirania *attracted the attention of Franklin, who brought him to Philadelphia. The work describes an idealized institution with emphasis on training for citizenship and for the "mechanic professions." It was included in Smith's* Discourses on Public Occasions in America, *a collection of Smith's writings published for a wider audience in Great Britain.*

metaphor, he exhorts those concerned with the college in New York to emulate their "noble sister," Philadelphia:

> Rise, nobly rise! Dispute the Prize with *Those*;
> As *Athens*, rivaling *Lacedaemon* rose!
> . . . .
> This nobler Strife, ye nobler Sisters feed
> Be yours the contest in each worthy Deed;
> . . . .
> Hence with your Names shall *Fame* perfume
>   her Wing;
> To her eternal Tromp your *Glories* sing.[2]

Franklin had the poem printed on his press and, from this time on, supported Smith's admission to the faculty of the Academy.

In *Mirania*, Smith describes a province of the New World in the utopian tradition of Plato and Sir Thomas More. It is inhabited by "a mighty and florishing [*sic*] people, in possession of an extensive country, capable of producing all the necessaries and many of the superfluities of life." Reflecting on the importance of securing their present and future well-being, the inhabitants decide to set about educating their youth in the distinction between the true and the false, "by directing their studies to such things as come more immediately home to their business and bosoms." He then sets forth a specific program of study in an institution erected for the purpose. At first, all students are to receive identical instruction in a "common school." After two or three years, the curriculum diverges: those bound for the learned professions receive five years of education at a Latin school, followed by a further four years of undergraduate study, while those who are to follow a trade spend six years at a mechanic's school. This provision for formal technical education was unusual for the time. As Smith informs the reader: "Public seminaries are almost universally calculated for the first class; while a collegiate class for the instruction of the latter is rarely to be met with. This class of people, by far the most numerous, . . . are overlooked."[3] Aspects of his scheme echo Franklin's practical proposals for an "English School" to which Smith does not fail to allude. He also draws upon his own college experiences in Aberdeen and his familiarity with recent educational reforms in Scotland. In essence, however, *Mirania* is based on an informed appraisal of the needs of the colonies. Although the title suggests a utopian plan, Smith translated some of his suggestions into actual practice, and certain of his arguments also foreshadow ideas on educational diversity of much later date.

It was at the Academy, soon to be the College of Philadelphia, and not in New York, that Smith's "general ideas" were put into effect. In an edition of his *Discourses* in 1762, he notes that his proposals are "a pretty exact reproduction of what the author is now endeavoring to realize in the seminary over which he has the honor to preside in another city." An *whom the Charge we are as follow*

Paul Jackson ? *M.*

Jacob Duché
Francis Hopkinson
James Latta
Samuel Magaw
John Morgan
Hugh Williamson

*B.
a*

Josiah Martin ? *Hon*
Soloman Southwick

The Class of 1757
From the copy of the *Discourses* which William Smith gave to John Morgan Hand-written list of the first graduates of the College of Philadelphia who received the "batchelor of arts" degree in 1757. Four of them, including John Morgan, founder of the school of medicine, became members of the faculty; Francis Hopkinson, signer of the Declaration of Independence, served as a trustee.

impression of the curriculum at the College of Philadelphia may be obtained from the schema which Smith published in the *Pennsylvania Gazette* in 1756.[4] In keeping with the reforms of Scottish realism, the students are seen to progress in the course of their undergraduate program from a study of the concrete and the particular to more abstract areas of consideration. In the first year, the student proceeds from Latin and English exercises and arithmetic to logic, Euclidian geometry, and logarithms. There are also extensive readings from prescribed classical authors. In what constituted a new departure in the education of the time, a list of modern writers, including Isaac Watts, John Locke, and the authors of contemporary treatises on mathematics, as well as a perusal of the *Spectator*, is recommended for the occupation of "Private Hours."

In addition to continued readings with emphasis on the theory of poetry and rhetoric in writings ancient and modern, second-year students begin moral philosophy and pursue their studies of logic and geometry, together with navigation, trigonometry, and "natural philosophy" (physics), "conic sections" (analytical geometry), and "fluxions" (differential calculus). During both years, a place is reserved for the oral arts of "declamation" and "disputation." In their final year at the College, students apply themselves to moral philosophy, natural law, and aspects of government and commerce which bear a relation to the modern disciplines of political science and economics. Scientific studies are continued in the third year with courses in physics and astronomy as well as in "natural history of animals" (biology), "natural history of vegetables" (botany), and chemistry. The third-year readings, prescribed as well as private, continue to reflect the subjects designated for study in the principal courses. During the entire period, the French language is offered as an optional extra, and the daily reading of the Holy Bible is compulsory.

The College's three-year curriculum was widely imitated by other colleges during the half century which followed. With its emphasis on science, the curriculum of the College of Philadelphia differed substantially from that of other colonial colleges of the time which continued to teach the classics almost to the exclusion of other disciplines. The nonsectarian character of the institution in Philadelphia is frequently taken as its distinctive mark, particularly in comparison with King's College—later Columbia University—which was founded in the same period by Anglicans. Yet, Smith was no less an Anglican clergyman than Samuel Johnson of King's College. If the colonial College of Philadelphia stood apart from the others, it was, according to Laurence A. Cremin, mostly on account of "the vision of its leadership and the urban context in which that vision was realized."[5]

The fortunes of King's College, New York, and the College of Philadelphia are intertwined at a number of points in their early colonial history. If Smith had initially been interested in heading the New York

Plan of Education in the College of Philadelphia

From the *Pennsylvania Gazette*, August 12, 1756

Outline for the detailed scheme of studies prepared by William Smith and published in Franklin's Gazette in 1756. The three-year program in the "Philosophy Schools," leading to the Bachelor of Arts degree, was the first arrangement in the colonies of a nonsectarian collegiate program freed from medieval tradition. Mathematics and science made up one-third of the course by which the student in the College of Philadelphia was "to be led through a scale of easy ascent till finally rendered capable of Thinking, Writing and Acting well, which is the grand aim of a liberal education." The curriculum of 1756 was retained by the College and University until well into the nineteenth century.

college, Johnson, who actually assumed the position, was eager for Smith to join him there. Franklin, in the meantime, was arranging for Smith to start teaching at the Academy. Some years later when Smith was in England soliciting contributions for the College of Philadelphia of which he was now provost, he was less than overjoyed to receive a call from Sir James Jay of King's College, whose business in London was manifestly the same as his own. Smith seemed to recollect having mentioned his fund-raising venture which had been approved by the Philadelphia trustees in 1761 on a visit to his associates in New York. Whatever had decided the trustees of King's College to follow suit, there was nothing for the representatives of the two colleges to do but to coordinate their efforts. Between them, they proceeded to raise an unprecedented sum of money: even after division had been made of the funds collected, Smith returned to Philadelphia with more than £7,000 sterling.[6]

On this occasion, Smith remained in England in the service of his college for a period of over two years before returning home. On an earlier visit, however, there had been personal reasons for his prolonged absence. Within a year of becoming provost, Smith had found himself under attack for his overt political sympathy with the proprietary party of the Penns, by then in a minority in the local Assembly. Opposition had come to a head in 1758 when he was suspected of having had a hand in publishing an attack on the Assembly in an article which had found its way into an influential German-language newspaper. Smith was cited for contempt along with the initiator of the derogatory remarks, Judge William Moore of Chester county, later to become Smith's father-in-law. The judge was now imprisoned for his penmanship.

When Smith declined to admit any complicity or to make an apology, he too was taken into custody. The "inconvenience from thence arising to the College" was satisfactorily remedied, according to the minute book of the trustees: "Mr. Smith having expressed a Desire to continue his Lectures to the Classes which had formerly attended them, the Students also inclining rather to proceed in their Studies under his care, They ordered that Said classes should attend him for that Purpose at the usual Hours in the Place of his present confinement."[7] That place was none other than the new Market Street "gaol" from which he was released after three months, only to be imprisoned once more and threatened, on regaining his liberty, with being locked up again when the Assembly met in the fall. The trustees hurriedly granted him a leave of absence and Smith departed for London to appeal to the Crown against the Assembly's action.

Not only was Smith vindicated as a result of his appeal: he received a further mark of the esteem in which he was held in the home country. In the Rare Book Collection of the University of Pennsylvania is a printed recommendation, signed by the Archbishop of Canterbury and five other

Anglican bishops, for the award of the degree of Doctor of Divinity from
the University of Oxford.[8] Such honors may have secured Smith's position
but they did little to improve his popularity in Philadelphia. In fact, even
the successful fund-raising mission of a few years later was viewed with
suspicion in some quarters because of Smith's favorable standing with the
Proprietors, the King himself, and, in particular, the princes of the
Anglican church.

Although the College's finances improved as a result of the provost's
fund-raising in England, its political position worsened. The College came
under attack for its connections with the proprietary party. As Revolutionary sentiment increased, Smith himself was viewed by many
republicans with mounting distrust. Although in his correspondence he
inveighs against the Stamp Act for impeaching the loyalty of the colonists,
his British birth as well as his ties with men of high station in England
brought him under suspicion as a royalist and sympathizer. Nonetheless,
there was sufficient rapport between the College and the new authorities for
the provost and trustees to invite the members of the first Continental
Congress to take part in the commencement exercises of 1775. On this
occasion, George Washington and the other delegates proceeded in a body
from the State House to the College on Fourth Street.

All the considerations which rendered Smith suspect of royalist
sympathies further exacerbated the difference of opinion between himself
and Franklin. As early as 1763, Franklin had written bitterly of his former
protégé: "I made that Man my Enemy by doing him too much Kindness.
'Tis the honestest Way of acquiring an Enemy. And since 'tis convenient to
have at least one Enemy, who by his Readiness to revile one on all
Occasions, may make one careful of one's Conduct, I shall keep him an
Enemy for that purpose."[9] Nonetheless, as president of the State
Constitutional Convention in 1776, Franklin was able to introduce an
article protecting charter rights which Smith had proposed "for religious
and scientific corporations," and this was adopted as a clause in the newly
framed constitution of the Commonwealth of Pennsylvania. Their foresight
was rewarded later on, although their proposal had little effect on the
immediate fate of the College after the Revolution.

In September 1778, after the last redcoats had departed from the city,
the College, which had been used as a military hospital by the army of
occupation, prepared once more to open its doors. A very large number of
trustees, faculty, and alumni of the College and the Academy served
their country with distinction during the Revolution. In the army, Major
General Thomas Mifflin (A.B., A.M., and trustee) and Major General John
Peter Gabriel Muhlenberg (graduate of the Academy and trustee) were but
two of the military leaders who had attended the institution, while the first
three professors of the department of medicine—John Morgan, William
Shippen, and Benjamin Rush—held high administrative posts in the army

as medical director and chief physician. The chaplain to the Continental Congress was the future Right Reverend Bishop William White (graduate of the Academy, A.B., A.M., D.D., and trustee), and, of some fifty graduates and trustees who were sometime members of the Continental Congress, twenty had very close bonds with the institution and no fewer than nine of these signed the Declaration of Independence.[10]

Hostility to the College had nonetheless grown in the legislature which suspected it of loyalism on account of certain Tory trustees and its Anglican provost. A committee was therefore appointed to look into the affairs of the College and to investigate accusations that the trustees had mismanaged its finances and infringed the religious freedom intended by its founders. On the pretext that they were not abiding by the conditions of the College's original charter, the board of trustees was accordingly dissolved and a new one appointed in its place.[11] The College in 1779 was renamed the "University of the State of Pennsylvania," a clear indication that, in future, it would find itself under domestic rather than foreign influence. It thus became the first institution in the English-speaking world outside Great Britain to receive the title of university.

Among the new trustees, officials of the state appeared in an *ex officio* capacity; an attempt was made at an equitable distribution of seats among the various Christian sects in the city. The perennial Benjamin Franklin was made a trustee of the new University, but he did not accept the honor. Instead, after returning from France in 1785, he set about reassembling the former board at his house. Meanwhile, the members of the faculty of the colonial College were relieved of their duties and, with them, Provost Smith, who had spent the years of tumult at his home at the Falls of Schuylkill. In other respects, the act of the legislature ratified all the existing charters and made provisions for the University to receive additional funds collected from estates which had been confiscated in the Revolution.

It was to be expected that this action would be bitterly opposed by the former trustees and particularly by William Smith who was well known for making his opinions heard. For almost a year, he refused to vacate the provost's house or to turn over the keys and seals of the College to his successor, the Reverend John Ewing. When he finally complied, it was only because he had been served with a writ for his eviction. Smith promptly moved to Chestertown in Maryland where he became rector of the parish church and took a few private pupils. It was not long before his life's work of improving education in the colonies was resumed, this time when he expanded a local school and obtained a charter for it from the legislature of Maryland. This institution was given the name of Washington College in honor of the nation's hero. Speculation in western land also occupied his time.

Acknowledging defeat in Philadelphia was, however, out of the

Francis Hopkinson (1737–1791)
by Robert Edge Pine
Historical Society of Pennsylvania
Member of the first class of the College of Philadelphia to graduate (1757), Hopkinson received an A.M. (1760) and an LL.D. (1790). He became a lawyer and was a delegate to the Continental Congress and signed the Declaration of Independence. Devoted to the arts, he wrote Seven Songs, *probably the first book of music published by an American composer (1788). At the time of the Revolution, he composed many political satires. He played the organ, invented a quill for plucking the harpsicord, and designed the first American flag (1777), the Great Seal of New Jersey and the original Orrery Seal of the University of Pennsylvania (1782).*

The Washington Diploma, 1783
*George Washington, who attended the
1775 commencement of the College of
Philadelphia along with other members
of the Continental Congress, was the
recipient of an honorary LL.D. eight
years later. The diploma of the University, "ambitious of enrolling your justly
celebrated name in the catalogue of her
sons" and bearing the pendant paper
orrery seal, is a hand-lettered parchment
now in the Library of Congress.*

question: for the next ten years, Smith continued to assail the legislature
of the Commonwealth with complaints and objections concerning their
arbitrary treatment of the colonial College. As time passed, the Revolutionary zeal of the men who had drawn up the most radical constitution of
any of the thirteen colonies gave way to a more conservative element in
the government. Smith's vehement protests against the "robbery," by
which he did not hesitate to imply that the earlier trustees had owned the
College, were at first ignored; but gradually, as changes took place in the
composition of the legislature, there was greater willingness to give him a
hearing. Chiefly as a result of Smith's persistent petitions, a committee was
formed in 1788 to open up the whole question once more. Smith
immediately published a new tract entitled, with no pretense at
moderation, *An Address to the General Assembly of Pennsylvania in the
Case of the Violated Charter, of the College, Academy and Charitable
School of Philadelphia*. The next year, it was finally decided that, in the
light of clauses in the state constitution of 1776 which Franklin and Smith
had been instrumental in putting on the books, the statute of 1779
contravened the law protecting the property rights and privileges of
existing corporations.

As a result of a new act passed by the Assembly, the former trustees and faculty were reinstated in the original College buildings. There were now two institutions of higher learning in Philadelphia with faculties which overlapped at some points, for, in the absence of judicial action at this or any other time, nothing prevented the University from continuing to exist side by side with the resurrected College. Forced to seek alternative accommodation, the University took up quarters in the building being constructed for the American Philosophical Society at Fifth and Chestnut Streets. Anomalous though it may seem, this situation continued for the next three years, by which time both the College and the University came to recognize the wisdom of joining forces instead of competing with one another.

Among the problems which had to be resolved at the time of union, none was more sensitive than the fate of William Smith. The new board of trustees represented a merger of the two previous bodies, with each responsible for electing twelve members. Despite his versatility as a teacher and his long experience since the inauguration of the College, there was considerable opposition to Smith among these men. When the board made its appointments to the faculty of arts, Smith was left out altogether. Amazed, he inquired of a member of the board whether "not voting *in* is the same as actually voting *out*, and is to operate as a *Discharge*," and he requested some indication that there was nothing dishonorable in his omission. The trustees then proceeded to reinstate Ewing as provost. Smith responded by making a statement of his financial claims against the University while still expressing eagerness to serve the institution in any capacity. A financial settlement was forthcoming, but Smith discovered the truth of his incredulous fear that "after all my Services, for near forty Years, in the Cause of Learning in Pennsylvania, I am now absolv'd from all future Duties and connexion with the seminary."[12] By a strange irony, William Smith, who had been associated with the College of Philadelphia since 1754, was destined not to hold a position when faculty were elected at the newly constituted University of Pennsylvania in 1792.

4

John Morgan and Benjamin Rush: America's First Medical School

John Morgan (1735–1789)
by A. F. King, after the portrait
by Angelica Kaufmann
Professor of the theory and practice of medicine at the College's medical department founded by him in 1765 as the first school of medicine in the colonies. Born in Philadelphia, and a member of the first class to graduate from the College of Philadelphia (A.B. 1757, A.M. 1760), he pursued his medical studies in London and Edinburgh, where he received his M.D. (1763). Before his return to Philadelphia, he was elected a fellow of the Royal Society and correspondent of the Académie Royale de Chirurgie. At the time of independence he was medical director of the Continental Army (1775–1776). Among his papers is A Recommendation of Inoculation, According to Baron Dimsdale's Method *(1776).*

When William Smith reprinted his *Discourses on public occasions in America* in 1762, he inscribed a copy and presented it to John Morgan whose "Genius and Application" he had observed while Morgan was a student at the College of Philadelphia.[1] Only eight years younger than Smith, Morgan himself was to make a tremendous contribution to higher education, for it was through his efforts that a medical curriculum was established in the American colonies. At the time, it was customary for colonial doctors to be trained in the course of a protracted apprenticeship with an established physician. In his proposals, however, Morgan did more than merely advocate organized teaching of the theory and practice of medicine: according to his forceful argument, the instruction must be given at the College as an adjunct to the sound education in language and the liberal arts already being taught there.

It was at the College of Philadelphia where he had taken his A.B. and his A.M. that John Morgan persuaded the trustees to set up this program modeled after some of the great European universities. In fact, when the institution obtained formal university status, the new title could be justified primarily because of the medical department which had opened in 1765. In Morgan's view, "the flourishing state of literature in this college, and the perfection in which the languages, mathematics, and polite arts are taught here, are strong inducements for such young men as propose engaging in the study of Medicine, to enter the college." While there had been previous suggestions for setting up external courses or founding an independent medical school, Morgan insisted that his was "a scheme for transplanting *Medical science* into this seminary."[2] In the firm belief that medicine should be taught as a part of the college curriculum, he was influenced, naturally enough, by his own experience at the University of Edinburgh, where he and the two other professors in the early years of the medical department had received their training. The Scottish university was generally accepted as the model for this new departure in medical education in the colonies. A few years later, Franklin wrote to Morgan from England: "Thank you for the inaugural Dissertations, and am pleased to see our College begin to make some Figure as a school of Physic, and have no doubt but in a few years, with good Management, it may acquire a Reputation similar and equal to that in Edinburgh."[3]

In the course of his education, Morgan had himself shown considerable interest in the liberal arts, and he had never restricted his studies to medicine alone. It was during his apprenticeship to Dr. John Redman, the most prominent physician in Philadelphia, that the College of Philadelphia first opened its doors and Morgan enrolled in the baccalaureate program. After graduating with the first class, he continued to investigate many branches of humanistic and scientific knowledge during his travels in the true spirit of an eighteenth century philosopher. While in Scotland for the purpose of studying medicine, he attended lectures in belles-lettres with the Reverend Hugh Blair, the eloquent proponent of the fictitious Gaelic bard Ossian. On that occasion, he received an amused comment on his "Enterprising Genius" from a medical student friend in London: "Thou won't be satisfied without being a Psychologist, Chemist, Physician & Rhetorician. Mercy upon us, where will you end?"[4]

The Grand Tour of Europe with which his five years of education abroad concluded further reflects the diversity of Morgan's interests. It included visits to hospitals in Paris, discussions with doctors in Italy, and courses on art and architecture and the collection of antiquities. In Rome he came into contact with the painter Benjamin West and posed for a portrait by the young Swiss artist Angelica Kauffmann. Not long before, he had been kindly received in Padua by the aged but active Giovanni Battista Morgagni who had established pathology as a branch of modern medicine by introducing post-mortem studies to supplement his clinical observations. Morgan's visit to this eminent anatomist marked a high point in his experience abroad and, before it was over, Morgagni not only inscribed a fine copy of his most important work for Morgan, but "claimed kindred with him from the resemblance of their names."[5]

On their way through Switzerland, Morgan and his friend Samuel Powel were entertained cordially by Voltaire at his estate outside Geneva, and, while in the Alps, Morgan noted the splendors of the view and the prevalence of goiter among the inhabitants. When he returned to America in the spring of 1765, John Morgan was a "compleat Man" of learning and cultivation, in addition to being a proven investigator into the medical sciences and a member of the leading learned societies of eighteenth century Europe. His international acceptance further appears in references to him as the "Scots doctor," by the Académie Royale de Chirurgie in Paris, while Voltaire introduced Morgan and Powel as "two English Gentlemen." In a letter to an Italian lady, the Philadelphian did not hesitate to identify himself as "J. Morgan, Cavaliere Inglese."[6]

It was with a significant list of accomplishments and distinctions to his credit that young John Morgan pronounced his *Discourse upon the Institution of Medical Schools in America*, composed in large part during

Benjamin Rush (1745–1813)
attributed to John Neagle
*First professor of chemistry (1769–1791)
at the College of Philadelphia and
University of Pennsylvania. Born in
Byberry near Philadelphia, he studied at
the College of New Jersey (Princeton)
and attended the first medical course at
the College of Philadelphia. He signed
the Declaration of Independence and
served as surgeon-general of the Armies
of the Middle Department during the
Revolution. As a member of the staff of
Pennsylvania Hospital, he reformed the
treatment of mental disease. President
of the Pennsylvania Society for Promoting the Abolition of Slavery (1803),
advocate of temperance, the abolition of
capital punishment, and the education of
women, he wrote many medical, political,
and moralizing works, including
America's first text on chemistry (1770)
and an autobiography (1800 but published later). Rush succeeded John
Morgan as professor of theory and
practice of medicine (1789–1813).*

his recent stay in Paris. Described as "a Magna Carta for American medical education," the address was given at the public anniversary commencement held at the College of Philadelphia on May 30 and 31, 1765.[7] In it, Morgan enumerated the potent reasons why a medical department should be immediately established at the College. Coming after years of the best available training, his appeal represented the culmination of his own career. The full significance of his ideals as he moved to establish medical education in the colonies appears in the evaluation of one of Morgan's twentieth century successors at the medical school, Professor Francis Wood: "If, during the succeeding 150 years, we in America had not deviated from the principles and objectives which John Morgan outlined, we would not have strayed from the road in medical education, and would not have needed the flogging administered by Abraham Flexner in 1910 to bring us back to the right path."[8] The proposals which he set forth were for the reform not only of the teaching of Physic but also of the practice of medicine itself. At the time, his lofty "discrimination" between true medicine and the trades of surgeon and apothecary appeared extraordinary to practitioners and to the general public alike. Despite the prophetic nature of his insights, it was many years before his recommendations would become common practice.

In broaching his subject, Morgan had first of all to acquaint those who heard or later read his *Discourse* with "the various branches of knowledge [which compose the science of medicine] Anatomy, Materia Medica, Botany, Chymistry, the Theory of Medicine, and the Practice." The Theory of Physic, he explains, usually known as the *Medical Institutions*, "comprehends the important doctrines of Physiology and Pathology. Of the former he declares: "The study of it is most entertaining, and also engages our closest attention from the many curious subjects with which it abounds," while the latter, by linking prognostication with indications of treatment, "forms a system of precepts in the art of healing."[9]

In his reference to system, Morgan speaks from the conviction that instruction must be based on a coherent medical theory rather than relying on the necessarily limited experience of the individual practitioner. For this reason, after having familiarized his listeners with the various branches of the science, he notes the importance of a systematic philosophy such as the one on which his own medical education at the University of Edinburgh had been based. There must be an underlying plan as well as coherence among the several courses of instruction, since the vastness and complexity of the subject make it "impossible to learn it thoroughly without we follow a certain order." Describing the interconnection between the various disciplines and the sequence in which they should be pursued, he makes a point of emphasizing the importance to the student of previous instruction, there being "no art yet known which may not contribute somewhat to the improvement of Medicine." In addition to the classical languages and liberal arts curriculum, already "taught in such perfection in this place," he singles out the value of learning the French language, as he himself had done, as well as of an acquaintance with mathematics and natural philosophy.[10]

Morgan now launches into the more controversial portion of his *Discourse*, after first repeating the opinion that the trades of surgeon and apothecary are beneath the dignity of the true physician. Earlier, a group of American students at the University of Edinburgh, most of them from Virginia, had vowed not to degrade their profession "by mingling the trade of apothecary and surgeon with it." Their conviction reflected a recent decision by the prestigious Royal College of Physicians of Edinburgh to exclude members of the Corporation of Surgeons from their number.[11] For his part, Morgan initially complied with these precepts on his return to Philadelphia by distinguishing the fee for a medical consultation from the apothecary's charge for medicine. But his patients were too accustomed to doctors who did everything for a single payment, and there was considerable resistance to change from his colleagues as well. Colonial physicians saw no alternative to performing surgery or mixing drugs according to their patients' needs, and Morgan found himself compelled to elaborate on his Scottish purism with an "Apology for attempting to introduce the regular mode of practising PHYSIC in PHILADELPHIA," which was printed along with his *Discourse*.[12]

More unwelcome to those already in medical practice was Morgan's lurid depiction of the state of colonial medicine. Although he took care in the *Discourse* to congratulate the population of certain American cities such as Philadelphia on the presence there of numbers of excellent physicians and surgeons "qualified by genius, education, and experience," many of these doctors had received no supplementary training after serving their apprenticeship. Morgan made it clear that he considered this course inadequate and pernicious, and he describes the nature of so restricted a foundation for medical practice:

> A contracted view of Medicine naturally confines a man to a very narrow circle, and limits him to a few partial indications in the cure of diseases. He soon gets through his little stock of knowledge; he repeats over and over his round of prescriptions, the same almost in every case; and, although he is continually embarrassed, he has the vanity to believe that, from the few maxims which he has adopted, he has within himself all the principles of medical knowledge, and that he has exhausted all the resources of art. This is a notion subversive of all improvement.

From an unflattering account of the disadvantages of such limitations, Morgan goes on to express pure outrage at their effects. Over a century later, a doctor's son, Gustave Flaubert, described how the operation on a club foot by the well-intentioned ignoramus Charles Bovary resulted in gangrene and amputation. Morgan had only to consult his own experience to evoke similar scenes, and he goes on to inveigh against the ignorance and incompetence of doctors: "Great is the havock which his ignorance spreads on every side, robbing the affectionate husband of his darling spouse, or rendering the tender wife a helpless widow; increasing the number of orphans; mercilessly depriving them of their parents' support." One of nine children who had been bereaved of both parents by the time he was thirteen, Morgan did not use entirely empty rhetoric when he excoriated this "remorseless foe to mankind," finally exhorting the doctor with the words: "Hold, hold thy exterminating hand."[13] At the end of the *Discourse*, there is a return to a more moderate tone as Morgan once again lauds the city and the College and reaffirms the positive advantages of his proposals. But after the preceding outburst, it must have appeared to his audience that medicine in the colonies was a threat to their health and that they should heed his words.

For all its idealism, Morgan's *Discourse* bore little relation to the medical course which was initiated that year at the College. Nonetheless, in putting forward these proposals, Morgan could draw on his own varied experience. When he criticized the teaching and practice of medicine in the colonies, he did not speak as an inexperienced graduate of a prestigious European university, for his own career before his departure for Britain had given him the right to speak out. If his European training had equipped him with the status necessary to voice his proposals and to become himself the first collegiate professor of medicine in the colonies, it was previous experiences in and around Philadelphia which enabled him to describe the state of American medicine with such feeling. It is therefore of some interest to return to his earlier activities and, at the same time, to see the way his horizons were widened and his ambition to found a medical school was fixed by his years abroad.

John Morgan's first contact with the medical profession as the apprentice of John Redman, had consisted of running errands and mixing drugs for his master and observing him at work. Redman, who became the first president of the College of Physicians of Philadelphia, had trained in London and Edinburgh before receiving his medical degree from the University of Leyden, the most famous center of medicine in Europe for a half a century longer than Edinburgh. But his training was the exception at a time when most of the physicians in Philadelphia had gone straight from medical apprenticeship to practicing on their own account. Although a great deal could be learned during an apprenticeship with a good master, there were many shortcomings, not necessarily of a medical variety, inherent in the situation. Benjamin Rush, another of Redman's gifted apprentices whom Morgan encouraged to go to Edinburgh after he had attended the first medical lectures in Philadelphia, points out the gulf separating teachers interested in the academic progress of the young men they are instructing and doctors whose students are also their apprentices. A barrier of status inevitably separates the younger man from the practicing physician whom he pays for the privilege of serving. Comparing his professor in Edinburgh, Joseph Black, to his master in Philadelphia, Rush wrote: "There are *teaching* and *ruling* masters. I cannot say I ever received a single idea from Dr. Redman, whereas I have received some hundreds from Dr. Black. I owe Dr. Redman no obligations. . . . But to Dr. Black I owe most of the knowledge I possess. He has conferred a thousand favors and marks of friendship upon me, although I never pounded his mortar or posted his books six long years to deserve them."[14]

If Morgan's longest exposure to an important aspect of colonial medicine was as an apprentice to a successful Philadelphia practitioner, he subsequently had the opportunity of seeing for himself just how bad medical treatment could be and experiencing the low esteem in which doctors were generally held in the colonies. Soon after he graduated from the College in 1757, he took a post as regimental surgeon, and it was only because a commission as ensign was procured for him by his friends that he was paid as an officer. Without a similar advantage, a simple surgeon might earn little more than a cook. Even so, Morgan frequently had to purchase supplies out of his own pocket. When, on one occasion, he asked for additional help, the response was to promote him to lieutenant after which he was expected to provide for his own assistant from the increase in his pay.[15]

The battlefield in the late fifties was the forest along the western frontier of Pennsylvania where war was intermittently waged against the French and the Indians. Further animosities involved the rival claims to land by the colonies of Pennsylvania and Virginia. In addition to the enemy who took their toll of men wounded in skirmishes, there were other potent foes to contend with: scurvy, dysentery, fevers, and the dreaded smallpox. With only one doctor covering a wide area and obliged to travel from post to post to tend to casualties, the sick and wounded were frequently left unattended or were cared for by others in their company. There was, moreover, little real understanding of how to prevent the havoc caused among the troops by infectious diseases and malnutrition. What Morgan experienced at the time was but a foretaste, mild in comparison with the medical horrors of the Revolutionary War when he found himself cast in the role of director general and chief physician of the Continental Army. For the moment, however, Morgan's internship with the military ended when the provincial forces disbanded in 1760 at the close of the French and Indian War. Faced with settling down to medical practice in the city, the twenty-five-year-old John Morgan elected instead to go abroad to continue his study of medicine in London and Edinburgh.

Morgan never surpassed the academic and social distinction which was his during the five years that he remained in Europe. Arriving in London with letters of introduction to Franklin and Penn, he gained immediate access to the group of influential men most concerned with the American colonies. It was understood that, in selecting a program of study, he would let himself be guided by the eminent physician, John Fothergill, who, although he never visited America himself, was representative for several colonies in which both his father and a brother had traveled as Quaker preachers. Fothergill had a particularly lively interest in the development of medicine in the New World, and he kept himself informed about all manner of other scientific discoveries across the Atlantic. Having understood the implications of Franklin's *Observations on Electricity* when it was communicated to the Royal Society in 1751, Fothergill had taken it upon himself to supervise its printing and had written a preface to the work. Another of his interests was botany, and he obtained plants from John Bartram in Philadelphia for cultivation at his country estate, later the largest private botanical garden in England.[16] So many were the claims on his time that it had become his custom to invite visitors to breakfast with him. In the 1760s, he successively received William Shippen, John Morgan, and Benjamin Rush in this manner—the men who later occupied three of the four original chairs in the medical department of the College of Philadelphia.

On Fothergill's advice, Morgan first became a student at St. Thomas' Hospital, which entailed little more than the right to watch surgeons at their work and to ask them questions. More important for his training was his connection with William Hunter, one of the most important teachers of the time, with whom he studied anatomy. Departing from the usual didactic method of teaching the subject, Hunter procured cadavers for the practical instruction of his students. He freely imparted the secrets of preparing anatomical specimens through the method of injection and corrosion, with the result that, during Morgan's later travels, he was able to demonstrate the technique to the doctors on whom he called in Paris and Padua, and he received considerable praise and attention for his skill from the great Morgagni.

Before leaving London to enroll at the University of Edinburgh, Morgan was joined by William Shippen, his former classmate, who had just received his medical degree from the Scottish university. While they were together, it seems more than likely that the two Philadelphians discussed the subject of introducing the study of medicine at the College in their home city. Medical education in the colonies was a live issue among the American students who met in Edinburgh, and the project for a school is mentioned in a letter Fothergill wrote to one of the managers of the Pennsylvania Hospital on Shippen's return home in 1762, and again three years later when Morgan arrived back in Philadelphia. While they were in London, Morgan and Shippen witnessed the coronation procession of George III from a vantage point opposite Westminster Hall. From that time

William Shippen (1736–1808)
attributed to Gilbert Stuart
First professor of surgery and anatomy at the College of Philadelphia (1765). Educated at the College of New Jersey and by his father, a prominent Philadelphia physician and a founder and trustee of the College. The younger Shippen studied obstetrics in London and, after receiving his M.D. from Edinburgh, he opened a course in anatomy in 1762, beginning a career during which he was frequently assailed by citizens who suspected early anatomists of grave-robbing. Shippen succeeded John Morgan as director-general of the Military Hospital and physician-in-chief of the American army (1777). After the Revolution, he served as professor of anatomy, surgery, and midwifery at the University until 1806.

on, however, they seem to have been perpetually pitted against each other
in situations of rivalry and acrimony. The royal celebrations of 1761 seem
also to have marked the end of civil social relations between the first
collegiate professors of medicine on the American continent, each a
Philadelphian and both of them on the faculty of the College.

With the crowning of its first English-speaking monarch in a great many
years, London was enjoying a heyday of power and wealth at the hub
of the largest commercial empire in the world. In this period, Edinburgh
was in the midst of an intellectual flowering unequalled anywhere else, with
such giants as David Hume and Adam Smith identified with the city and
the university. In the course of its forty years' existence, the school of
medicine had come to rival the University of Leyden where a number of
eminent Scottish physicians had trained at the end of the seventeenth
century before returning home to set up the Royal College of Physicians in
Edinburgh. The medical school, founded in 1726, immediately attracted
able and well-trained men and, by the time Morgan and other idealistic
young Americans arrived on the scene, William Cullen was proposing a
systematic theory of medicine which had a profound effect on Morgan and
the subsequent systematization of medical science by John Brown in
Scotland and Benjamin Rush in Philadelphia.

Much of the intellectual stimulation which Morgan enjoyed at
Edinburgh was the result of his unanimous election to the prestigious
student Medical Society, a membership so highly regarded that it gave him
an entrée to the highest scientific circles on his later travels in Europe. A
paper he prepared for this society on the formation of pus was the subject
of the thesis that he defended with the customary formality in public and
entirely in Latin, in order to qualify as an M.D. Soon after receiving his
degree, Morgan departed for the continent on the Grand Tour without
which no young gentleman's education could be considered complete.
Reflecting the paradoxical sentiments of many a tourist after him, Morgan
wrote afterwards to William Smith: "I am glad 'tis over. I would not have
missed the scenes I have gone through within this twelve month for a good
thousand, nor would I have to go through them again for as much more."[17]
In the same letter, he congratulates himself on the company he has kept:
entertained as part of the retinue of the King's brother, the Duke of York,
in Leghorn, he had further received an audience with the King of Savoy in
Turin. Despite a warning in the Bible of his mother's Quaker family against
priestcraft and holy water, John Morgan had even been received privately
by the Pope.

At the same time, he had worked assiduously to gain admittance to the
most eminent learned societies in Europe. In the course of his travels, he
had been invited to join the Roman literary society of the Accademia degli
Arti and been made correspondent by the French Académie Royale de
Chirurgie. Back in London, he was elected to the Royal Society after being

sponsored by an eminent group of men, and he sought and gained membership in the Royal College of Physicians of both London and Edinburgh. Clearly, his success in the British Isles was sufficiently known for him to have remained in London and started a successful career there had he so desired. But his loyalties and his ambitions tied him to his homeland. Loaded with honors from the Old World, he returned to Philadelphia with the international prestige necessary for his aim of immediately founding a medical department at the College in that city.

Among the first medical students in the year 1765 was Benjamin Rush, a graduate of Princeton, known at the time as the College of New Jersey. That year, and for some time to come, the entire curriculum in medicine was taught by two professors who occupied, in the ancient wisecrack, not chairs, but settees. William Shippen, although slighted by Morgan's brief and frosty mention of him in his *Discourse*, nonetheless applied for the professorship in anatomy and was duly elected to that position by the trustees. The *Pennsylvania Gazette* announced that Shippen would lecture on anatomy at the College, while Morgan would teach materia medica, a subject to which he appended a brief survey of chemistry. Students were admitted to the lectures on the purchase of a ticket of instruction, and, in the first years, these took the form of playing cards endorsed with the signature "John Morgan, M.D., FRS & Profr of Medicine," accompanied by his seal.[18] Of the local apprentices who enrolled in the lectures, ten went on to become the first recipients of a medical degree in America. At the commencement of 1768, they were awarded the Bachelor of Medicine, the traditional British degree in the profession. The defense of a Latin thesis was considered an essential requirement for the doctorate.

The year that the first medical degrees were awarded in the colonies, Rush received his M.D. from the University of Edinburgh. He had followed in the footsteps of his two Philadelphia professors by studying in London and Edinburgh. Rush's first school had been the West Nottingham Academy in Maryland, where both John Morgan and William Shippen had preceded him. In *Travels Through Life*, qualified as "an account of sundry incidents and events in the life of Benjamin Rush" and penned half a century later for the "Use of his Children," Rush leaves a most favorable impression of the methods and principles of his teacher, the Reverend Samuel Finley, who was also his uncle by marriage. In addition to academic studies and training in manners and morals, Rush recalls with approval the instruction in "practical agriculture" at the Academy: hay-making time at West Nottingham was an introduction to an aspect of education which Franklin and others considered particularly important in the colonies. Rush writes that the activity "begat health and helped to implant more deeply in our minds the native passion for rural life."[19]

Rush left for Princeton at the age of fifteen and graduated the year

Caspar Wistar (1761–1818)
by Samuel B. Waugh, after the portrait by Bass Otis
Successor to Rush in the chair of chemistry (1789), adjunct professor of anatomy and midwifery and surgery (1792–1808), and successor to Shippen as professor of anatomy at the University of Pennsylvania (1808–1818). Born in Philadelphia, Wistar graduated from the University (M.B. 1782) and completed his medical education in London, Dublin, and Edinburgh, where he received his M.D. (1786). President of the American Philosophical Society and the Society for the Abolition of Slavery and author of the first American textbook in anatomy (1811), he possessed a collection of anatomical specimens which was presented to the University on his death. The wisteria vine introduced from China by his friend Nuttall, the botanist, was named after him.

before Finley was elected its president. In other associations with the College of New Jersey, he was happily married to the daughter of an influential trustee and, while studying in Scotland, he was instrumental in persuading John Witherspoon (and particularly Mrs. Witherspoon) to leave Paisley and take up the presidency of the college.[20] Many years afterwards, Rush's principles obliged him to withdraw his oldest son from the college after the "poor deluded boy" had been caught gambling on the sabbath.[21] On his own graduation, the opinion was expressed that he was well suited for the law and would "make a better figure at the bar, than in the walks of a hospital." Samuel Finley, however, advised him to fast and pray before coming to any decision, and soon afterwards, Rush became the apprentice of John Redman, the Philadelphia physician.[22]

In his autobiography, Rush goes on to describe his life as a medical apprentice and his years of study abroad. A little advertised aspect of journeying to the Old World in the pursuit of education emerges from his account of the voyage across the Atlantic. Although he allayed Mrs. Witherspoon's fears about the crossing, Rush "suffered much from sea-sickness" himself and took laudanum as an antidote. Describing the discomforts of both the outward journey and the voyage home, he quotes Franklin as saying that " 'there were three classes of people who did not care how little they got for their money, viz. school boys, sermon hearers, and sea passengers.' "[23] The *Travels* give little account of the sights of Europe, descriptions he gladly left to others. His early observations as well as the remarks in the commonplace books he kept in later life indicate that Rush was mainly concerned with the personalities of the men of learning and position with whom he became acquainted.

If the son of Lord Auchinleck, James Boswell, had disagreeably characterized John Morgan as a humorless coxcomb after traveling with him through Holland, Rush redresses the balance by quoting remarks made by Samuel Johnson about his biographer at a dinner party given by Sir Joshua Reynolds. Johnson described Boswell on this occasion as "much given to asking questions . . . not always of the most interesting nature," an example being a query about the difference between apples and pears. On the same occasion, Rush records that Johnson himself was given to speaking in a commanding manner and treated the "gentle and unoffend-ing" Oliver Goldsmith with great rudeness.[24]

One celebrity Rush frequented in London is of particular interest to Pennsylvanians. The somewhat tenuous association between the Reverend George Whitefield and the University of Pennsylvania is impossible to overlook on account of the lively statue of the renowed evangelist which stands in the Quadrangles. As a boy, Rush had heard him preach in Philadelphia, possibly in the New Building itself. He had personal connections with Whitefield since his uncle, Samuel Finley, was one of the leaders of the "New Lights" branch of the Presbyterian Church started by

The House of Dr. Philip Syng Physick (1768–1837)
Maintained by The Philadelphia Society for the Preservation of Landmarks
The finest surviving house of an early faculty member is the Federal period mansion at South Fourth Street occupied from 1815 by Dr. Philip Syng Physick (A.B. 1785), a member of the medical faculty for thirty years and known as "the Father of American Surgery." Here are displayed gifts from grateful patients including Joseph Bonaparte and Chief Justice John Marshall (LL.D. 1815). Restoration was made possible through the generosity of another alumnus, University trustee, the Honorable Walter H. Annenberg.

Whitefield after he diverged from the Methodist Revival of John Wesley. Referring to the latter as "Mr. Westley," Rush declares that he was the more learned of the two, although he describes Whitefield as being more eloquent. Franklin attests to this characteristic when he recalls the effect of Whitefield's oratory on a firm and rational intention on his part not to contribute to a charity "preach'd up" by Whitefield. ". . . I silently resolved he should get nothing from me. I had in my Pocket a Handful of Copper money, three or four silver Dollars, and five Pistoles in Gold. As he proceeded I began to soften, and concluded to give the Coppers." But in the end "he finished so admirably, that I empty'd my Pocket wholly into the Collector's Dish, Gold and all."[25] By all account a good man as well as an eloquent one, Whitefield informed his young visitor that he owed his continued existence to the prayers of twelve widows maintained at his expense near his church in the Tottenham Court Road. Rush was greatly struck by this remark. He also noticed the biblical verses concerning food and drink inscribed on the preacher's crockery, and years later he remembered the words written on the cup from which he had formerly taken his tea in Whitefield's parlor.[26]

When Rush left the College of Philadelphia for Edinburgh, John Morgan had suggested that he should make a particular study of chemistry in order to qualify himself for the position of professor of chemistry on his return. Rush corresponded with Morgan on the vicissitudes of his proposed election and describes himself as following "the plan you proposed to me when I left Philadelphia." His letters are full of "the great Dr. Cullen . . . [who] daily exhibits such surprising efforts of genius and learning that I am no longer surprised that you used to call him the Boerhaave of his age."[27] Rush returned from Edinburgh an enthusiastic follower of Cullen's System, and he attributed his later unpopularity to the fact that he had rejected the more practical teachings of Boerhaave, the great Dutch physician, on which the colonial doctors had been raised. In actual fact, most of the opposition he encountered centered on his heroic treatment of yellow fever during the epidemics which raged in Philadelphia towards the end of the eighteenth century.

During the summer of 1793, Rush's letters are full of the dreaded disease. He labored unstintingly for the sick and lost three of his dedicated apprentices at a time when most Philadelphia physicians were more interested in leaving town. Philip Syng Physick, the father of American surgery, attributed his recovery to Rush's treatment during which he lost "176 ounces of blood by 22 bleedings in 10 days."[28] Not surprisingly, some people balked at these measures; even Ebenezer Hazard, one of Rush's oldest friends, comments: "He is a perfect Sangrado, and would order blood enough drawn to fill Manbrino's helmet, with as little ceremony as a mosquito would fill himself up on your leg." When one of Rush's patients, having felt his own pulse, objected to further bleeding, Hazard reports:

Dr. John Morgan's Lectures, 1770
The founder of the medical department indicated his fellowship in the Royal Society on tickets issued for his lectures. Morgan's student, Jonathan Easton, introduced inoculation against smallpox to Newport, Rhode Island, in 1772.

"The Dr. pronounced 'this opinion as one of the most dangerous symptoms in the case; the disorder extremely critical; not a moment to be lost; send for the bleeder directly—if you are not *bled* today, I shall not be surprised to hear that you are *dead* tomorrow.' The patient declared he would lose no more blood; the Dr. declared he would no longer consider him as his patient, left him to *die* and the man *got well*."[29]

Rush was further involved in a dispute over the origins of the yellow fever: was it imported from the West Indies or, as he believed, of local origin, generated by the unsanitary conditions of the harbor and the sewage of the city itself? Rush bitterly describes his opponents as intent on "destroying the influence of a man who had aimed to destroy the credit of their city by ascribing to it a power of generating the yellow fever."[30] William Cobbett, the English essayist, never known for the moderation of his prose, made Rush the target of a damaging attack in his *Porcupine's Gazette*. After a successful libel suit had been brought against him, Cobbett used the final issue of his paper to report how Washington's attending physicians "took 9 pounds of blood from General Washington, who was *sixty-eight* years of age, while, during the same space, they gave him *three doses* of CALOMEL, or *mercury in powder*."[31] The President died on the "fatal day" on which Cobbett was also convicted for slandering Rush whose methods he considered very similar to those responsible for the President's death. Smarting under a $5,000 fine for his "squibs, puns, epigrams and quotations from Gil Blas," Cobbett set out to earn the judgment against him in good earnest by publishing several volumes of personal invective from the safety of New York in a journal expressly entitled *The Rush-light*.

Some of the opposition to Rush could, nonetheless, be ascribed to the "new" theories he had brought back with him from Edinburgh. Although he denied authorship of newspaper articles ridiculing Boerhaave and proclaims that the toast ascribed to him, "Speedy interment of the System of Dr. Boerhaave, and may it never rise again," was a calumny, he considered it indisputable that "Dr. Cullen's System . . . was built upon the ruins of Dr. Boerhaave's which was then the only prevailing system of medical principles and practice in America." Rush claims to have been introduced to republican sentiments during his student days at Edinburgh, and he came to see some relation between his politics and his medical views: "To the activity induced in my faculties by the evolution of my republican principles by the part I took in the American Revolution, I ascribe in a great measure the disorganization of my old principles of medicine."[32] When in turn he rejected Cullen's System, it was in line with his renunciation of all authoritarian systems in science and his profession as in politics.

One of the most interesting chapters in Rush's *Travels* is certainly his account of "political and military events in the years of the Revolution."

Rush gained prominence as a member of the Provincial Conference, and this body in turn elected him to the second Continental Congress. In this way, he ultimately came to be one of the signers of the Declaration of Independence. He had come to public attention, however, as a result of what he describes as "the frequent use I have made of pen and ink."[33] After being appointed to the first chair of chemistry in the colonies in 1769, Rush had composed *A Syllabus of a Course of Lectures in Chemistry*, the earliest American work on the subject. The beginning of a career in public affairs in Philadelphia was also marked, as he informs us, by numerous articles under a variety of pseudonyms, few of which have been identified. In one that was, the subject of patriotism—about which he wrote with deep feeling in private letters from abroad—is the occasion for an exhortation to his countrymen which appeared under the pseudonym of "Hamden" in the *Pennsylvania Journal* in 1773.[34] In this article, he inveighs against the enslavement threatened by the East India Company and the approaching chests of taxed tea. Rush also made notes for a tract on the separation of the colonies. When he met with Tom Paine, newly arrived from England, he played an important part in persuading the radical pamphleteer to write *Common Sense*, a work for which Rush himself chose the title.[35] In 1780, Paine received an honorary A.M., the first to be granted to an outsider, from the newly constituted University. Until this time, the degree had been reserved for faculty and trustees, the only other recipients being a few members of the clergy.

By the time the first Continental Congress assembled in Philadelphia, Rush had gained access to most of its members. He rode to Frankford to meet the Massachusetts delegates, and conversed with John Adams. Using a technique he had learned in London, he inoculated Patrick Henry, whom he describes as "amiable in his manners," against smallpox. By the following year, when Rush became a member of the Congress, he had become an ardent believer in the inevitability of separation.

In an entry in Washington's diary before his new responsibilities as commander-in-chief of the American armies put an end to such writing for the duration of the war, there is a habitually terse note for the date June 18, 1775: "Dined at Mullen's upon Schoolkill."[36] Rush elaborates on the events of the night when Washington was toasted in his military capacity for the first time since his appointment three days earlier. The tableau is no less powerful for the quarter century which had elapsed since Rush witnessed the event on the banks of the Schuylkill:

> The whole company instantly rose, and drank the toast standing. This scene, so unexpected, was a solemn one. A silence followed it, as if every heart was penetrated with the awful, but great events which were to follow the use of the sword of liberty which had just been put into General Washington's hands by the unanimous voice of his country.[37]

This is but one example of Rush's masterful use of his pen, which he did not employ exclusively in the service of medicine or politics. Salient personal detail for the purpose of heightening the dramatic quality of the events he records appears again in his account of the circumstances surrounding the Battle of Princeton. He makes only brief allusion to Washington's success in crossing the Delaware, choosing instead to elaborate on a minor incident which he had observed while in the company of Washington that Christmas day of 1776: "While I was talking to him, I observed him to play with his pen and ink upon several small pieces of paper. One of them by accident fell upon the floor near my feet. I was struck with the inscription upon it. It was 'Victory or Death.' " It was only later, after Washington's successful venture against the Hessians, that Rush discovered that these very words had been the password at the surprise attack on Trenton. During the engagement, Rush was impressed by the quality of the leadership around him, General St. Clair smiling calmly in the expectation of battle, General Mifflin in a blanket coat appearing to be "all soul." But, with his physician's eye for relevant detail, he was also profoundly afflicted by the horrible wounds of the soldiers, and all too aware of the tragic circumstances of the war.[38]

Rush gives an insight into the nonheroic aspect of the fighting through a personal anecdote. One of the enemy was a Scottish nobleman whom Rush had known in Edinburgh. His friend died in action, and his body was ignominiously thrown on a baggage wagon. It was only after a letter was found on him in which Rush had recommended a safe-conduct to Philadelphia from Generals Washington or Lee if he should be captured by the Americans that the young lord was buried with the full honors of war. The following year, Rush erected a stone over his friend's grave in Pluckemin, and he later retells his feelings as he picked a blade of grass from it. The poignancy of the episode is revived six years later in a letter to the fallen man's sister, in which Rush alludes to a love affair with her dating from his student days in Scotland.[39]

Although Rush was an ardent Whig and bitterly opposed to the Tories, he did not approve of the radical constitution adopted by the Commonwealth of Pennsylvania in 1776. He became a member of the Republican society which was made up of the moderate "anti-constitutionalists" who ultimately regained control in the state. Unlike many of the men of his day, Rush did not allow his judgment to be clouded by the emotions of Revolutionary politics. For this reason, his influence declined after Independence. While a member of a committee of inspection reporting to Congress, he opposed the intolerance he saw displayed by his party towards opponents of the war. In his autobiography, he ridicules the diehard or "furious Tory," but he is equally critical of their irresponsible fire-brand counterparts whom he derides as "furious Whigs."[40]

In 1776, he wrote gleefully about the discomfiture of his former

College of Philadelphia, 1790

A COURSE of LECTURES

On the

THEORY and PRACTICE of MEDICINE,

BY

BENJAMIN RUSH, M. D.

For Mr. *David Hosack*

Teacher and Student, 1790
Ticket of admission issued the year before the College of Philadelphia became the University of Pennsylvania. David Hosack (M.D. 1791), later a teacher at the College of Physicians and Surgeons in New York and a founder of Bellevue Hospital there as well as of the New York Botanical Gardens, was the first to ligate the main artery to the leg to reduce pressure and prevent bursting. He was the attending physician at the Burr-Hamilton duel in 1804.

associate, Provost Smith, whose "insolence and villainy" could no longer find party protection.[41] But he expressed opposition to the arbitrary treatment of the College of Philadelphia by the Commonwealth, and he initially refused to accept a position at the reorganized University of the State of Pennsylvania. In 1783, he relented and resumed his post as professor of chemistry; but he supported Smith's battle with the legislature, and shifted from the University to take up his old position when the College was reinstated in 1789. With Smith's position on the property rights of the former trustees Rush appears to have been in full accord: he remarks in passing on the fact that "the College of Philadelphia was finally thro' the industry and perseverance of its former Provost restored to its *just owners*."[42]

Rush suspected sectarian motives behind the reconstitution of the College on the part of the predominantly Presbyterian members of the legislature. Their move affected his own behavior in two ways: he suggested that a Presbyterian institution should be established in Carlisle, and this came about with the establishment of Dickinson College in 1783, named for the president of the Supreme Executive Council of the State of Pennsylvania. At the same time, Rush quit the First Presbyterian Church where the Reverend John Ewing was pastor in protest against the clergyman's appointment as provost of the newly organized University of the State of Pennsylvania.[43]

After the Revolution, Rush continued to play a part in other affairs of public concern. Ever since his return from abroad, he had been an ardent abolitionist, a fact which had initially brought him into contact with Tom Paine. If his opposition to capital punishment originally had the support of but three persons in Philadelphia, he had the satisfaction of seeing it become the prevailing view, particularly of the Society of Friends.[44] Throughout his life, however, Rush dedicated himself first and foremost to the practice and improvement of medicine.

One of his most original contributions was his approach to mental illness. For thirty years, while on the staff of the Pennsylvania Hospital, Rush kept careful records of the "lunatiks" among the patients. From the start, he protested against the inhuman conditions in which the insane were housed, in opinions expressed first to the managers of the hospital, then in public. In 1792, he was responsible for an appropriation in the state legislature for $15,000 for the construction of a special wing at the hospital which, for the first time, included bathing facilities. Rush ascribed mental illness to physiological causes and among the remedies he prescribed were purges and bleeding. Along with these, however, he advocated "acts of kindness" and the provision of useful occupations. On the subject of enforced idleness he wrote: "Man was made to be active. Even in paradise he was employed in the healthy and pleasant exercise of cultivating a garden. Happiness consisting in folded arms, and in pensive contemplation, beneath rural shades, and by the side of purling brooks, never had any existence, except in the brains of mad poets and lovesick girls and boys."[45] A year before his death in 1813, Rush published his last work, *Medical Inquiries and Observations, Upon the Diseases of the Mind*, which remained the only comprehensive treatise on the subject for seventy years.

In addition to his fame as a teacher and writer on medical subjects, Rush was also recognized as the most distinguished physician in Philadelphia, and probably the country. He complains in his autobiography about opposition from his colleagues which, on more than one occasion, almost caused him to move to New York, and he also remarks on the ingratitude of poor patients whom he tended *gratis* and who afterwards deserted him on gaining a measure of wealth. Nonetheless, just after his confrontation with Cobbett had been concluded in his favor, he wrote:

> With all the folly and indiscretions in my life, with all the odium
> to which my opinions in medicine, politicks and religion have
> exposed me, . . . I believe I did more business, and with more
> profit, between the years 1769 and 1800 than any contemporary
> physician in Philadelphia. Thus it is the providence of God
> often blesses men in spite of themselves, and finally protects
> them from the evils to which an adherence to the dictates of
> their judgments, and well meant endeavors to promote knowl-
> edge and public happiness expose them.[46]

In acknowledging the rightness of his own judgment while admitting to a rather exaggerated tenacity, his evaluation throws light on the brief yet enigmatic appraisal of himself included among his *Characters of the*

Dear Sir   Washington Oct. 13. 08.

This will be delivered you by my grandson Th Jefferson Randolph who goes to Philadelphia to attend a course of lectures in natural history Anatomy, & Botany. he will also attend the lectures in Surgery, but as an amateur, and with a view to the care of a family when he shall have one, in a country situation where we have no surgeons & want them every day. he may then recollect and apply what he will have heard & seen in his attendance on the lecturer. the museum of mr Peale, the garden of mr Hamilton, the anatomical preparations & dissections give to Philadelphia advantages in these branches of science not to be had elsewhere in america. for his mathematics, chemistry &c he will go to Williamsburg where they are well taught, & where he will be making acquaintances among his own countrymen whose friendships will [add to his] happiness through life, more than if contracted in another state. tho' none of these pursuits, while in your city, will bring him within your cognisance, yet I could not let him go there without making his bow to you, as a testimony of my esteem for you, as well as a future gratification to him to have seen & been known to you. at the same time I must deprecate those notices & attentions to him, which would be trou[b] (giving him a taste for company would) blesome to you, & withdraw him from those pursuits which are the object of his journey, & for which he will have little time enough. accept the assurances of my constant friendship & respect.

Dr Rush   Th Jefferson

Thomas Jefferson's Letter to Dr. Benjamin Rush, 1808
The author of the Declaration of Independence sent his grandson to the department of medicine at the University of Pennsylvania because of his conviction that it was unsurpassed in America.

Revolutionary Patriots. Along with a careful characterization of each of those men who signed the Declaration of Independence, he remarks for his own part: "BENJAMIN RUSH. He aimed well."[47]

If John Morgan's ambition on his return to Philadelphia had been to institute medical instruction at the College, Rush was more interested in the treatment of patients although, as he notes, his academic position served to bring him to the attention of the public. Despite the benefactions of William Allen and his association with prominent men, including Franklin who had insisted on a loan to prevent him from running short of money on the Continent, Rush adamantly maintains that he started out without the benefit of name or connections in the city. As a result he began a practice among the poor, often working without payment. Many were the "risques" he took in making his calls, climbing up ladders and sitting on beds which threatened him with vermin as well as infectious disease. In acknowledging an obligation to tend the lowly as a part of his Christian duty, he gives an interesting account of a dream he had after recovering from a fever:

> . . . I dreamed that a poor woman came to me just as I was getting into my chair in Penn Street, and begged me to visit her husband. I told her hastily, that I was worn out in attending poor people, and requested her to apply to another Doctor. "O! Sir (said she, lifting up her hands), you don't know how much you owe to your poor patients. It was decreed you should die by the fever which lately attacked you, but the prayers of your poor patients ascended to heaven in your behalf, and your life is prolonged only upon their account." This answer affected me so much that I awoke in tears.[48]

Unconsciously or not, Rush perhaps recalled Whitefield's observation about the effect on his life and health of the grateful prayers of the widows he supported.

At the same time, Rush was certainly well aware of the enormous value to a student of medicine of the accompanying opportunities for observing disease along with the effect of prescribed remedies. But there is nothing coldly calculating about his heartfelt testimony on the subject: "If I have rendered any services to my fellow citizens or added any facts or principles to that part of the science of medicine which relates to Epidemics, I owe both to the knowledge I acquired by my familiarity with diseases among the poor, in whom they appear early, and in a simple state. To my unfettered prescriptions in their diseases I owe likewise much of my knowledge of the doses and effects of medicines."[49] In his appreciation of the advantages of such a practice for the advancement of medical knowledge, Rush was no different from Boerhaave, Fothergill, and Cullen himself, all of whom had treated the poor in the cities where they were later to make their mark. Rush's relation to the College of Philadelphia was also similar to that of Boerhaave in Leyden and Cullen in Edinburgh. In 1805, a

doctoral thesis was defended at the University of Pennsylvania entitled
"Remarks on the Medical Theories of Brown, Cullen, Darwin and Rush"
(some indication of the regard in which Rush's own system was held at the
time). His ideas had been crystallized under the obligation of composing a
new set of lectures when he succeeded to the professorship of the theory
and practice on the death of John Morgan in 1789.

Rush brought distinction to this new position by formulating a system
based on his own critical evaluation of his former tenets and influenced, as
he claims, by his conversation with students. Although it cost him sleepless
nights, he accomplished the task through the dedication which he brought
to every new challenge in his life. Students flocked to hear him from all
over the country, increasing from less than 50 in 1790 to 369 in 1810. His
lectures were described as "uncommonly eloquent, correct and interesting,"
and more students registered in his classes than in those of any contemporary. James Rush calculated that almost three thousand attended his
father's lectures in the years after his election to the senior chair.[50]

On succeeding to the chair previously occupied by John Morgan, Rush
had paid suitable tribute to the founder of the medical school.[51] The events
gave him pause, however, for, as Morgan's fortunes and health deteriorated,
he had given up teaching and, widowed and childless, had progressively
withdrawn from the world and from his medical practice. Rush also
recorded Morgan's tragic end, at the age of fifty-four, in his commonplace
book where he writes:

> October 15. This afternoon I was called to visit Dr. Morgan, but
> found him dead in a small hovel, surrounded with books and
> papers, and on a light dirty bed. He was attended only by a
> washerwoman, one of his tenants. His niece, Polly Gordon,
> came in time enough to see him draw his last breath. His dis-
> order was the Influenza, but he had been previously debilitated
> by many other disorders. What a change from his former rank
> and prospects in Life! The man who once filled half the world
> with his name, had now scarcely friends enough to bury him.[52]

The tributes to Rush when he died were very different in tone, and bear
witness to a life which more than fulfilled its early promise. They came
from his contemporaries who had helped shape the nation's history. On
hearing of his death, Thomas Jefferson chronicled his qualities of mind and
spirit in a letter to John Adams: "Another of our friends of seventy-six is
gone, my dear Sir, another of the co-signers of the Independence of our
country. And a better man than Rush could not have left us, more
benevolent, more learned, of finer genius, or more honest."[53] A year after
Rush had been laid to rest in the churchyard of Christ Church, fifty yards
east of the grave of Benjamin Franklin, Adams in turn reflected on the life
of Benjamin Rush: "As a man of science, letters, taste, sense, philosophy,
patriotism, religion, morality, merit, usefulness, taken all together, Rush
has not left his equal in America; nor that I know in the world."[54]

5

James Wilson, Justice

In the 1967 edition of the works of James Wilson, three-quarters of the
pages are taken up with the law lectures which he gave or planned for
delivery at the University of Pennsylvania, beginning in 1790. In presenting Wilson's writings, the editor, Robert G. McCloskey, comments on
the almost complete obscurity which now surrounds their author. The
variety of the contributions of this little remembered founding father of the
University and of the American Republic makes his fall into oblivion all
the more astonishing. For, as McCloskey states, Wilson was: "a signer of
the Declaration, one of the primary figures in the Constitutional
Convention, the leader of the ratification movement in Pennsylvania, the
architect of the Pennsylvania constitution of 1790, one of the six original
justices of the Supreme Court, the new Republic's first law professor, and
the only founding father to essay a general theory of government and
law."[1] To this list of Wilson's major accomplishments can be added a
number of other roles and titles, and these complete the picture of a
forceful and energetic representative of revolutionary and early federal
America: delegate to the second Continental Congress, elected colonel in
the Pennsylvania militia, proponent of the first Bank of North America and,
throughout his career, rapacious speculator in land.

Wilson employed his energies and talents untiringly in the service of
the Republic. At the same time, he was set on procuring both fame and
wealth for himself. One result of his personal ambition was that, during
his lifetime, his enemies often attributed his actions to aristocracy and
self-interest; and if history has failed to accord him his proper place in its
annals after his death, this may also be attributed to the disrepute of his
last years. In his confident optimism about the course of American
democracy and his predictions on this subject, Wilson showed greater
prescience than any of his contemporaries.[2] Yet, perhaps because of the
events connected with his financial collapse he seems not to have received
even the credit most certainly due him for his contributions to American
law and his part in setting up the new government of the United States.

During his life, Wilson associated with the great men of the time.
Because of the heroic dimension accorded to the founding fathers, there are

elements of a classical tragedy in the peripeteia of his disgrace and downfall. The dénouement with its disastrous ending was brought about by his relentless pursuit of material reward, and it has been described as a "peculiarly American tragedy."[3] On the human level, his fate would undoubtedly have been interpreted as the wages of his overweening pride by the strict Calvinist family he had left behind in Scotland. In a letter from Coul in 1769, his brother remarks: "Mother says it would give her more pleasure to see evidences of your being bound on the way to Zion and set out for the Celestial Country than to hear of your purchasing the greatest fortune." It must be added that even these dour, straight-laced Scots were favorably impressed by Wilson's position and influence, for the letter goes on," at the same time she thinks she has reason to bless God for countenancing you in your secular affairs."[4]

Wilson was born in 1742 in Fifeshire, on the windswept eastern shore of Scotland where every owner of rent-free land, however small, could call himself a laird and, most likely, boast among his possessions of: "a puckle [grain] of land, a lump of debt, a doocot [dovecote], and a law plea."[5] As the son of a farmer, when he won a scholarship to St. Andrews, Wilson entered the university as a "terner"—one of the third or common rank. His father died before he had completed his studies for the ministry in the strict "Associate Presbytery" to which his parents adhered. Forced to help support his sisters and younger brothers, he took a position, first as a tutor and later in accounting. An interesting sidelight on the determined character of the young Scot, already marked for success, appears in the description of his first game of golf. An Edinburgh merchant, Thomas Young, invited him to a few rounds, and Wilson proceeded to rout his host although he had never played before in his life.[6] Small wonder if he felt hampered by the narrow scope of employment open to a farmer's son as well as by the Presbytery's sanctions against the sin of pride. Not without difficulty, Wilson succeeded in gaining his mother's consent and incurred his first debt by borrowing from relatives to pay for his voyage to the colonies. In 1765, he arrived in America, vowing never again to make the stormy crossing from Glasgow to New York.

Wilson traveled on to Pennsylvania with a letter of introduction to Richard Peters, one of the trustees of the College of Philadelphia. He was immediately taken on as Latin tutor since men with his training were rare in the colonies. In the fall of that year, he taught Greek, Latin, grammar, and rhetoric and was rewarded at the commencement of 1766 with the honorary Master of Arts degree, reserved primarily for faculty, which he had requested. On the same occasion, the recently appointed professor of medicine, John Morgan, received a medal for a political essay. Having found his feet in Philadelphia by this time, Wilson foresaw that it would be advantageous for him to embark on the study of law. Another loan from a prosperous relative who had gone to school with him in

Scotland before settling down in Pennsylvania permitted the young immigrant to enter the law offices of John Dickinson, one of the most respected legal minds of the time. Dickinson would later play a prominent part in state politics and, together with his Scottish student, in the earliest independent government of the United States.

In less than a year, Wilson was admitted to the bar. He started practicing on his own in 1768, choosing to set himself up first in Reading and later in Carlisle. These were frontier communities where his adroit handling of land litigation cases brought him recognition and the beginnings of a fortune. During this time, he married an heiress for love, and under the influence of Dickinson, whose *Farmers Letters* had been a literary success, he contributed moralizing essays to the *Philadelphia Chronicle*. Written in collaboration with his friend Billy White, the articles were signed pseudonymously by "The Visitant." The identity of this personage was warmly debated in Philadelphia where few suspected that one of the two authors would later become the first Episcopal bishop of Pennsylvania, while the other would be among the original justices of the Supreme Court.[7]

In these years, Wilson continued to find time to lecture in English literature at the College of Philadelphia. From the beginning, however, his skills in writing and law were employed for political ends. As early as 1768, he composed one of the most cogent and lucid statements on the causes of the Revolution in a pamphlet entitled *Considerations on the Nature and Extent of the Legislative Authority of the British Parliament*. He was advised against publishing what amounted to an attack on Parliament; when it was finally distributed six years later, the atmosphere was one of defiance occasioned by the Boston Port Act. Wilson seems to have had the misfortune of being in the van of circumstances and announcing new ideas before the time was fully ripe. On this occasion, his statement that Parliament should have no voice in the affairs of the colonies was a radical sentiment although, when he had written it, Wilson was still convinced that there could be perpetual union with the mother country in a looser association under the crown. But it was many years before the British government came up with the idea of according dominion status to colonial possessions. By the time Wilson became a delegate to the Continental Congress, his standpoint had become that of a conservative Whig. His initial reluctance to vote for total independence caused a delay, and his resistance at this point was never forgotten. Yet it was principally occasioned by his own consistency in the face of rapidly changing circumstances.

The "Revolutionary patriot" recognized by so few Americans today was characterized in glowing terms by Benjamin Rush. No doubt Rush's memory was further enhanced by Wilson's eloquent defense of the Constitution for which both Pennsylvanians later labored unstintingly:

JAMES WILSON. An eminent lawyer and a great and enlightened statesman. He had been educated for a clergyman in Scotland, and was a profound and accurate scholar. He spoke often in Congress, and his eloquence was of the most commanding kind. He reasoned, declaimed, and persuaded according to the circumstances with equal effect. His mind, while he spoke, was one blaze of light. Not a word ever fell from his lips out of time, or out of place, nor could a word be taken from or added to his speeches without injuring them. He rendered great and essential services to his country in every stage of the Revolution.[8]

Having passed from radical to conservative views by staying in the same place, Wilson found himself in strong opposition to the Pennsylvania constitution of 1776. He became an active member of the Republican society and was ousted from Congress in 1777. Nonetheless, with business interests second only to his vigorous political activities, he moved his family to Philadelphia where he promptly gained notoriety and unpopularity by defending a number of wealthy Quaker loyalists, two of whom were executed for treason. Wilson's defense involved a thorough investigation of the nature of treasonable acts and provided a new and more limited definition which gave the individual citizen considerably greater protection against capricious and arbitrary accusations of treason. It is likely, too, that Wilson's adaptation of English law to the American situation in this instance provided the basis for the treason clause later introduced into the Constitution, since it was submitted to the Federal Convention by the Committee of Detail of which he was a member.[9]

In another development which raised the suspicions of his adversaries and produced a long and heated battle with the Pennsylvania radicals, Wilson saw a need to establish a national bank. Its first function would be to provide funds for the provisioning of the army. Wilson had read the work of Sir James Steuart, and had been struck by the similarity between the situation dealt with by the Scots economist and the state of affairs at home.[10] In America as well, he felt, it should be possible for notes to be issued on land and other securities since, as in all new countries, cash for further development was in short supply. Wilson acted as legal adviser to the Bank of North America and spoke eloquently in its defense; he "also became, quite promptly, its most persistent debtor."[11]

Throughout his public life, Wilson speculated in land, making huge purchases in the south and west as well as in the state of Pennsylvania. A small deposit was all that was required in order to procure a "warrant" or preliminary title to land which could then be surveyed. Clear title could be obtained later on payment of the balance. In order not to forfeit his original investment, Wilson engaged in all manner of complicated arrangements for raising money and, as land values rose, he was continually tempted to acquire greater areas than he could reasonably hope to redeem. Towards the end of the century, new settlers were failing to arrive in their hoped-for numbers to buy up the surveyed land, while investments from the Old World began to be diverted to finance the wars in Europe. It was then that Wilson suffered financial ruin along with a number of other prominent Philadelphians. The financier, Robert Morris, wrote: "I am seriously uneasy, for W—l—n's affairs will make the vultures more keen after me."[12] In his commonplace book, Benjamin Rush records 150 failures in the city over a period of six weeks at the end of 1796. He comments on the extreme measures taken by some victims of this crash and adds, with disapproval: "Judge Wilson deeply distressed; his resource was reading novels constantly."[13]

For a surprising number of years, however, Wilson managed to keep disaster in his personal enterprises at bay. In fact, during these years he made his greatest contribution to public affairs, playing a major role in drawing up the Constitution and achieving ratification by the State of Pennsylvania. At the Federal Convention, Wilson was one of the two men most familiar with the subject of political economy and thus in a position to judge the central problem of dual sovereignty. In most instances, he and the other principal proponent of federation, James Madison, agreed with each other. Wilson argued for a central government upon a broadly democratic base. As he was to describe it in his law lectures: "The pyramid of government— and a republican government may well receive that beautiful and solid form—should be raised to a dignified altitude; but its foundations must, of consequence, be broad, and strong, and deep. The authority, the interests, and the affections of the people at large are the only foundation, on which a superstructure, proposed to be at once durable and magnificent, can be rationally erected."[14] He favored direct popular election for the President as well as for both houses of Congress but later compromised and was instrumental in working out a plan for the electoral college.

Wilson was not only committed to popular rule but optimistic about the effect the will of the people would have on government. This faith in a relatively untried venture in democracy may have had its seeds in his background and upbringing. The area of Scotland where he had been raised was relatively poor but it was also egalitarian in the way property was distributed among social classes. Wilson was also influenced by the Scottish philosopher Thomas Reid, who had subscribed to the notion of a benevolent human nature. Given this view, it was possible to see men's behavior in society as being moral and not molded by self-interest alone.[15] While both Adams and Hamilton drew back from granting too much power to the common people, Wilson believed in universal manhood suffrage.

Wilson was one of only six men who signed both the Declaration and the Constitution, the only delegate to the ratifying convention of the State of Pennsylvania who had also been a member of the Federal Convention.

As such, he was not only called upon to explain the proposed Constitution but also became its most eloquent defender. The radicals, who were losing their hold in the state, still imputed aristocratic motives to Wilson's defense, although it was on the grounds of legal weakness that he had opposed the state constitution of 1776, and not because of the democratic principles on which it was based. A pamphleteer proffers the following ironical "receipt" for a stinging anti-Federalist attack. It must include forty mentions of MR. WILSON, along with "*Well-born* nine times, *Aristocracy,* eighteen times . . . and lastly GEORGE MASON's *Right Hand in a Cutting Box,* nineteen times." In defense of Wilson's stiff bearing which caused this Scottish commoner to be repeatedly accused of "aristocracy," a Federalist friend explained Wilson's "lordly carriage" as being the result of an effort to keep his spectacles from falling off his nose.[16]

Wilson's speech before the ratifying convention was widely read in the other colonies. On receiving a copy of it, Washington expressed the wish for it to be printed and circulated. The example of ratification by the large and influential State of Pennsylvania was of importance to the other states, and it had been achieved in large part through Wilson's efforts and eloquence. Ratification constituted a defeat for the western radicals in the state legislature whose influence had been gradually waning, with opposition from the Republican society which included men as diversified in interests and politics as Rush and Wilson. The experience Wilson had gained in drawing up the national Constitution stood him in good stead when, in 1790, he had the task of framing a new state constitution which closely followed the national model.

In the years since his service as tutor at the College of Philadelphia, Wilson had remained in touch with William Smith. He sympathized with the provost's claim that the statute of 1779 had been an abrogation of the original charter. Elected a trustee that year, he almost immediately found himself in the position of being "retained as Council [*sic*] and . . . required to undertake the Defence of the Charter Rights of this Institution before the House of Assembly."[17] At that time, his eloquence fell on deaf ears but, ten years later, he played a part in restoring all its former rights to the College. Not long after the restitution of the charter, Wilson made his most notable contribution to the history of the University.

In the first week after the trustees resumed their meetings in March 1789, they received a petition from "a Number of young Gentlemen Students in Law, who have formed themselves into a Society for their mutual improvement," for permission to hold their meetings in one of the rooms in the College. The request was granted, and the next year the time seemed ripe to Charles Smith, Esquire, to transmit the following opinion to the trustees through his father, Provost Smith: "That among the many other Improvements of the Plan of liberal Education in this College, the Institution of a Law Lecture or Lectures has been considered as very

necessary and essential." The petitioner was ready to offer his services to
the College as professor of law or, if this course of action was not
approved, to start lecturing anyway in the hope of receiving such
recognition thereafter. But, if the trustees were fully prepared to act on the
proposal for a professorship in law as they had been when they elected the
first professor of medicine, Charles Smith had not armed himself with the
credentials of a John Morgan.

A committee of three was appointed, including Wilson and Edward
Shippen, Esquire, and a report was promptly submitted on the purpose of
a "system of Law lectures in this country." A prime function would be to
explain the Constitution of the United States, so recently framed, and "to
ascertain the merits of that Constitution by comparing it with the
Constitutions of other states—with the principles of Government and with
the Rites [sic] of Man." The proposal for a history of the law from the
earliest times and the place allotted to a full explication of the common
law indicate the scope of Wilson's intended lectures. According to the
minutes, the plan was approved on Friday, 14 August, and on the following
Tuesday "Mr. Wilson, by a Ballot taken for choosing a Professor of Law,
was unanimously elected."[18]

Law had been taught for over a decade at William and Mary by
Jefferson's preceptor, George Wythe, while Judge Tapping Reeve's law
school in Litchfield, Connecticut, had been in operation for six years. The
importance of the lectures at the University of Pennsylvania, however, was
that they were systematic. Since they were the first to be inaugurated in the
Federal period, they presented Wilson with an excellent opportunity to
examine the Constitution. Delivered by a lawgiver who had achieved
prominence in the Federal debate and whose intellect and eloquence were
so generally admired, the lectures were an event of major importance in the
Republic.

In 1790, Philadelphia had just become the seat of government and
would remain the capital city for a decade. That year, Congress
reconvened in the city in time to attend the lectures on December 15. The
audience which assembled at the College Building at Fourth and Arch
was both prominent and, in Wilson's own words *"fair,"* for Martha
Washington had accompanied her husband and Vice-president Adams, and
there were other women present. The lectures were heard by members of
Congress and of the state legislature along with professional lawyers and
students, and the entire board of trustees who entered their invitation and
acceptance in the Minute Book. Some of the people in the audience had no
legal training, and this was in line with the purpose of the lectures, as
originally stated, to "furnish a rational and useful entertainment to
gentlemen of all professions, but particularly to assist in forming the
Legislator, the Magistrate, the Lawyer."[19] Wilson's claim to speak to the
layman as well as to the specialist appears in a rhetorical statement of the

people's role in democratic government: "The science of law should, in some measure, and in some degree, be the study of every free citizen, and of every free man. Every free citizen and every free man has duties to perform and rights to claim. Unless, in some measure, and in some degree, he knows those duties and those rights, he can never act a just and independent part."[20]

If John Morgan's *Discourse* at the foundation of the medical department occurred at the apogee of his career, Wilson's delivery of his first law lectures also appears as something of a climax to his professional life. Wilson took the event as proof that, in a land of lawyers, he was accepted as the most learned and profound legal scholar of his generation.[21] This certitude led him to join other office-seekers in proposing himself to George Washington as chief justice of the Supreme Court. When it came, his nomination was only as an associate justice. But the lectures provided him with an opportunity, only a short time afterwards, of laying the foundation for a system of American jurisprudence.

The lectures proposed by Wilson included nothing less than a complete survey of systems of law past and present, culminating in one adapted to the needs of the new Republic. Conscious of the importance for America of the English common law for which he had very great respect, Wilson nonetheless drew analogies with the great democracies of the past, for "government, founded solely on representation, made its first appearance on this, and not the other side of the Atlantick."[22] Like many before and after him, he emphasized the love of the American people for liberty and law; but his particular contribution at that moment in history was the synthesis he proposed between the two. The hard-nosed attitude of some of his contemporaries made them ready, at this point, to sacrifice many aspects of universal liberty to the rule of law. Wilson firmly believed that these ideals could coexist harmoniously in a democratic state. In this, he demonstrated a faith in popular democracy uncommon at the time.

The law lectures were intended to be given over a period of three years. With his customary energy, Wilson set about preparing compendious notes which amounted to a dissertation on the nature of law and encompassed epistemology and political theory, a study of natural law, common law, and the law of nations, as well as including the promised treatment of constitutional law with respect to the government of the United States and the Commonwealth of Pennsylvania. Not content with one vast project alone, he also began work on a complete digest of the laws of the state and the nation. As it turned out, Wilson actually delivered only about half the lectures he composed. He terminated the course after the second winter, and, although he was unanimously elected as professor of law when the College and the University of Pennsylvania were united, he never taught again. Bird Wilson, who assembled and published his father's writings in 1804, states the facts without further elucidation: "The causes of these circumstances are not within the Editor's knowledge."[23] It is certain, however, that, along with a preoccupation with his duties on the Supreme Court, there was also increasing pressure on him in these years from his business affairs. At the time when he had touched a high point in his life as legislator and scholar, his compulsive speculation was catching up with him. It is possible that his debts had already jeopardized any chance he might have had of becoming chief justice during his lifetime; now they were to lead to an ignominious end, not only to his temporal and material ambitions, but perhaps to his hopes of being remembered by posterity.

After 1797, there was no escape from his creditors. While he was out of Philadelphia on the business of the Supreme Court, Wilson was arrested and thrown into debtor's prison. Released on bail, he fled to North Carolina where he was jailed for a second time and also suffered an attack of malaria. Although money was somehow again procured to post bail, there were insufficient funds to feed and clothe the family. His young second wife, who occupied squalid rooms in the Hornblow Tavern in Edenton with him, writes of being unable to go out for want of shoes, and her youngest stepchild, in a letter from school in Pottstown about his papa's health, comments pathetically: "I am hardly fit to be seen my trousers is so bad."[24] Resisting to the last the idea of dismembering his vast empire of encumbered land, Wilson suffered a stroke during the torrid summer of 1798. Ruined in mind and body, goods and reputation, he died on August 21 and was buried far from the scenes of his triumph by the waters of Albemarle Sound.[25]

Even the law lectures which were assembled and printed after his death did little to restore Wilson's tarnished reputation. They had been intended for oral delivery, and, in some cases, all that he left were notes. The solidity of the content suffered from the incomplete form in which he had abandoned his ambitious project for establishing a new jurisprudence in America. In this way he lost the chance of being remembered as "the John Locke of America's Glorious Revolution."[26]

It was not until a hundred years later that a portrait of the University of Pennsylvania's first professor of law was painted for the new law building at Thirty-fourth and Chestnut Streets.[27] Copied from a miniature, now in the Smithsonian, it shows a man of ruddy complexion with a neat white wig who peers out from behind heavy spectacles perched on his snub nose. Another portrait looks down on the justices of the Supreme Court of America, a body whose function Wilson foresaw as vital to the government of the United States. Few of the men of 1776 played a greater role in establishing that government than the stiff Scottish lawyer, teacher, and University trustee who since his death has been almost completely forgotten by Pennsylvania and the rest of the country alike.

Pioneers of American Science

My grandson Th. Jefferson Randolph . . . goes to Philadelphia to attend a course of lectures in Natural history Anatomy & Botany. He will also attend the lecturer in Surgery. . . . The museum of M^r. Peale, the garden of M^r. Hamilton, the anatomical preparations and dissections give to Philadelphia advantages in these branches of science not to be had elsewhere in America.

Thomas Jefferson
to Benjamin Rush
October 13, 1808

6

David Rittenhouse

From the beginning, the College of Philadelphia had a scientific bias unusual at the time of its foundation. Of all the colleges which existed in the colonies prior to the Revolution, Philadelphia alone had introduced a course of study which put as much as one-third of its time into science and practical study.[1] Nonetheless, in the colonial period, men of science remained "amateurs" in the manner of the eighteenth century—observers and investigators who pursued their interests in private rather than attached to any institution. John Bartram, the first American botanist, is reputed to have left his plow to study the natural world around him. He started a botanical garden on the Schuylkill near the present grounds of the University of Pennsylvania and corresponded with Linnaeus and the European followers of that eminent Swedish scientist. His son, William, who continued his father's work, was an alumnus of the Academy. In 1782, he was elected the first professor of botany at the College, a position he never filled because of ill health and the need to absent himself on journeys of exploration and identification.

Another self-educated investigator of even greater distinction was David Rittenhouse: clockmaker, mathematician, and astronomer. Like Bartram, he is said to have first given an indication of his future interests while at the plow on his father's farm in Norriton, Pennsylvania. His brother recalled seeing "not only the fences at the head of many furrows, but even his plough and its handles—covered with chalked numerical figures."[2] With some unwillingness, Matthias Rittenhouse gave in to his elder son's bent and allowed him to set up as an instrument-maker in a workshop on the family property. In addition to being a respected craft, the clockmaker's trade was one known to involve skills in arithmetic and geometry, and it was not uncommon for gifted artisans to go on to achieve prominence in science and mathematics.

During his lifetime, David Rittenhouse achieved the highest acclaim for his science, his mechanical and inventive skill, and his steadfast character as a public figure and a politician. In the latter role, the modesty and virtue for which he was noted served to keep him almost entirely above the enmities of the partisan politics of the time. In fact, his association with the radical state government of 1776 and the Constitutionalists, before they were finally defeated in 1790, was one of that party's chief boasts. During the Revolutionary years he lent stature to an otherwise undistinguished group of political novices in the Commonwealth of Pennsylvania rather than becoming himself a target for the almost general abuse lavished on his associates.

In the *Eulogium* he delivered on the death of Rittenhouse, Benjamin Rush chose to emphasize the unlettered background from which this native genius had risen to a position of international fame. Far from being a drawback, his want of a formal education had permitted him to escape "the pernicious influence of monkish learning." Had he been subjected to the antiquated training suited to the European schoolmen of the fifteenth century, "instead of revolving through life in a planetary orbit, he would probably have consumed the force of his genius by fluttering around the blaze of an evening taper."[3] Rush was pleased to observe that the subject of his eulogy did not waste time in "composing syllogisms, or in measuring the feet of Greek or Latin poetry." Unfortunately, it was not a moment in history when men could profitably dedicate themselves to science alone, and even if he did not suffer the effects of the narrow education of his day, Rittenhouse's talents were nonetheless squandered later on in life. Patronage for independent research was not forthcoming in the Revolutionary period. Instead, Rittenhouse served as the treasurer of the State of Pennsylvania for thirteen years, as well as conducting numerous surveys for boundaries and border disputes; for "talents so splendid, & knowledge so practical in mathematicks are like mines of precious metals. They become public property by universal consent."[4]

In a letter to Rittenhouse, Thomas Jefferson deplores the wastage involved, however advantageous to the new country such patriotic service may be. With men such as Rittenhouse and Franklin in mind, he declares: "I am also satisfied there is an order of geniusses above that obligation [to government] & therefore exempted from it, nobody can conceive that nature ever intended to throw away a Newton upon the occupations of a crown." He goes on: "I doubt not there are in your country many persons equal to the task of conducting government: but you should consider that the world has but one Ryttenhouse, & that it never had one before." Although a patriot, Jefferson, the man of science, could nonetheless lament the loss to "the erudition of the world" necessitated by "the commonplace drudgery of governing a single state."[5]

The emphasis placed by Rush on Rittenhouse's unlettered background did not sit well with the astronomer's nephews. Their father, the Reverend Thomas Barton, had been responsible for recognizing and encouraging the genius of the slightly younger man, and the bond between them was cemented when Barton married Rittenhouse's sister. After his brother-in-law's premature death, Rittenhouse looked on his nephews almost as his

The House and Garden of John and William Bartram
Drawing by Edward C. Smith, reproduced with permission from the John Bartram Association
The first native American botanist and naturalist, John Bartram (1699–1777), named Royal Botanist to George III, laid out a botanical garden on the banks of the Schuylkill River in 1728 and built himself a stone house, still standing. The garden was enlarged by his son William who was named the first professor of botany at the University of Pennsylvania.

William Bartram (1739–1823)
by Charles Willson Peale
Independence National
Historical Park Collection
*Son of John Bartram, born in the house
built by his father on the Schuylkill and
educated at the Academy of Philadelphia.
He accompanied his father in journeys of
exploration in the Catskills (1755) and
the St. John's River (1765–1766) and
explored the southeastern part of the
United States (1773–1777). Elected professor of botany at the University of
Pennsylvania in 1782, he never filled the
position because of his travels and also
ill health. His book,* Travels through
North and South Carolina, Georgia, East
and West Florida, the Cherokee Country,
the Extensive Territories of the Musco-
gulges or Creek Confederacy, and the
Country of the Choctaws *(1791) was
widely read by naturalists abroad and
had a great influence on the Romantic
writers Chateaubriand and Coleridge.*

own sons and, when they became distinguished members of the faculty of the University of Pennsylvania, they did not respond favorably to the romantic but somewhat derogatory references to their maternal grandparents in whose simple household, it was presumed, David Rittenhouse had undergone a process of self-education similar to that of Franklin or Rousseau. William Barton refutes Rush and describes his grandfather, Matthias, as holding "the highly respectable station of an intelligent, independent farmer."[6] At the same time the younger Barton had no wish to detract from the genius of his uncle by attributing his scientific perspicacity to anyone else. The one exception was his own father who, by taking an appointment at the Philadelphia Academy on his arrival in the colonies from Ireland, had been in a position to provide Rittenhouse with valuable reading matter from an early date in their friendship.

There are few firm facts known about the astronomer's early education. At the age of seven, he is credited with having built a replica of a water mill of the sort he had seen at his grandfather's paper mill on the Wissahickon where he was born in 1732. Another tradition has him constructing a wooden clock while only a child. It is quite possible that Rittenhouse showed such skill at an early age, but another reason that much is made of these exploits in accounts of his boyhood is that his contemporaries wished to think of him as the American Newton. It was well known that the English genius from Grantham, Lincolnshire, had built a model windmill as well as a water clock and a sundial during his childhood. In another neat parallel which occurred in later life, Newton and Rittenhouse were both appointed director of the mint in their respective countries. In Jefferson's opinion, the talents of each were squandered equally in the service of the state or the crown.

Through Thomas Barton, Rittenhouse came to the notice of Provost William Smith of the College of Philadelphia. In his eulogy, Benjamin Rush divided the credit for discovering Rittenhouse between them, but William Barton corrects that misapprehension in his father's favor: "Perhaps it might be said, with greater strictness, that the 'discovery' here spoken of, belonged solely to Mr. Barton; by whom it was communicated, very early, to his learned and reverend friend, Dr. Smith."[7] At all events, the provost soon came to benefit from the association. Smith had been instrumental in introducing a curriculum at the College of Philadelphia which reflected his interest in science. Now, in his energetic pursuit of excellence, he labored for a number of years to bring the astronomer to Philadelphia. Even before Rittenhouse moved to the city in 1770, Smith maintained close scientific contact with the country genius.

An opportunity to enhance scientific knowledge as well as Smith's own reputation was presented by a rare astronomical occurrence on June 3, 1769. Smith appealed to Thomas Penn who donated a two-foot Gregorian

IXEA CÆLESTINA.
*Rad. bulbosa subrotunda. Caulis
teres, vaginatus Foliis lineari-
lanciolatis, cuspidatis. Floribus
expansis magnis cæruleis.
vid. Journ!
l.ª 184.*

Ixea Celestina
Botanical plate from
William Bartram's *Travels*
(Philadelphia, 1791)
*In addition to making drawings, the
author wrote lyrically of the Florida
vegetation "seemingly unlimited in
extent and variety; how the dew-drops
twinkle and play upon the sight,
trembling on the tips of the lucid, green
savanna, sparkling as the gem that
flames on the turban of the Eastern
prince; see the pearly tears rolling off the
buds of the expanding Granadilla [May-
Apple); behold the azure fields of
cerulean Ixea!"*

reflector for observing the transit of Venus, "a phaenomenon . . . which would never be seen again by any person then living."[8] The next transit of Venus would take place 105 years hence, and this event had important astronomical significance. Calculations of the solar parallax could be made by timing the course of the planet as it crossed the face of the sun from various places on the earth's surface. These data could then be used for computing the distance of the sun from the earth, and from this relation all other distances in the solar system could then be accurately derived.

If valuable for the advancement of scientific knowledge, the observations which were to be made from the Rittenhouse farm in Norriton had the further advantage of supplementing—as well as vying with—those sponsored by the American Philosophical Society, the scientific and scholarly association that Franklin helped found in 1743. These competing observations were conducted in Philadelphia by Vice-provost Ewing who, although outmaneuvered on this occasion by William Smith, later supplanted him when he became provost of the reorganized University after the Revolution. Ewing's equipment had been purchased from England with funds obtained from the Pennsylvania Assembly while Smith received an excellent reflecting telescope from Penn. Everything else needed for the observations of Smith and Rittenhouse were constructed by the astronomer. Among these instruments was an equal altitude instrument of simple but elegant design, a meridian telescope, considered the first of its kind to be built in America, and, of course, a clock. Among the lenses placed at his disposition were some which had been sent from England and were destined for Harvard's observations in Newfoundland. The lenses arrived in Philadelphia too late to be forwarded to Cambridge in time for the transit of Venus. Seven months later, on the occasion of a transit of Mercury, they were still serving a useful purpose at Norriton. Meanwhile Franklin in London was at a loss to explain their disappearance to John Winthrop, the Harvard astronomer.[9]

The superiority of the observations made by Rittenhouse and Smith, together with some machinations on the part of the latter, enhanced Rittenhouse's already growing reputation. By a maneuver too effective to be attributed to chance, Smith privately communicated the Norriton results to Thomas Penn so that they appeared through unofficial channels in the fifty-ninth volume of the *Philosophical Transactions* of the Royal Society. Meanwhile Ewing's account of the observations from the State House square was held up by a motion sponsored by none other than Smith in which it was resolved that the first official publication of both sets of findings should appear together in the American Philosophical Society's own *Transactions*. In this way, Rittenhouse's account alone achieved recognition by the Royal Society to which he would be elected in the last year of his life.

A year before Rittenhouse achieved international recognition as an astronomer, Smith had prevailed on the trustees of the College of

Philadelphia to award him an honorary Master of Arts degree. Apart from his role in some early surveys which had brought him to the provost's attention, Rittenhouse's skills were still practically unknown at that date. Even after his move to Philadelphia, his reputation was primarily as a clockmaker and manufacturer of fine instruments. About the time of his honorary degree in 1767, however, he started to work on a project which would not only test his knowledge and skill to the utmost but was of a nature to bring him national repute. In the first scientific paper delivered before the American Philosophical Society after it was refounded in 1768, Smith, as secretary, introduced a description of an orrery to be constructed by the Society's newly elected member David Rittenhouse.

The mechanical planetarium which Rittenhouse proposed to build would provide conclusive evidence of his preeminence as a mathematician and craftsman. Called after the title of Charles Boyle, 4th Earl of Orrery, for whom a mechanical planetarium had been constructed earlier in the century, the Rittenhouse orrery would exceed all existing models in ingenuity. Thomas Barton had done much to encourage his brother-in-law in this venture, even offering to indemnify him for his expenditures in the unlikely event that the orrery should not find a buyer. An early twentieth century professor of mathematics at the University has suggested that this agreement marked the first research fund to be set up in the State of Pennsylvania.[10]

Barton provided Rittenhouse with books on the subject; nonetheless, he insisted that the astronomer should rely principally on his innate genius: "I would have you pursue your Orrery in your own way, without any regard to an ignorant or prevailing taste. All you have to study is truth, and to display the glorious system of Copernicus in a proper manner;— and to make your machine as much an original as possible."[11] Rittenhouse was hardly in a position to receive detailed information about instruments constructed in distant lands. Besides, he followed his usual mode of procedure which was to present himself with the appropriate questions and then work out the proper solutions in solitude. The Rittenhouse orrery promised to be unique, a hope reflected in the endorsement by the American Philosophical Society: "If it shall answer his Intention, which they have the greatest reason to expect from his known abilities, they are of opinion that it will do honor to himself and to this Province."[12]

For a long time, the Rittenhouse orrery appeared on the seal of the University. It is described in the trustee minutes for 1782:

> The seal to be 2 Inches in diameter; The Device a front view of the Orrery belonging to the University, invented and made by David Rittenhouse, Esqr. Above the orrery a Star of the first magnitude in full Radiance, being one of the Thirteen Stars in the arms of the United States Representing the State of Pennsylvania. The inscription, Sigillum Universitatis Pennsylvaniensis.[13]

The Rittenhouse Orrery
The mechanical planetarium commissioned from David Rittenhouse by the College of Philadelphia in 1771 as it stands today in the Van Pelt Library, enclosed in a Chippendale case. After Rittenhouse was appointed professor of astronomy (1779), the orrery was used by his pupils at the University to study the movement of the heavenly bodies.

Nonetheless, the University did not gain its symbol without a battle, in the course of which the orrery ceased to be unique, becoming instead one of two identical planetaria.

Rittenhouse found himself committed to the construction of a second orrery after having been persuaded to sell the first to the College of New Jersey. On a visit to the astronomer in 1770 shortly before Rittenhouse moved to Philadelphia, President John Witherspoon of Princeton was entranced with the ingenious device. Aware of the importance of this wholly American achievement, he proceeded to offer Rittenhouse £300 for his creation even though the sum exceeded all the funds allotted by his college for scientific apparatus. When Smith read in a newspaper report about this coup on the part of a rival institution, he pronounced himself "mortified." Although he had not yet raised money for the purpose, he thought Rittenhouse had understood his intention to procure its purchase by either the Commonwealth or the College. As he declares: "This state is willing to honour him as her *own*." Fortunately, Governor John Penn was

The Orrery Seal, 1782
The device of the old College of Philadelphia, a pyramid on a table-top of seven books representing the branches of knowledge, was replaced by a new seal designed by alumnus Francis Hopkinson (1782), showing the Rittenhouse orrery. The use on the corporate device of this fine piece of scientific apparatus created by the University's professor of astronomy emphasized the eminence of science and reason in the view of the new "Revolutionary" board of trustees. The orrery seal was used intermittently until 1847.

in complete agreement with Smith's indignant complaint that Rittenhouse "should think so little of his *noble* invention, as to consent to let it go to a village; unless he had first found, on trial, that his friends in this city had not spirit to take it."[14] A compromise was worked out and it was agreed that the Princeton orrery should not be delivered until after a second planetarium had been completed.

In 1771, Princeton gained possession of its orrery although it arrived without the lunarium specified for the side panel. For some reason, the University of Pennsylvania's orrery which now graces the Van Pelt Library did not in the end enrich its creator. This fact appears in the characteristically self-effacing letter that Rittenhouse addressed to the trustees of the University at a time when the institution was attempting to clarify the financial claims against it by the first provost of the College. Rittenhouse mildly discloses the disparity between the sum he had received and the grandiose payment which had figured in resolutions by the legislature of the State of Pennsylvania in its first enthusiasm to support a work of American genius. Of the £109.10 received by Rittenhouse, £65 went immediately to Parnell Gibbs and John Folwell, joiners, for the Chippendale casing. Rittenhouse's only remuneration was the difference between these amounts, and he had had to share "the drudgery of raising it" by lecturing on the subject of the orrery.[15]

The tone of the letter is unruffled even though it appears that Smith was attempting to recoup the sum paid for the orrery as though he had financed its purchase out of his own pocket. Despite the very different politics of the two men, their scientific interests long prevented their personal association from coming to an end, and Smith's standing was undoubtedly enhanced by his friend's contributions. Rittenhouse's most substantial connection with the University, however, began at the moment of eclipse of Provost Smith. At the time that the provost was forced to step down in 1779, Rittenhouse became a trustee. He had been elected treasurer of the Commonwealth in 1777 and his position made him an ideal selection for an appointment at the new University of the State of Pennsylvania. Thus began an affiliation which the astronomer had long enjoyed almost by proxy. Both Ewing and Rittenhouse resigned as trustees shortly afterwards on being appointed provost and vice-provost of the University.

Arrangements were made for the former rivals to share in the instruction of natural philosophy. As professor of astronomy, Rittenhouse would join with Ewing, and their combined efforts would represent a further advance in the scientific evolution of the University. Rittenhouse had already given lectures on his orrery as well as acting as an unenthusiastic demonstrator of scientific apparatus during a former absence of Smith from the College. Apparently, he took little pleasure in public speaking although the oration on astronomy which he delivered before the American Philosophical Society in 1775 was a dazzling success. On that occasion, it seems, the scientific and philosophical weight of his discussion compensated for his style of delivery. For he reportedly pronounced the "sentiments," described as "ingenious, original, and in some instances sublime," in a feeble voice, and "without the advantages of oratory."[16]

Rittenhouse resigned his professorship in 1782, whereupon he was immediately reappointed a trustee. In this post he remained till his death, despite an attempted resignation which was accompanied by the gift of a rare one-handed regulator clock with the main dial calibrated in minutes— an early example of a digital clock—which today stands in the president's office. When the restored College and the University combined in September 1791, the astronomer was among the dozen trustees whom the University of Pennsylvania inherited from the short-lived University of the State of Pennsylvania.

David Rittenhouse was, in the estimation of his contemporaries, the natural heir to Franklin. He regarded the older man with respect and, with Franklin's friendship after his return to Philadelphia, Rittenhouse achieved the status of a revered figure in America. Again like Franklin, he was a scientific genius who served his country through politics—although Rittenhouse was more of a scientist than Franklin, who remains an eminent example of a philosopher in the eighteenth century sense of the word. The two men's differences and similarities are epitomized in the words of Rittenhouse's biographer, Brooke Hindle:

> The two men had been separated by a large gulf of years and a larger gulf in most of their characteristics: Franklin was easy and brilliant in the company of men while Rittenhouse was diffident. In science, Franklin was an intuitive, experimental genius without knowledge of mathematics while Rittenhouse was a fastidious observer, an inventive experimenter, and a master of the mathematics required for the pursuit of astronomy. Yet both had begun as mechanics, and both had remained true to their heritage which included the dream of a republic of virtue where the welfare of the people came first.[17]

As to public office, Rittenhouse often followed in Franklin's footsteps. His first entry into politics was in 1775 when he was elected to fill Franklin's unexpired term in the Pennsylvania Assembly, at which time he proceeded to add duties on the Committee of Safety to other calls made upon his scientific expertise by the war. On an intellectual plane, he succeeded Franklin as president of the American Philosophical Society, an event related in another sample of the verse of Provost Smith:

> What busy Mortal told you—FRANKLIN's DEAD?
> What though he yields to JOVE's imperious NODD?
> With Rittenhouse, he left his MAGIC ROD!

While he was in a position to do so, Provost Smith had energetically striven to provide Rittenhouse with a source of income which would have permitted him to devote himself to his science. Instead, his later life was burdened with the politics and projects of the Commonwealth, and it is astonishing that he succeeded in finding any time at all for the scientific investigations which constantly occupied his mind. In 1781, the legislature voted a few hundred pounds for an observatory, a far smaller sum than had been proposed prior to Independence. Nonetheless, the Commonwealth continually called on him to use his technical skills in its service, sending him off into the forest to survey boundaries between Pennsylvania and its neighbors. From these lengthy and hazardous treks into the literally uncharted wilderness, Rittenhouse returned with notebooks full of diversified observations. What remained behind was an astronomically accurate survey, and, on the astronomer's death, Rush was moved to exhort future generations who would benefit from Rittenhouse's labor in these words: "Philosopher or naturalist, whosoever thou art! that shalt hereafter traverse the unfrequented woods of the state, forget not to respect the paths, first marked by the feet of this ingenious, and faithful servant of the public."[19]

In the following century, various scientists at the University of Pennsylvania would follow Rittenhouse in making important contributions to knowledge. Among the most eminent of these was a descendant of Franklin whose surveying work was accomplished on a vast national scale. But Alexander Dallas Bache also went far towards establishing a position of mutual advantage between government and science. Through the efforts of Bache and his circle, the energies of creative scientists ceased to be frittered away. The importance of scientific research came to be recognized and supported, permitting scientists to serve society and simultaneously contribute to the universal world of ideas.

7

Alexander Dallas Bache

If nineteenth-century Philadelphia continued to be regarded as the
scientific capital of the nation, its position of eminence was an inheritance
of the original investigative minds of the eighteenth century, when, in
addition to the University, "the conjunction of the American Philosophical
Society, William Bartram's botanic garden, Rittenhouse's observatory, and
Charles Willson Peale's museum gave Philadelphia a good claim to being
the cultural center of the new republic."[1] At the turn of the century, when
the University of Pennsylvania moved to the building at Ninth and Market
Streets originally constructed by the Commonwealth as a residence for the
president of the United States, it was in a position to benefit from its
location even though its fortunes were at a low ebb at the time. In the
first decades of the century, problems of finance and discipline were
plaguing all the institutions of higher learning so proudly established in the
colonial period. At the University of Pennsylvania, the problem was
compounded by the unequal weight of a prestigious, self-perpetuating
board of trustees and an ill-organized faculty of four or five professors,
with no president—as there was elsewhere—to adjust the balance.
Meanwhile, American colleges in general were acquiring a reputation for
"riots and rebellion . . . and unpunished dissipation."[2]

Frederic Beasley who became provost in 1813 realized that much of the
indiscipline could be attributed to the extreme youth of the students. He
proposed that the age of students entering the University should be raised
from fifteen to sixteen as well as suggesting minimum entrance requirements—an innovation at the time. The University course was extended to
four years in 1826. Despite all efforts at improving the situation,
disciplinary action against student ring-leaders was difficult everywhere.
Nonetheless, Harvard expelled forty-three students after the "Great
Rebellion" of 1823, and expulsions and withdrawals also occurred at Yale,
where the dying behest of one president was that "discipline may be
preserved."[3]

In 1828, the Pennsylvania trustees took radical action by vacating
all the professorships in the department of arts. The faculty was
so small that the reorganization did not have an overwhelming impact

although it did permit the trustees to pension off the fifth provost. His indignation on being removed from office is reminiscent of the complaints of the first provost, William Smith. "Am I to be considered as responsible," protested Beasley, when the structure of the University was "acknowledged on all hands to be so radically defective in itself . . . operating in the midst of a population so unconcerned about its interests?"[4] Fair or not, the reorganization was beneficial to the University. One of the new faculty was Robert Adrain, the most gifted mathematician in America, who had previously taught at Princeton and Columbia. Among his original contributions, he gave the first proof of what is now known as Gauss's exponential law of error, which, had the work been done in Europe, would almost certainly have been named after Adrain.[5]

Another result of the trustees' action in 1828 was the appointment of a young Philadelphian to the professorship of natural philosophy and chemistry, a position which had been held in turn by the two scientifically oriented provosts, Smith and Ewing. The new professor, Alexander Dallas Bache, was only twenty-two at the time of his election, having graduated from West Point in 1825. A member of one of Philadelphia's most distinguished families, he was the bearer of a notable tradition in both science and politics. Some years later, at a time when Bache became the most influential regent of the newly established Smithsonian Institution, his uncle, George Mifflin Dallas, was the Vice-President, and one of his wife's uncles was a Senator who later became Secretary of the Treasury, a position formerly held in Madison's cabinet by Professor Bache's namesake, Alexander Dallas. His most celebrated ancestor, however, was his great-grandfather, Benjamin Franklin.

The young professor was well aware that his famous forebear had been associated with all the institutions where he, in turn, was carrying on his own investigations, and he made a point of underlining Franklin's priority in a number of scientific observations.[6] Even though Bache himself made great contributions to science and to its organization on a professional basis in the United States, his contemporaries constantly alluded to his intellectual genealogy. Thus his famous Swiss colleague, Louis Agassiz of Harvard, addressed him as "the learned *Grandson*," in the same way that his West Point classmate, Jefferson Davis, hesitated between grandson and great-grandson in his memoir.[7] Throughout his life, Bache encountered reactions similar to that of an elderly German savant: "Mein Gott, now let me die, since I have lived to see an emanation of the great Franklin."[8]

Alexander Dallas Bache grew up in Philadelphia during the University's most difficult days. With his family background of government service, both civil and military, he was sent, before his fifteenth birthday, to Sylvanus Thayer's young but already distinguished United States Military Academy. He graduated first among a distinguished group of cadets, and his classmates later recalled, with more enthusiasm than accuracy, that

John Fries Frazer (1812–1872)
Photograph by M. P. Simons
Vice-provost of the University of Pennsylvania and professor of natural philosophy and chemistry following Bache. Graduate of the University of Pennsylvania (A.B. 1830), he went on to study medicine as well as law. He published scientific papers on the subject of light and heat and was interested in mathematics as applied to mechanics. A founding member of the National Academy of Sciences, he displayed a continuing taste for contemporary French and English literature as well as the classics. He died the day after College Hall was opened in West Philadelphia while he was engaged in showing it to visitors.

"during the whole term of his course at West Point, he never incurred a single mark of demerit." Although this exemplary record has found its way into the *Dictionary of American Biography*, the Academy's conduct book, nonetheless, registers a number of minor infractions on his part.[9] It appears, however, that Bache was liked and respected from his earliest youth, and throughout his life he continued to be highly regarded as an original investigator, a gentle, persuasive educator, and a hospitable and tactful politician whom Benjamin Peirce, the Harvard mathematician and astronomer, sometimes addressed in his flowery letters as "My Darling Chief."

With the appointment of Bache, the trustees acquired a professor with a brilliant academic record, and a small amount of previous teaching experience, who, for some reason, encountered none of the disciplinary problems experienced by many of his contemporaries. In a eulogy in 1872, his lifelong friend, the physicist Joseph Henry of Princeton and the Smithsonian, wrote:

> His pupils could not fail to be favorably impressed by his enthusiasm and influenced by his kindness. He always manifested an interest not only in their proficiency in study, but also in their general welfare. They regarded him with affection as well as respect, and while in other classrooms of the university disorder and insubordination occasionally annoyed the teachers, nothing was to be witnessed in his, but earnest attention and gentlemanly deportment.[10]

During his tenure at the University there is no record of any complaints against Bache in the Minute Book. His practice appears to have been in keeping with his stated approach—one whose value was by no means widely recognized at the time:

> The strictest discipline is, in my opinion, consistent with kindness of feelings and mildness of action. Punishments are, no doubt, necessary in a school; and the good sense of a community of young people recognises, at once, when punishment is applied as a means of correcting bad habits and propensities; or when administered in the spirit of revenge.[11]

In his second year at the University of Pennsylvania, Bache became secretary to the faculty. In this capacity, he was obliged to record the many complaints arising from lack of discipline in the classroom. The problem was usually one of rowdy behavior, in which lectures were interrupted by odd noises or drowned out by the shuffling of feet or, occasionally, by eggs being thrown at the professors. Bache also signed the letter of acceptance sent to the parents of the twenty-eight freshmen admitted in 1829. As an official communication from the secretary, it gives a good idea of the priorities of the era. Punctuality and diligence and orderly conduct in chapel are demanded of the student, who is "required to demean himself respectfully to the officers of the College at all times," and "to abstain from injuring the buildings of the University by breaking, cutting, marking, or in any way defacing them." By asking the prospective student to sign and return a copy of these regulations, the authorities hoped to commit him to observing the rules.[12]

Bache was thus soon involved in the details of University administration. At the same time, the city to which he now returned remained, according to a contemporary account, "the Hot-Bed of Sciences, the nursery of the Arts and the Home of Philosophy."[13] In these surroundings, he was able to pursue his scientific investigations at the institutions of learning and research founded by his great-grandfather. Close to the University at which he taught daily was the Franklin Institute where, as principal director of scientific research, Bache took charge of experiments in heat and magnetism and made observations on meteorological phenomena. One problem on which he worked in these years is particularly significant in view of his later role in obtaining government support for research and in organizing technology in the service of the nation. The investigation concerned explosions in boilers, and it was carried out at the direct request of the Treasury Department of the United States. It set a precedent for future projects in which the government recognized the value of its support for applied research.

The subject which held the greatest fascination for Bache, in common with many scientists of the age, was terrestrial magnetism, which he continued to investigate throughout his life. In 1830, he built a small observatory in his Philadelphia garden where some of the data were collected for him by John F. Frazer who later succeeded to his professorship at the University. Frazer became interested in science as a result of taking part in these experiments at the age of eighteen. In later years, Bache set up the first magnetic observatory in the United States at Girard College after first convincing the American Philosophical Society, of which he was a member, that it was important to collect magnetic data. At Bache's prompting, it was resolved: "That in the opinion of the American Philosophical Society, it is highly desirable that the combined series of magnetic observations now in progress under the direction of the British government, should be extended to the United States, by the establishment of Magnetic Observatories at suitable places."[14]

Bache's own experiments were never limited to the laboratory. In collaboration with Edwin H. Courtenay who was, for a time, professor of mathematics at the University, readings were taken "upon a marble column in the yard of Professor Bache's dwelling, in Chestnut street near Schuylkill Sixth Street," or on another column in West Point "to the north of the residence of Professor Courtenay," and even "in the yard attached to the Hamden Coffee-house Hotel in Springfield, Massachusetts."[15] On his departure to Europe in 1836, Bache carried with him portable instruments

Henry Vethake (1792–1866)
Photograph by M. P. Simons
Professor of mathematics and then of moral philosophy (1855–1859), and vice-provost and provost of the University of Pennsylvania. Born in British Guiana, A.B. Columbia University (1808), he was professor of mathematics and natural philosophy at Queens College (Rutgers), the College of New Jersey, New York University and president of Washington College, Lexington, Virginia, before coming to the University of Pennsylvania. Trained as a mathematician and astronomer, he wrote two pioneer treatises, an Introductory Lecture on Political Economy *and* The Principles of Political Economy. *In his economic studies, he dwelt on the law of diminishing returns.*

for measuring the dip and intensity of terrestrial magnetism, and during his travels he acquired apparatus designed by Gauss himself.

By this time, Bache had already published papers on the variation of the magnetic needle in the *American Journal of Science* and the *Journal of the Franklin Institute*. His study of magnetism led later to his appointment as superintendent of the United States Coast Survey in which an immense triangulation from Maine to Florida was only the point of departure for a vast range of projects. On the other hand, early experiments concerning heat came to a premature end. According to the University of Pennsylvania chemist Provost Edgar Fahs Smith, his paper entitled "Inquiry in relation to the alleged Influence of Color on the Radiation of non-luminous Heat" is a scientific classic.[16] As recounted by his friends, however, the story behind the termination of this project bears witness principally to his self-control and sweetness of temper:

> One room on the sunny side of his house was appropriated to these experiments; the various thermoscopes and all the subsidiary apparatus were arranged there, and the apartment was held sacred to scientific investigation. One evening, while he was attending a session of the Philosophical Society, an alarm of fire broke out in the neighborhood. His mother, then a member of his family, heard the alarm, and hastily entered the room without a lamp, to look from the front window. A crash reminded her, too late, of the inconsiderateness of her movements.

On learning of the accident, Bache went out again, "white with emotion," but he returned shortly afterwards and consoled his mother for the effects of her clumsiness.[17]

It appears that Bache's equable temperament was responsible for his ease in handling students. Since disorders continued to plague the classrooms of many professors regardless of their field, his success cannot be attributed merely to the fascinations of the subjects of physics, chemistry, and geology.[18] In fact, Joseph Henry compared him with such notable contemporaries as Priestley, Davy, Dalton, and Faraday as an example of how "it is precisely among the most celebrated explorers of science of the present century that the most successful and noted teachers have been found." Bache was at all times engaged in a broad variety of experiments and investigations, and his case refuted the view that researchers do not make good teachers.[19]

Because of a keen interest in education in general, Bache was willing to give up his work at the University and in experimental laboratories to undertake an investigation of school systems in Europe. In 1832 an enormous sum of money had been left by Stephen Girard to endow a college for orphan boys. Bache was elected president of Girard College at a time when he had already been a professor of the University of Pennsylvania for eight years and a trustee of the proposed new college for three; by then, he was thirty years old. Girard College was not to open until eleven years later and Bache had resigned from his position long before that time. Nonetheless, he completed a thorough study of methods of education abroad. For two years, Bache spent time visiting the major school systems in Europe. On his return, he volunteered to organize the public school system in Philadelphia, and his vast experience helped to produce the best system of free education in the country. Indeed, Central High, the degree-granting school of which he became the first principal, was known for a time as the Bache School.

The educational approaches he observed during his travels abroad ranged from the methods of Pestalozzi in Switzerland to those of Thomas Arnold of Rugby. Although he was not permitted to attend a class in any of the English public schools, he found much to interest him in the British schools for younger children. He recommended German secondary education, notably the system he found in Prussia, but preferred the training given to teachers in the normal schools of France. In a general comment he assailed the amateur status given to theories of education at the time: "Few persons claiming to be enlightened go to those unlearned in medicine for advice; & still fewer do not resort to the lawyer when litigation is to be commenced or avoided, but every one erects himself into judge of what may be taught in schools & how it must be taught."[20] In his own approach to the subject, Bache displayed the analytic approach of the scientist. When the trustees of Girard College demanded an interim report, he pointed out that this could not be furnished by an objective investigator who, as he did not start out with preconceived opinions, was also averse to jumping to premature conclusions.

Not only did Bache acquire a particularly favorable impression of education in the German states, he returned with a lasting attachment to hock. His German wines were an element of some importance in his well-known hospitality in later life. As a visitor from Philadelphia, he further noted that Unter den Linden in Berlin was "wider than Market Street." In addition to the notes of his 666-page *Report on Education in Europe to the Trustees of Girard College for Orphans*, Bache kept journals in which, like many of his traveling countrymen, he recorded impressions of men and places. Among these is an amusing portrait of a nineteenth century "American tourist." Bache classified him according to his bearing:

> He talked to every one who could speak his vernacular, and spoke to every one who would give his broken French an answer. His meals were bolted down in haste. He fidgeted lest he should lose anything of the moon or sun rise, and actually, turned out to witness the former in regular Kickapoo style, wrapped in a blanket. . . . He was off among the first in the morning, and after the day's journey we met him in the evening at Meyringen, still talkative as ever, and his tones certifying that he came from east of the Hudson; so far, the very beau-ideal of the American figured by tourists.

Robert Adrain (1775–1843)
Artist unknown
Professor of mathematics and vice-provost of the University of Pennsylvania, having previously taught at Queen's College (Rutgers), Columbia, and elsewhere. Born in Ireland, he started teaching at fifteen, being entirely self-taught after this age. Forced to flee after the Irish Rebellion of 1798, he was recognized for his mathematical genius in the United States where he accomplished the first original work in pure mathematics, a deduction of the law of probability of error in observation. This appeared in the Analyst, a publication edited by him (1808). His books and manuscripts were presented to the library in 1925.

In pursuing the subject more attentively, Bache discovered that "this *undoubted* American was last from Thread and Needle Street, and had been born and bred in the old country." Apparently, even in the nineteenth century, European stereotyping and American self-consciousness led to false generalizations on national characteristics.[21]

One unequivocal impression which Bache brought back with him from Europe was the low status accorded there to American science. This had been equally evident to Joseph Henry, whose European tour had coincided with that of his friend. Henry had read a paper before a learned society in London and had encountered unwarranted skepticism. The suspicion with which data coming from the United States were viewed was, unfortunately, not without foundation. Some time after his return to Princeton, Henry wrote to Bache:

> ... The charlatanism of our country struck me much more disagreeably when I first returned than before or even now. I often thought of the remark you were in the habit of making that we must put down quackery or quackery will put down science. ... I am now more than ever of your opinion that the real working men in the way of science in this country should make common cause and endeavour by every proper means unitedly to raise their own scientific character.[22]

To this endeavor Bache would dedicate his influence and judgment when he set out on a second career as superintendent of the Coast Survey.

A promising student at Central High School who was afterwards employed in the Coast and Geodetic Survey as it was later named, suggests that Bache had some thought of becoming provost of the University of Pennsylvania when he resigned as principal of Central in 1842 to resume his position as professor of natural science.[23] The direction of his talents was radically altered, however, by his call to Washington two years later. John F. Frazer who, although only a few years younger than Bache, often addressed him in letters as "Grandpa," served the University as the eleventh vice-provost and succeeded to his friend and mentor's professorship. During years devoted to educational research and administration, Bache had neither "relinquished or deferred the scientific pursuits to which the habit of his mind and the bent of his genius continually impelled him."[24] Now, this advocate of basic research found himself in the employ of the federal government, in charge of the largest practical application of scientific principles ever sponsored by government funds.

Under his tutelage, the magnetic survey became a continuing study: it was extended from the Atlantic Coast to those of the Pacific and the Gulf. Telegraphy was developed in its service, and it included astronomical research, the measurement of mountains, and investigations of the Gulf stream and the tides. Allotment of funds for these ever-widening projects was violently attacked in Congress—and defended with equal vehemence. Jefferson Davis, although sick, "was taken in a close carriage up to address the Senate on an appropriation for the coast survey," for, he said," 'It is for the good of the country and for my boyhood's friend Dallas Bache, and I must go if it kills me.' "[25] The Coast Survey not only became a model for large-scale scientific investigation sponsored by government: with the arrival in Washington of a scientist to head the organization, pure science became both antecedent and ancillary to applied science.[26] The end product was practical and justification enough for government financing. But under Bache, numerous scientists were engaged in developing new methods and exploring phenomena of basic scientific interest.

Having dominated the scientific scene in Philadelphia, Franklin's descendant now became the acknowledged "Chief" of an eminent group of investigators in Washington as well as at the universities. These men all shared a common ambition: that of developing a community of professional scientists in America. Shortly after his arrival in Washington, Bache was instrumental in persuading Joseph Henry to leave Princeton, where he was professor of geophysics, to become the first secretary of the Smithsonian Institution. The intimates of Bache and Henry, who were for the most part involved with the physical sciences, soon became the dominant influence of the newly formed American Association for the Advancement of Science. This society superseded the Association of American Geologists which Henry D. Rogers, the first professor of mineralogy and geology at the University of Pennsylvania, had helped organize in Philadelphia in 1840. Bache was the second president of the AAAS when it held its first formal meeting in September 1848 in the Hall of the University of Pennsylvania. In the speech he made on retiring from this position in 1851, he emphasized the need to give "pre-eminence to research over the literature of science." On the same occasion, he advocated government patronage and the establishment of a responsible body which would serve to screen proposals and prevent the government from investing in irresponsible projects.[27]

The threat to science from quackery which Bache and Henry had recognized in the thirties continued and by the time of the Civil War was seen as a real danger. At that time, Benjamin Peirce took up the cudgels in an attack on "charlatanism" and "old fogeyism" by underlining the menace to the government from "amateurs and tinkerers."[28] Peirce foresaw a disastrous fate for true science. "Amid the din of war, the heat of party, the deviltries of politics, and the poisons of hypocrisy," he protested, "science will be inaudible, incapable, incoherent and inanimate."[29] A society of like-minded scientists calling itself the Florentine Academy had been formed in Harvard, and this soon became part of a national movement under the leadership of Bache. One of the stated purposes of this unofficial body was "once per winter" to consume "one outrageously good dinner together."[30] Its members became known as the scientific Lazzaroni, after a society of Neapolitan beggars.

In their search for government support for science these beggars of Lazarus were accused of elitism and sometimes referred to as a Cambridge clique. In fact, under the leadership of Bache, they included among their number scientists from Philadelphia, Cambridge, Albany, New York, and New Haven—the people Henry had meant when he wrote of "the real

Henry Darwin Rogers (1808–1866)
Drawing; artist unknown
First professor of geology and mineralogy at the University of Pennsylvania (1835–1846). State geologist (1835–1842), he conducted the first geological survey of Pennsylvania and New Jersey, mapping much of the Appalachian Mountain system at a time when his brother, William, founder of M.I.T., was head of the Geological Survey of Virginia. At the end of his life, he was professor of geology and natural science at the University of Glasgow (1857–1866). Founding member of the Association of American Geologists (1840) which was superseded by the American Association for the Advancement of Science.

"The President's House"
Steel engraving by Traversier, 1837
Collection of Mrs. Martin Meyerson
*The French traveler J. B. G. Roux de
Rochelle included this view of the Uni-
versity on Ninth Street in his book on the
United States published in Paris by Didot
Frères. Depicted is "The President's
House," erected for but not used by
President John Adams while Philadelphia
was the national capital and purchased
by the University in 1800. Architect
Benjamin Henry Latrobe designed the
wing on the left to house the medical
department. The handsome Adam-style
mansion was demolished and replaced by
a new building in 1829.*

working men in the way of science." Only a small number of biologists
belonged to the group, but few dominant figures in the physical sciences
remained outside it. Most of the research in progress at the universities
or elsewhere was in the hands of their associates. Their ultimate goal of
respected professionalism and recognition by government was achieved in
1863, the year the National Academy of Sciences was founded in response
to their efforts. Although Henry was not a party to the final establishment
of this body, finding the concept "something at variance with our
democratic institutions," he was included as one of the fifty original
members after the proposal had been skillfully pushed through Congress
by Senator Henry Wilson of Massachusetts.[31]

Problems naturally arose because certain deserving investigators were
omitted from the body while nonscientific men from the army and navy
were included. But the event was seen as recognition of the relation of
science to government and, more important, the need for a central body
to screen the scientific soundness and content of proliferating inventions,
the result of a developing technology. After the legislation had been signed
into law, Louis Agassiz, the renowned Swiss scientist and one of the few
naturalists among the Lazzaroni, wrote gleefully to Bache: "My dear young
Chief, Yes there is a National Academy of Sciences." He went on to
propose arrangements for its inaugural meeting:

> Now let us proceed to organize in such a way, that our action
> shall bear the nearest scrutiny. I wish our first meeting would
> have some solemnity. It were best to gather for the first time in
> Philadelphia in some of the hallowed places of Revolutionary

memory. The learned *Grandson* of Franklin must be our first
President, and here shall the old man be pardoned for not
introducing a clause in the Constitution favorable to Science, as
he left a better *seed.*[32]

During his lifetime, Bache earned the reputation of being a worthy
descendant of his great forebear. If Agassiz accused Franklin of a notable
omission in the service of science, it was one which Dallas Bache was to help
rectify. Building on the legacy of the eighteenth century when science was
an area for amateur investigation by the enlightened philosopher, Bache
and his associates raised it to a level of scholarly professionalism and
heralded its position in the modern world. Bache survived the foundation of
the Academy by only a few years, and, in the early days, it did not live
up to the hopes of its first supporters. The advisory capacity which he had
envisaged was slow to be recognized, and the projects channeled to it for
investigation were few and far between. Yet, in the same way as he had
striven to set up this symbol of high-level science during his life, Bache
continued to promote its fortunes at the time of his death. He willed the
National Academy of Sciences the bulk of his estate. Another important
development was Joseph Henry's decision to accept the presidency as a
debt of friendship to Bache. By converting its aims from government
service to the support of research, Henry helped place the National
Academy on a secure scientific footing and assured its future of significant
service which had been the cherished object of Bache and the Lazzaroni.

8

Joseph Leidy

Joseph Leidy (1823–1891)
Photograph by M. P. Simons
Professor of anatomy (1853–1891) and director of the department of biology (1884–1891). Studied medicine at the University of Pennsylvania (M.D. 1844). Pioneer of vertebrate paleontology in America, he corresponded with Darwin whose Origin of Species *was corroborated by Leidy's own research which ranged over a wide variety of subjects and resulted in over 600 publications. Identified the parasite* Trichina spiralis *in pork. Received the Lyell medal of the Geological Society of London (1884) and the Cuvier medal of the Institute de France (1888).*

Whenever a body of specialists is established, it seems inevitable for some worthy people to be unaccountably excluded. Although Bache endeavored not to become embroiled in personal rivalries, he found himself on the defensive and confessed: "I have been obliged to admit—that there are some men too mean to bring into our Academy."[1] The reverse problem seems to have occurred in the form of opposition in some quarters to the election of Robert Empie Rogers, professor of chemistry and dean of the medical faculty, as one of the fifty founding members of the National Academy of Sciences. He was one of four brothers associated with the Academy and the University, another of whom was the founder of the Massachusetts Institute of Technology. Yet another Pennsylvanian, included through no effort of his own, was Joseph Leidy, professor of anatomy for 38 years in the medical school. Nothing could have been more foreign to the nature of the man generally regarded as the founder of American vertebrate paleontology than the political maneuvering of the Lazzaroni group. With his dedication to research and the natural world, Leidy was indifferent to reputation and declared himself "too busy to theorize or to make money."[2]

On hearing of his election to the National Academy of Sciences, he commented that it was "an illiberal clique, based on Plymouth Rock." Perturbed by the exclusion of Frederick Hayden, professor of geology at the University, he consoled his friend and collaborator with the observation: "I think it will turn out to be a grand humbug, and I intend to have nothing to do with it."[3] Such political concerns lay outside the all-encompassing scientific interests of an investigator who wrote to friends on the question of priority for a geological observation: "I am too little ambitious to give myself any trouble about such a case as that you mention. Even should any one pass unnoticed more important things I may have done, I shall feel no regret about the matter."[4]

The University of Pennsylvania provided this unassuming scientist with the setting in which he pursued his studies for almost half a century. His contentment appears in his unwillingness to move when, on the death of Louis Agassiz, he was offered the Hersey professorship at Harvard.

Leidy was considered the most prominent naturalist at the time, and a special emissary was sent to Philadelphia on this occasion. Leidy gently persisted in declining the position and, soon afterwards, accompanied the disappointed Cambridge courier to the door of his house in Filbert Street. Stepping outside, he scraped a piece of moss from the wall and examined it closely, reportedly adding: "When I have exhausted all the possibilities found here at my own front door I may reconsider my refusal."[5]

Joseph Leidy's long association with the University of Pennsylvania began as a student. After receiving his medical degree in 1844, he became the assistant of his preceptor, Paul B. Goddard, and also worked in the laboratory of Robert Hare, the distinguished chemist. A few years later, he served as prosector to the professor of anatomy, William Edmonds Horner. Apart from one brief period as demonstrator of anatomy at Franklin Medical College, Leidy remained at the University of Pennsylvania for the rest of his life. As a result of strong support from students and faculty, he was elected chairman of anatomy on Horner's death in 1853. He was well qualified to succeed the distinguished anatomists Shippen, Wistar, and Physick in one of the two senior chairs of the medical school; at thirty-one, his youthfulness was another point in common with the earlier professors of anatomy.

In one respect, however, Leidy was an exception. After a few years in private practice, he abandoned medicine altogether in order to devote himself entirely to his researches. William Hunt, who was his demonstrator for ten years, considered it a great tribute to Leidy's personal qualities and his teaching ability that "for thirty-eight years he filled without objection a practical chair in an essentially practical medical school for science and science alone."[6] In 1891, Provost William Pepper declared: "In the death of Joseph Leidy . . . the medical profession in America lost its most loved and honored member, and American science its most illustrious representative."[7] At the time, an amused observer commented that since Leidy had not practiced medicine for the past forty-five years "it was rather like telling an assembly of all the tanners of the United States that, in the death of General Grant, they had lost the most beloved member of the trade."[8]

In later years, Leidy recalled that Sir Charles Lyell, author of the influential *Principles of Geology,* had urged him to give up medicine and concentrate on research. In 1884, Leidy was awarded the Lyell Medal by the Geological Society of London, at which time he commented on the advice he had received from the award's namesake: "I feel as if Sir Charles himself was expressing satisfaction in consideration of my having complied with his wish, when thirty years ago in my own home here he said he hoped I would devote my time to palaeontology instead of to medicine."[9] Leidy was characterized at the time of the award as "careful in observing, accurate in recording, cautious in inferring." An enemy of speculation, he

William Wood Gerhard (1809–1872)
Photograph by M. P. Simons
*Medical alumnus of the University of
Pennsylvania and lecturer in the insti-
tutes of medicine (physiology) where he
introduced his students to the study of
disease based on clinical diagnosis and
postmortem examinations (1838–1872)
After receiving his M.D. (1830), he spent
two years in Paris and collected material
on the pathology of smallpox, pneumonia
in children, cholera, and tuberculous
meningitis. His most famous publication
was on typhus, which he distinguished
for the first time from typhoid fever
(1837), and his papers on the diseases of
the chest (1842) remained classics for
many years.*

favored scrupulous amalgamation of accurate data over conjectures based on inadequate evidence. For this reason, he was often called the Cuvier of America and, appropriately enough, he received the medal commemorating the great French zoologist from the Institute de France shortly before his death.[10]

The thoroughness and objectivity so typical of his life's work were already apparent in his childhood interests. As a boy, Leidy was fascinated by all aspects of nature and showed an unusual gift for depicting the minutest of observed details. While growing up in Philadelphia, he would often play truant from school where he was bored by study of the classics. He found more to interest him while wandering on the banks of the Schuylkill and the Wissahickon, collecting specimens of stones, plants, and insects. At ten his beautiful freehand drawings of shells led his father, a Philadelphia hatter, to conclude that his second son might consider being a sign painter when he grew up. Joseph's stepmother, to whom he always recognized a debt of gratitude, had other ideas on the subject, and the young Leidy proceeded to study medicine instead. During his early years on the medical faculty, Leidy's skill as a draftsman proved advantageous for both him and the school. In 1851, he and George B. Wood went to Europe where Leidy assembled models and preparations and made drawings to illustrate Wood's lectures. As the newly elected professor of theory and practice, Wood was responsible for bringing medicine at the University out of the eighteenth century. From the first, Leidy's own scientific publications were illustrated by beautiful plates reproduced from his detailed drawings.

Joseph Leidy's situation as a scientist with a faculty appointment—a man trained as a physician, but whose financial support came entirely from his teaching position—pointed towards future developments in science and academic medicine. On the other hand, the encyclopedic range of his scientific interests made him one of the last of that breed of nineteenth century naturalists who regarded the whole of nature as their hunting ground. Leidy was in the first place a comparative anatomist: his medical thesis of 1844 was on the comparative anatomy of the eye of vertebrated animals. The following year, he read a paper on the anatomy of the winkle and one on fossil mollusks before the Boston Society of Natural History and the Academy of Natural Sciences of Philadelphia. He was promptly elected to each at the age of twenty-two. In a textbook, *An Elementary Treatise on Human Anatomy,* first published in 1861, the anatomical nomenclature was simplified for the benefit of students by the substitution of English terms for the traditional Latin. As usual, the work was illustrated with Leidy's original drawings of his own dissections.

Although he was neither a mineralogist nor a botanist and published nothing on these subjects, he nonetheless devoted considerable time to these aspects of natural history. Every Sunday found him spending a few

Robert Hare (1781–1858)
by John Neagle,
finished by I. L. Williams
*Professor of chemistry (1818–1847). Born
in Philadelphia, he showed interest in
chemistry at an early age. Invented the
oxyhydrogen blowtorch (1801), as well
as improving the voltaic pile and finding
a process for denarcotizing laudanum. A
cannon made by him for demonstrating
the explosiveness of hydrogen and oxygen
continued to be used for many years in
chemistry classes at the University. Hare
wrote moral essays under a nom de plume
and, in his last years, became interested
in scientific evidence on spiritualism,
publishing his* Experimental Investigation of the Spirit Manifestations *in 1855.*

hours in the mineral cabinet of the Philadelphia lawyer Richard Vaux, who claimed to be the only American to have danced with Queen Victoria. At the Centennial Exposition in Philadelphia, Leidy recognized that a mineral labeled as beryl was, in fact, an unusual topaz of considerably greater value. He later detected a bogus specimen of quartz in the University Museum.[11] Throughout his life, specimens of all kinds were sent to him for identification, and it was not uncommon for ladies of fashion to visit him to ask his opinion on their gems. A collection of precious stones which he brought back with him from Europe was sold during his lifetime, and the gems in his possession at the time of his death were purchased by the government for $2,800 and preserved in the National Museum in Washington.

Another subject of great interest to Leidy was helminthology—the study of worms—and flukes and thread worms were often sent to him by his fellow researchers.[12] In 1847, Leidy made an observation in this area which proved to have considerable medical significance: he provided the earliest indication of the source of trichinosis in man. This parasitic organism had been discovered in humans the previous decade and named by Richard Owen in London. When Leidy identified some whitish specks in a piece of ham as the cysts of *Trichina spiralis*, he also had a short-lived effect on the exportation of American pork. "Though the most ancient of lawgivers declared swine to be unclean," observes one of Leidy's memorialists, "it does not seem supposable that he anticipated Leidy and knew that the pigs of his time were infested by this microscopic parasyte."[13] The medical implications of the observation were not immediately so clear as they were later to become. Leidy terminates an otherwise impersonal article on the subject in Pepper's *System of Practical Medicine* with the telling remark: "The writer may add that it was in a slice of boiled ham, from which he had partly made his dinner, that he first discovered trichina in the hog."[14]

Around the time he was appointed to the chair of anatomy, Leidy was beginning to be identified with ideas on evolution. With his almost pathological distaste for controversy, and his inability to make enemies, he was particularly hurt by the way his research was used against him for political ends. "All those things which you would think would recommend me to the trustees my opponent is using against me," he wrote to a friend on the subject of his proposed election. "I am shamefully abused as being an atheist, an infidel. It has been positively asserted that I seek to make *proselytes to infidelity,* and that in my writings I have tried to prove that geology overthrows the Mosaic account of the creation. You may judge my feelings."[15]

In preparing *The Origin of Species,* Charles Darwin was able to draw upon a body of information supplied to him by American investigators, notably his correspondent Asa Gray of Harvard. Fully expecting his book to create an unprecedented furor, Darwin documented his theories to the fullest possible extent. Leidy avoided becoming embroiled in the dispute on this side of the Atlantic in which Gray defended Darwin against vehement opposition from Agassiz. Soon after *The Origin of Species* was published, however, Leidy wrote to Darwin enthusiastically and enclosed some of his own papers. Darwin thanked him graciously in a letter in which he went on to say:

> Your note has pleased me more than you could readily believe, for I have during a long time heard all good judges speak of your palaeontological labours in terms of the highest respect. Most palaeontologists (with some few good exceptions) entirely despise my work; consequently, approbation from you has gratified me much. All the older geologists (with the one exception of Lyell, whom I look on as a host in himself) are even more vehement against the introduction of species than are the palaeontologists. . . . Your sentence, that you have some interesting facts "in support of the doctrine of selection, which I shall report at a favorable opportunity," has delighted me even more than the rest of your note.[16]

One possible contribution to the theory of species was the material Leidy had published on the strange case of the American fossil horse. Without theorizing on the subject, he had described remains proving that there had, indeed, been such an animal, since become extinct. With the arrival of European settlers, horses were reintroduced, and these proceeded to flourish in the environment which had formerly ceased to support the American species. In view of his personal observations, Leidy was more than ready to accept Darwin's doctrine of selection and, on reading his work, he describes feeling "as though I had hitherto groped in the darkness and that all of a sudden a meteor flashed upon the skies."[17] Leidy recommended Darwin's election to the Philadelphia Academy of Natural Sciences which became one of the first institutions to honor him after *The Origin of Species* was published in 1859.

The theory of evolution which Darwin was finally emboldened to print by the threat of being preempted by a rival did not come as a complete surprise to some of the men working in the field. Just such an explanation of life had been making headway in scientific circles, and Leidy himself had published remarks of a very similar kind in 1853, six years before the appearance of *The Origin of Species* and five years after meeting with Darwin in England. In the introduction to Leidy's article, "A Flora and Fauna within Living Animals," the author first dismisses the theory of spontaneous generation which was prevalent at the time. Before treating the microscopic organisms which are his subject, he speaks from his knowledge of geology and paleontology, describing the nature and conditions of life in general:

> The study of the earth's crust teaches us that very many species
> of plant and animals became extinct at successive periods, while
> other races originated to occupy their places. This probably was
> the result, in many cases, of a change in exterior conditions
> incompatible with the life of certain species, and favorable to
> the production of others. But such a change does not always
> satisfactorily explain the extinction of species.

At this point he refers in a footnote to the American fossil horse. He then
goes on:

> Probably every species has a definite course to run in con-
> sequence of a general law; an origin, an increase, a point of
> cumulation, a decline, and an extinction. . . . Of the life, present
> everywhere with its indispensable conditions, and coeval in its
> origin with them, what was the immediate cause? . . . There
> appear to be but trifling steps from the oscillating particle of
> inorganic matter, to a *Bacterium*; from this to a *Vibrio*, thence
> to a *Monas*, and so gradually up to the highest order of life!

Although fossils provide evidence that the more complicated forms of life
existed alongside the simpler organisms, Leidy hypothesizes that "life may
have been ushered upon earth, through oceans of the lowest types, long
previously to the deposit of the oldest palaeozoic rocks as known to us!!"[18]
With his aversion to speculation, Leidy attempted to modify his claim for
evolution through the expedient of exclamation marks. It is nonetheless
clear from this early statement, quoted from a work accepted for
publication in 1851, that Darwin's theories were in accordance with
conclusions which Leidy had drawn in the course of his own studies.

In the field of paleontology, Leidy laid the foundation for investigations
on a larger scale by ambitious younger men. Othniel Marsh was attached
to Yale's Peabody Museum, an institution endowed by his uncle, while the
Philadelphia Quaker Edward Drinker Cope was a student of Leidy and
professor of geology and mineralogy at the University of Pennsylvania
from 1889 to 1897. With new arrivals in the field, the father of American
paleontology found himself squeezed out by these ruthless rivals in the
"Battle of the Bones."[19] Leidy was unable to compete with two men of
independent means for the specimens which had formerly been sent to
him *gratis*. He sorrowfully withdrew from the scene of one of the grand
scientific controversies of the century which, in the seventies and eighties,
embroiled Congress as well as all the major scientific institutions. Concerns
for priority and reputation, most often disregarded by Leidy, soon
dispelled the courteous tone of the letters in which Cope at first addressed
Marsh as "thee." Not long afterwards, he was writing "as a man of honor
I request of you . . . to correct all statements and innuendoes you have
made to others here and elsewhere."[20]

Before Leidy bowed to necessity and removed himself from a field he
described as no longer fit for a gentleman, he had added no fewer than 375

Edward Drinker Cope (1840–1897)
by Clarence A. Worrall
Professor of geology and mineralogy and then professor of zoology and comparative anatomy at the University of Pennsylvania (1889–1897). Born in Philadelphia, Cope entered the School of Medicine but dropped his medical studies to pursue independent investigations at the Academy of Natural Sciences. He worked at the Smithsonian and with Joseph Leidy whom he joined in describing fossils from the Hayden Survey collected by professor of geology Frederick Hayden in Wyoming. The results of his paleontological and geological explorations were published in 600 articles and books.

genera and species to the 98 previously known.[21] As a teacher of anatomy, Leidy eagerly pursued specimens of a rather different kind to which Cope's bon mot, "de mortuis nil nisi *boneum*," seems particularly applicable. In fact, William Hunt attributes the only dishonest action on Leidy's part that he ever witnessed to the anatomist's desire to supplement the collections now in the Wistar Institute and the Mutter Museum of the College of Physicians in Philadelphia. In each collection there is an example of an adipocere body, that is, a body preserved because the degenerated fatty tissues have been transformed into a wax-like substance. Two petrified bodies from the epidemic of 1793 had been reportedly uncovered at an old burying-ground which was being cleared for improvements, and, in pursuit of these specimens, Leidy and Hunt went to call upon the caretaker. The superintendent mumbled something about "violated graves," but he added that he was able to release bodies to relatives. "The doctor immediately took the hint. He went home, hired a furniture wagon, and armed the driver with an order reading, 'Please deliver to bearer the bodies of my grandfather and grandmother.' " Hunt caps this anecdote with an appropriate rhyme:

> So the posters don't worry as to tuum or meum,
> But take the specimens for the museum.[22]

It was not until after the Civil War that an anatomy act governing the use of unclaimed bodies was passed by the Pennsylvania legislature, and only many years later were students at last able to do their own dissections or to study tissues under the microscope. At the time when Leidy had received instruction from Goddard, ability to use a microscope was still considered an uncommon accomplishment. The instrument with which Leidy did his later work had only two lenses, and was purchased for the grand sum of $50. With the emphasis at medical school still on didactic demonstration, Leidy continued throughout his teaching career to describe anatomical details from the "bull pit" to four hundred students perched on benches above him. According to one of his most illustrious students, George A. Piersol, Leidy nonetheless provided them with "the first glimpse of a most adequate conception of nature" and sent them forth "with the old fetters of thought shattered for ever."[23] When a department of biology was established at the University of Pennsylvania, Leidy was appointed professor of biology in the faculty of philosophy. A separate faculty of seven was appointed in 1884, and Leidy then became the first director of the biological department, agreeing to give up a professorship at Swarthmore College with which he had supplemented his income for fourteen years.

In addition to the many prizes and honors which he received during his life, Joseph Leidy was immortalized among the natural phenomena which had fascinated him from his earliest youth. On a trip to the Luray Caverns

**Professor Koenig's Class
in Mineralogy, 1886**
*Black-bearded George Augustus Koenig,
professor of mineralogy and metallurgy,
taught Towne School students in his
"mineral cabinet" in College Hall.
Koenig, who held a Heidelberg Ph.D.,
was brought to the University of Pennsylvania at a time when it was also
attracting faculty trained at Göttingen,
Marburg, Tübingen, and other German
universities.*

of Virginia in 1881, his adopted daughter was furnished with a bottle
filled with clear water from one of the pools in the cave. At the appropriate
moment, the torches of the assemblage were held aloft, William Hunt made
a brief speech, the bottle was broken, and a column and a stalactite were
named in Leidy's honor. As early as 1854, the University of Pennsylvania
alumni, explorers Elisha Kent Kane and Isaac Hayes, discovered two polar
capes on the east coast of Grinnell Land during their arctic expedition and
named them: Cape Joseph Leidy and Cape John Frazer, the latter for the
founder member of the National Academy of Sciences who became
vice-provost of the University in 1855. In addition, Ferdinand Hayden
called a peak in the Rockies after the scientist whom he had supplied with
specimens in the early years of paleontological investigation. Hunt reports
that "with the exception of the Tetons, Mount Leidy is the finest object in
the neighborhood, snow-capped and rising in solitary grandeur above the
plain."[24] At the University of Pennsylvania, where a chair was endowed in
his memory in the department of anatomy, his name is inscribed on the
biology building now known as the Leidy Laboratories. Furthermore, the
great men of medicine whose names decorate the walls of the main
reading room of the Philadelphia College of Physicians begin with
Hippocrates and end with Leidy.

　　When the bibliography of this prodigious investigator was assembled
by his nephew, Joseph Leidy, Jr., it included some six hundred titles. Not
listed among these serious works is a little book which was read to his
daughter and nephews at a party in celebration of his fifty-ninth birthday.

It is simply called *A Fairy Tale*, and it gives an account of the birth of a blue-eyed baby fifty-nine years before and the gifts he received from the fairies. After the usual perfections have been bestowed, "a sweet but grave fairy said 'with these eyes he shall see what man never before has seen; floras and faunas within and without; wings of grasshoppers and how they can move them, worms of the earth, of man and of cattle, fossils whose years are numbered by millions, and to them jelly like drops shall grow to rare beauty.' "

The fairies come back, fifty-nine fairy days later, to look for evidence of their gifts. They are greeted by a spectacle which would have frightened anyone but fairies:

> First came the great *Hadrosaurus*, his years quite a million—
> *"I am his servant, and proud of my master."* Next came the
> *Megalonides* and *Megatheria*, huge creatures, in size like to
> elephants: then great troops of *Wild Horses* and herds of *Wild
> Oxen. "We were long dead, and he gave us new being."*
>
> Then, little *White Ants, all their Parasites with them.*
>
> Then beautiful banners with rare pictures on them; great groups
> of *Polyps*, the *Corallium* leading them. Then wonderful
> *Sponges*; and *Floras* and *Faunas*; delicate *Rhizopods*, once mere
> drops of jelly, and then great leaves of Book Lore, *all having the
> baby's name on them.*[25]

Joseph Leidy was eminently modest, although he could be eloquent when speaking of his discoveries in the naive assurance that his enthusiasm must be shared. In the *Fairy Tale*, his virtue and scientific genius are ascribed to supernatural powers. Although he had no intention of subscribing to this view of Leidy's fairy-tale prowess, his memorialist William Hunt proclaimed: "Dr. Leidy was a giant in intellect, a saint in disposition."[26]

Elisha Kent Kane (1820–1857)
Medal by G. H. Lovett
Physician and explorer of the Arctic, he received his medical degree from the University of Pennsylvania (1842). As an assistant surgeon in the United States Navy, he served in China, West Africa, and Mexico, during which time he contracted rheumatic fever and typhus which left him in poor health. The remainder of his short life was devoted to discovery: he went on two expeditions to the Arctic in search of the lost explorer Sir John Franklin, commanding the second in his brig Advance. *He named two capes after professors at the University, and Kane Basin was named for him. At his death, he was regarded as a national hero, and his body lay in state at Independence Hall. A lunar crater near the moon's north pole was named after him, and a surveying ship, the* Kane, *was launched in November 1965.*

Transition

Only in the latter part of the nineteenth century did the colleges and universities of the country begin to assume forms that are at all recognizable today. . . . The determination to make available a higher education in America no less distinguished than any in Europe provided some of the impulse for reform; there was, however, much that was indigenous to the country itself that did not depend on European example. Major steps were taken to provide for the education of women; important measures were elaborated for the education of the newly-liberated blacks; curricula were largely transformed, losing their earlier bias in favor of the classics and gaining new emphases, sometimes practical or technological; a whole system of instruction, recitation, and examination, characteristic of pre-Civil War days, was gradually obliterated.

A First Report
January 1971
American Academy of Arts and Sciences
The Assembly on University Goals and Governance
Martin Meyerson, Chairman
Stephen R. Graubard, Director of Studies

Charles Janeway Stillé (1819–1899)
Student caricature as the University
peacock in *The Record*, 1880
*Graduate of the Academy, A.B. Yale
(1839), professor of belles-lettres and
English literature at the University of
Pennsylvania and provost (1868–1880).
Called the "Moses of the Exodus" to
West Philadelphia. During his tenure,
the University established the dental and
Towne schools, adopted the elective
system, and admitted its first women
students. Opinionated and proud—qualities which were evidently recognized by
his students—Stillé was limited in power
by the structure of the University, but
many of his proposals were implemented
by his successor, William Pepper.*

9

Charles Janeway Stillé and William Pepper: Creating the Modern University

William Pepper (1843–1898)
Student caricature,
The Record, 1883
Lecturer on morbid anatomy, professor first of clinical medicine and then of theory and practice of medicine (1868–1894), provost of the University (1880–1894) where he had been educated (A.B. 1862, M.D. 1864). Pepper instituted curricular reforms, encouraged new academic programs, and secured lands and funds for expansion. One of the forces behind the first university-owned teaching hospital in the country as well as a founder of the University Museum, he continued his research and practice in medicine throughout his career as an administrator and was prominent in medical circles in this country and abroad.

The period around 1870 has been described as "almost the 'Anno Domini of educational history' in the United States." After the Civil War, the colleges found themselves in a precarious plight financially, with traditional education increasingly coming to be regarded as superfluous by growing numbers of practical, self-made men. By the turn of the century, however, the transformation which had taken place "made the former college seem like a boys' school in contrast."[1] The University of Pennsylvania did not benefit from the Morrill Act of 1862 by which the federal government granted aid to states for the provision of instruction in agriculture and the mechanical skills. But the forces of change were clearly at work during the last third of the nineteenth century at the small private institution in Philadelphia. Between 1868, when Charles Stillé became provost, through the tenure of William Pepper and his classmate Charles C. Harrison, the progress of the university movement in the United States was reflected at the University of Pennsylvania in the reforms, the expansion, and the physical growth of the campus in its new location west of the Schuylkill.

There had been attempts earlier in the century to introduce graduate studies at American colleges as educators looked to Germany for examples of research-oriented institutions catering to advanced students. There were, however, strong feelings about the attempt to " 'Germanize' our American colleges."[2] At the University of Pennsylvania, the response to proposals put forward by Bishop Alonzo Potter, a trustee who had been a professor at Union College, epitomizes the opposition in the country at large. The argument used to counter his demands in 1852 for a more distinctive course of education for mature students at the college level was typical of those being heard at other institutions: that there was no present demand for any expansion in higher education. At the University of Pennsylvania opposition came from Henry Vethake, the mathematician who was to become provost in 1854. One of the first political economists in the United States, he had been a zealous reformer in his youth. At the age of sixty, however, he took the view that the average American expected to be earning a comfortable living as head of a family by his middle twenties, not occupying a subordinate position as a student. It was a mistake, he declared, "to think men *want* to be taught literature or science."[3] Another professor, George Allen, later helped Stillé extend the curriculum by finding instructors in modern languages, but he also opposed what he saw as a transplanting of a European plan of education to America. "It is not unreasonable to presume," he declared, "that if we are ever to have an American *University*, it must be the development and modification of the American *College*—it must be a *supply*, naturally shaping itself to meet a real (and not factitious) *demand*."[4]

To these objections was added the very real problem of lack of endowment at the time of the attempted reforms. Although his proposal was shelved, Bishop Potter made a contribution to the future of graduate education in the United States by adopting a position somewhere between those men who rejected such education on the grounds that there was no demand for it and those who ignored this lack as a matter of no account. In Potter's view, the demand could and should be deliberately stimulated by inducements such as prizes and other distinctions. With his moderate opinion he paved the way for developments in the future when men of influence came to recognize that the time was right to promote education on a graduate level.[5]

At a later date, the ideas and efforts of Charles Janeway Stillé similarly provided the impetus for the reforms of his successor, William Pepper. Moreover, if the West Philadelphia campus assumed its recognizably modern form under Charles C. Harrison, this was possible because of the earlier provost's decision to relocate the institution. In general, however, Stillé tends to be overshadowed by the more obvious successes of the men who followed him. In light of the changes taking place in higher education in the last decades of the nineteenth century, Stillé should receive credit for being the first provost at the University of Pennsylvania to take an accurate reading of the times.

Writing of William Pepper who figures so prominently in any account of the expanding University, Sir William Osler gives a detailed account of the activities of his friend and colleague. Without actually mentioning him, Osler may also have had Stillé in mind as the reformer of the contrary type who provides something of a foil for the portrait of Pepper.

> There are two great types of leaders: one, the great reformer, the dreamer of dreams—with aspirations completely in the van of his generation—lives often in wrath and disputations, passes through fiery ordeals, is misunderstood, and too often despised and rejected by his generation. The other, a very different type, is the leader who sees ahead of his generation, but who has the sense to walk and work in it. While not such a potent element in progress, he lives a happier life, and is more likely to see the fulfillment of his plans. Of this latter type the late Professor of Medicine at the University of Pennsylvania was a notable example—the most notable the profession of this country has offered to the world.

Charles Custis Harrison (1844–1929)
Student caricature
by Roy D. Bassette ('08)
in *Punchbowl*, December 1907
*Graduate (1862) and trustee of the
University of Pennsylvania (1876–1929),
Harrison succeeded his classmate William
Pepper as provost (1894–1911) after
many years in business. Born in Philadelphia, he was the grandson of John
Harrison, the chemist. During his tenure
as provost, the campus trebled in size as
did the assets of the University, while
the student body doubled and many
buildings were erected. The principal
fund-raiser for construction. his own
financial contributions were large.*

Pepper appears in Osler's account as the shrewd pragmatist, a "modern Machiavelli" to some sedate Philadelphians.[6] Although not named by Osler, Stillé might be gratified to be cast in the role of the other leader—the man of vision more than a little responsible for the laurels of his successor.

When Charles Stillé was elected professor of English and belles-lettres at the University in 1866, he had no experience as a teacher. A graduate of the Philadelphia Academy, he had studied at Yale and belonged to a well-established family which gave him ready access through its bonds and friendships to the trustees responsible for the governance of the University. During his years as a professor, followed by his appointment as provost in 1870, Stillé became aware that the board members who gathered at the sparsely attended monthly meetings resembled nothing so much as a body without a head. These men came to their position by virtue of family and social status, and most of them had little appreciation for the function of a university and small interest, Stillé thought, in furthering its ends. They nonetheless had absolute control over all the activities of the University, including the teaching programs, for which faculty opinion was not even consulted.

In a letter explaining his resignation in 1880, Stillé spelled out what he saw as the absurdity of the situation. "As well might you look for advice worth taking on matters of Banking and Insurance from our Professors," he complained, "as to suppose that the members of the Board could manage intelligently the details of our University work over which they now have full power." The provost himself had practically none. He was nominal head of only the faculty of arts while the departments of medicine and law were autonomous; he had no right to attend board meetings and, when he did make an appearance before the governing body for the purpose of imparting essential information to them, Stillé notes his anomalous position as "that strange nondescript, in college organization, 'an organ of communication.'"[7]

Much pain and disillusion might have been avoided had Stillé been satisfied with the inertia of his predecessors. But he was not prepared to accept the answers he had received when, as a newly elected professor, he had questioned several prominent men about the role of the University. The Reverend Daniel R. Goodwin, who preceded him as provost, had assured him "that there were in this city about one hundred young men who were disposed to avail themselves of the opportunity of getting a College education." Goodwin seemed perfectly satisfied with the existing state of affairs and his accompanying prognosis that the number was unlikely to increase. The professor of English literature, Henry Coppée, whose departure to become president of Lehigh University had resulted in Stillé's first appointment, explained the stagnation at the University of Pennsylvania by informing the new young professor of the indifference of the board to educational reforms and their lack of sympathy with any initiative stemming from the faculty. In what Stillé held, throughout his administrative tenure, to be its major function, the board was also a signal failure. "For more than eighty years previous to my election," writes Stillé, "it had received but one donation or legacy . . . the income of which was to be devoted to and in the instruction of drawing, an instruction, by the way, then not given in the university."[8]

In 1868, Provost Goodwin was forced to retire from the position in which he had served part time throughout the Civil War while also holding a chair at the Philadelphia Divinity School, an Episcopal institution unconnected with the nonsectarian university. Despite all warnings about the attitude of many trustees, Stillé viewed his election to succeed Goodwin as a vote in favor of reform. The elective system introduced by President Eliot at Harvard had been instituted at the University of Pennsylvania with good response from the students. Entering the perennial debate between ancient as opposed to modern languages on the side of Benjamin Franklin, Stillé engaged in procuring instructors in German, French, Spanish, and Italian, while using his personal influence to begin raising an endowment fund. He had already initiated the move which would lead to the foundation of a scientific school.

Immediately after becoming provost, Stillé proposed to the board that his position should be vested with actual executive power. The title he held was nominal, and since all other successful institutions were governed through a presidency, Stillé felt that precedent as well as common sense favored his suggestion that the provost should become *ex officio* chairman of the board of trustees and head of the other faculties of the University. When inaction by the board forced him to renew his appeal, he won the support of a committee appointed to consider his position. The motion was defeated, however, because of strong opposition from the medical faculty who feared that a legacy promised by a retiring physician would be jeopardized by any change in governance. When it came, the legacy in question amounted, in Stillé's account, to "a remote interest in a cranberry patch in Jersey."[9]

With the move of the campus to West Philadelphia in 1872, Stillé found himself faced with animosity or indifference on the part of the city and of some members of the University community as well. There had been much opposition to the University's original plan to acquire land on the Blockley Farm from the city at a nominal sum. In the final event, the University received less land at far greater cost than anticipated. Even so, the transferral was marked by suspicions on the part of men "utterly incapable of comprehending the grandeur of the scheme," who feared that selfish motivation was involved in the transaction. John Welsh, chief among the few trustees who actively engaged in fund-raising, appointed United States minister to Great Britain in 1877. On his return, he was

The Kiosk Quick Lunch Co.
A piece of brightly hand-decorated Americana, the forerunner of today's flotilla of mobile sandwich-men, served students short-order lunches and "Temperance Drinks of All Kinds" in the early 1900s.

greatly surprised to learn that the money had not been raised during his absence to pay for the new buildings which had been constructed on the west bank of the Schuylkill. Through his exertions, the University's property at Ninth and Chestnut Streets was sold to the U.S. government for its post office, and it became possible to complete the buildings without further loans. The lack of endowment remained a problem, however, and the debts of the University continued to grow at an alarming rate.[10]

It was not the financial trials of the University which finally led to Charles Stillé's resignation in 1880. In an exercise of power which, in Stillé's opinion reduced the gentlemen of the faculty to mere "employees," the board overrode the faculty in a disciplinary question. Stillé felt that this action clearly represented a reversal of the provisions of the University's charter although the trustees chose not to understand that he was protesting an action of theirs. In his memoir, *Reminiscences of a Provost,* he later spelled out the causes for his dissatisfaction which, he believed, proceeded from the anomalous organization unique to the University of Pennsylvania, where there was no president or head executive and the trustees were either not involved at all or were engaged in endless detail.

Stillé's case is somewhat weakened by historian Edward Potts Cheyney, who draws upon his personal recollections of him, "white and glowering with anger at disorder in the college chapel." If Stillé points to the way the trustees tended to side with their relatives in the student body against the faculty, Cheyney detracts from the provost's position of righteous administrative anger by relating the rather minor act of insubordination at the root of "the Price case." He elaborates on the disciplinary problem and prints "the piece of doggerel which, sung in the basement of College Hall and overheard by the Provost, put Provost, College Faculty, and Trustees, by the ears and caused the expulsion of the composer:

> Pomp and Stillé had a fight.
> They fit all day and they fit all night,
> And in the morning they were seen
> A rollin' down the bowlin' green."[11]

Stillé's supposed adversary, Pomp, was the attractive steward of College Hall for many years. The composer and culprit, Eli K. Price, Jr., was the grandson of a trustee and went on to obtain the A.B., the LL.B., as well as a gift for the University from his family. He finally became a trustee on his own account.

Stillé was disappointed in some of his greatest hopes for the University, but he still saw his period of tenure as "the most important era in the annals of the University of Pennsylvania." The University had come a long way from its somnolent posture between the Civil War and the American Centennial, and his own contributions were considerable. He oversaw the removal of the campus to its present location, and during the

Veterinary School Ambulance for Small Animals, 1909
Injured animals were brought to the veterinary school in one of two horse-drawn vans. The one used for small animals is seen standing in front of the building constructed as a result of the efforts of Dean Leonard Pearson (completed 1912). As state veterinarian, Pearson secured the passage of many laws for the control of communicable diseases of domestic animals. Some 13,000 animals are treated here annually.

time that he was provost the first important benefactions were made to the University. The department of arts was reorganized, women were admitted to some of the lecture courses, and scholarships for students from Philadelphia were established in return for land given to the University of Pennsylvania by the city. A new scientific school was instituted, and the department of music and the school of dentistry were organized. These were tremendous achievements considering that, at the time Stillé became provost, "the course of study in the College Department was substantially that which had been introduced by Dr. Smith into the old College of Philadelphia in 1755."[12]

The gains of his administration were the harbingers of further advances which would occur after he was succeeded by William Pepper. Towards the end of his memoir, Stillé points out that the formal adoption by the trustees of the improvements he had sought "was made by my successor an indispensable condition of his accepting the office of provost."[13] Indeed, the new provost's situation was facilitated by his success in gaining from the board of trustees all those prerogatives which, although "more or less an obsession with him," Stillé had not been granted.[14] As Stillé notes, the board "found no difficulty in providing by a simple *by-law* of the corporation in January, 1881, that 'the Provost shall be *President pro tempore* of the Board of Trustees, shall preside at the meetings, etc., appoint all committees, and generally perform all other duties which pertain to the powers and duties of a presiding officer.' "[15] Entertaining bold ambitions for the University he loved, Charles Janeway Stillé accomplished much but resigned because of his lack of true power and the seemingly insuperable indifference he faced in his attempts at reform. To carry on his work, a special kind of successor was necessary. As Horace H. Furness, the eminent Shakespearean scholar, rhetorically inquired: "Do you think such Provosts are as plenty as blackberries?"[16] The man who succeeded Stillé brought energy and determination to a situation which existed because the former provost had paved the way.

In reviewing the role which individuals have taken in the founding and reorganization of America's older colleges and universities, a former president of Western Reserve University remarks that no name is more significant in the shaping of a modern institution of higher learning than that of William Pepper. In another passage William Pepper is described as "the first really great university president [*sic*] of the land." The man who held the title of provost from 1881 to 1894 is quoted as saying: "After the days of Benjamin Franklin the University went to sleep. It slept in peace till I came one hundred years after. When I came it woke up and there was trouble—and there has been trouble ever since."[17]

The name "William Pepper" was prominently associated with the University for many years, and the provost was the second of three generations of the same name to serve the institution. In 1884, during his term as provost, he succeeded to the historic chair of theory and practice of medicine which had been held until 1864 by his father. Only shortly before his death, the first William Pepper had signed the medical diploma of his son, who, as provost, signed that of William Pepper III, professor of medicine and dean of the school of medicine for 33 years. He, in turn, signed the diploma of his son, D. Sergeant Pepper, who became a trustee.[18] Not only were the Peppers famous in Philadelphia as a family of physicians: the provost's grandfather had been one of the richest entrepreneurs of the city in the early nineteenth century. In addition, his wife was descended from Franklin.

William Pepper exerted his energies in an effort to develop a university which could consider itself a fitting inheritor of the dreams of Benjamin Franklin. He used his professional and social weight to further his plans: eloquent in expressing ideals for higher education, he also persevered in searching out what Furness describes as "the exact location in every rich man's body of the *pocket-book* nerve . . . so as to excite the largest reflex action."[19] In benefactions to the University, William Pepper took the lead, making liberal donations out of his own pocket. He refused remuneration for his services as professor and provost and, in a letter to the board of trustees, dated December 1887, he writes: "I have scrupulously returned to your Treasury all and more than all that I have received either for teaching or for administration."[20] His ceaseless activity is epitomized in the anecdote about the four-year-old boy at a holiday resort who disturbed the sleep of all the staid Philadelphians by "marching down the hall, armed with two sticks, and alternately beating on the doors and shouting at the top of his lungs: 'No one shall sleep in this house this afternoon, I say, if I can help it!' It was William Pepper. Fifty years later the story was told to some friends, one of whom added: 'And no one has slept in Philadelphia for years because of that same William Pepper.' "[21]

Even before he became provost, Pepper had demonstrated his organizational acumen in a variety of ways. Chief among these was his role in establishing at the University of Pennsylvania the first hospital in the United States owned and operated by a university. The part he played while still a member of the medical faculty already indicated the devotion to his goals which would be characteristic of his career as provost. At the time when the idea of relocating the University campus to West Philadelphia had first come up, one of the principal objections to such a move had been the distance which would then separate the medical department from the Pennsylvania Hospital where the clinical lectures and demonstrations had always been given to students. In addition, Children's, Episcopal, Howard, and Wills Eye hospitals were all located in the east of the city. While the Philadelphia Hospital, formerly the Almshouse, was situated in Blockley Township to the west, instruction

Joseph Wharton (1826–1909)
by Frederick Gutekunst
Founder of the Wharton School of Finance and Commerce (1881). Born in Philadelphia, he started as a dry-goods clerk and became director of the Bethlehem Steel Company and owner of the Gap nickel mine. At the time he provided his endowment, he pronounced the belief "that adequate education in the principles underlying successful business management and civil government would greatly aid in producing a class of men likely to become more useful members of society." He was awarded an honorary degree by the University (D.Sc. 1902). His Speeches and Poems were published in 1926.

Kenijiro Matsumoto (1870–1963)
President for many years of the University of Pennsylvania Alumni Association of Japan (1936–63), Matsumoto was a member of the Wharton School class of 1895. Born in Fukuoka, he returned home to head the Japanese Coal Mining Association. He was a member of the House of Peers, a director of the Meiji Technical College in Kyushu, and an owner of the Meiji Coal Mining Corporation. In 1930, he returned to the University for the fourth time and received from his classmate Owen J. Roberts a prize as the alumnus who had traveled the longest distance. He was awarded an honorary LL.D. by the University (1956).

there had more than once been ended as a result of political and personal dissension.

When the University purchased the land of the Almshouse farm in West Philadelphia, a proposal to build a hospital attached to the school of medicine became a serious consideration. The idea was unprecedented in the United States, and it was soon taken up by a trio of enthusiastic young graduates of the medical school with William Pepper the most vocal supporter of the plan. He had previously praised the medical department for having "the best and most complete system of dispensing clinical teaching in connection with any school," a situation that he believed would be jeopardized in the approaching move from Ninth Street.[22] Nonetheless, by the following year, Pepper was enthusiastically pushing the idea of building a hospital as part of the new campus.

When the Pennsylvania Constitutional Convention met in Philadelphia in January 1872, Pepper persuaded the University trustees to invite the legislature and the convention to a reception at the newly erected College Hall.[23] This provided an occasion to win many prominent men to the cause of the hospital. It is interesting to note that Stillé, who was still provost at the time, opposed the plan which he saw as a competing attempt to raise $500,000, a sum badly needed for the endowment fund for the University. From his point of view, the trustees' sanction of the hospital plan was another blow to his hope of improving the other departments of the University.

Before setting out to gain the support of local philanthropy, Pepper first made an investigation of the situation in Philadelphia with regard to hospital beds. In comparison with New York which had over 6,000 free beds for a population of 900,000—a ratio of one bed for 1,500 people—Philadelphia, the principal city of a state which was becoming increasingly industrialized, had only one free bed for every 7,000 people. A campaign was mounted to gain the support of the state legislature. As the result of much persuasion on the part of Pepper and his colleagues, the Assembly voted a grant of $100,000 on the condition that the University should raise matching funds. Within a few years similar petitions were made by other institutions; in fact, the University later failed to obtain continued financial aid, because so many had followed its successful tactic in appealing for Commonwealth funds.[24]

After considerable discussion as to location, the trustees finally purchased additional land from the city on Spruce Street in West Philadelphia. When two years later, in 1874, the first buildings were dedicated at ceremonies presided over by the governor of Pennsylvania, the structure consisted of a central unit for staff and students and a ward for 146 patients, the first of three projected wings. This was but the beginning of various projects for providing the University with major new facilities, but Pepper's interest and support for his first undertaking

continued unabated after he became provost. In 1883, the Gibson wing
for chronic disease was added to the Hospital as a result of a benefaction,
and, in one of a number of bequests to the University, Pepper's relative,
Henry Seybert, willed $60,000 to the Hospital.

Personal experience of disease and suffering was in part responsible for
Pepper's own financial contributions, particularly the grant of $50,000 he
made toward a laboratory of pathology. Both his father and a brother, who
"wore themselves out in the service of humanity and science," had fallen
victims to pulmonary consumption. Friends of Pepper's, among the most
promising young men in the medical school, had succumbed early in life
to chronic disease. "You cannot wonder," wrote Pepper in 1895 to a new
director of the University Hospital, "that I registered a vow to do what
I could to secure the erection and endowment of a special department of
the University Hospital for chronic disease of the lungs and heart, and a
laboratory of clinical medicine to promote original research into the causes
and the nature of disease."[25] The William Pepper Laboratory of
Clinical Medicine was named for Provost Pepper's father, a distinguished
physician who had trained under Pierre Louis in Paris. The great
Frenchman had also influenced another graduate of the medical department,
William Wood Gerhard, who, on his return from studying abroad, had
ushered in a new era of medicine based on clinical observation in place of
didactic reasoning. Before his death, the younger Pepper had the
satisfaction of seeing his initial project of raising a three-quarter-million-
dollar endowment for the Hospital far exceeded by the public response.

An early demonstration of Pepper's abilities had taken place when he
served as medical director of the international exhibition held in Fairmount
Park for the American Centennial. Alive to any advantage to be gained
from the correct handling of circumstances of dignity and pomp, Pepper
made the most of this and similar events which occurred during his
term as provost. In 1788, after New Hampshire became the ninth state to
ratify the Constitution, the Fourth of July celebrations had been organized
by a member of the first graduating class of the College of Philadelphia,
"Signer" Francis Hopkinson. One hundred years later, Pepper played a
major role in planning the festivities. At his suggestion, the parade and
industrial display originally devised by Hopkinson in honor of the
promulgation of the Constitution were recreated.

Not least among Pepper's motivations for promoting the centennial was
the important role which Philadelphia's learned institutions had played in
1788 and the prominent place occupied by the University on that occasion.
The official ceremonies held in 1888 assembled some of the most influential
persons of the nation in Philadelphia and lasted three days, closing at a
banquet given by the seven learned societies of the city.[26] Pepper presided
at the final dinner held at the Academy of Music "with President Cleveland
on his right and ex-President Hayes on his left."[27] A few years later, he

Eadweard Muybridge (1830–1904)
by Elsa Koenig Nitzsche
*Pioneer of motion pictures, born Edward
James Muggeridge in Kingston-on-
Thames, England, he photographed
animals in motion, first on Leland
Stanford's stud farm, then under a grant
at the University of Pennsylvania (1884–
1886) where he perfected a timing
mechanism. The pictures taken with his
zoöpraxiscope were published in* Animal
Locomotion: An Electrophotographic
Investigation of Consecutive Phases of
Animal Movements *(1872–1885), eleven
volumes.*

John Henry Towne (1818–1875)
by William Merritt Hunt
*Iron founder born in Pittsburgh, Towne
took great interest in the new department of science (1872) while trustee of
the University of Pennsylvania (1873–
1875). By a resolution of the trustees, the
name was changed to the Towne Scientific School after a bequest to the school
was made in his will.*

saw an occasion to make the centennial of the union of the College with the
University of the State of Pennsylvania an opportunity for a fund-raising
drive aimed at the alumni who, were thus prominently brought into
University affairs for the first time.

Despite his work as administrator and fund-raiser, Provost Pepper
nonetheless also remained a highly successful medical practitioner
throughout his life. At the height of his career, it was not uncommon for a
special train to take him to attend his more distinguished patients elsewhere
in the country—his care of General Sheridan, for which he refused
remuneration, being a case in point.[28] He was equally concerned with a
large clientele of poor people, and his former colleague at the medical
school, Sir William Osler, illustrates his habitual sympathy for the individual sufferer by describing how Pepper sent a former patient to him at
the Johns Hopkins with a handwritten letter of introduction.[29]

Frequently, Pepper was able to use his professional position in the
service of the University. In 1893, when Pepper was elected president of
the Pan-American Medical Congress held in Washington, he took charge
of the minutest details to insure that this significant event of medical
cooperation in the Western hemisphere should be a success. And equally
typical of his *modus operandi* was his care to reap benefits for the University at the same time. In a letter describing his busy time in Washington,
Pepper expresses a hope of using his South American ties to secure artifacts
for the University's growing archaeological collection. In concluding, he
notes that he is making arrangements to entertain the prominent members
of the international community at the University: "We go to Philadelphia,
where I will give all the foreign delegates a big time at the University. It
may do some good."[30]

The changes that took place during William Pepper's tenure continue to
affect the University of Pennsylvania. At the time of his inauguration, for
example, the new provost was able to announce a gift of $100,000 from
Joseph Wharton for the endowment of a department of finance and
economy, thus establishing the oldest collegiate school of business in the
United States. Wharton had expressed the hope that education at the
University in "the principles underlying successful business management
and civil government would greatly aid in producing a class of men likely
to become most useful members of society, whether in private or public
life."[31] In Wharton's opinion, these ends were not being satisfactorily
served by the so-called commercial colleges of the day; his foresight is
demonstrated by the fact that similar schools were subsequently established
at other institutions, assuring the place of management education at
universities and leading, later on, to the creation of graduate schools of
business administration. Foreign students, always a presence at the
University, were increasingly attracted by such new departures. A

prominent Japanese graduate who remained active in University affairs as the long-time president of the alumni association of Japan was Kenjiro Matsumoto, who attended the Wharton School in the class of 1895 as well as being awarded an honorary L.L.D. in 1956.

In another new departure, James McKean Cattell established a Psychological Laboratory in 1887. Based on the German model, it was the first of its kind in the United States.[32] Under his successor, Lightner Witmer, the Psychological Clinic was opened. Reorganized in 1909, it was viewed with great interest by Edwin S. Slosson during his researches at that time for his book on the great American universities. The early scientific bias of the College and the prominence of its department of medicine made it almost a foregone conclusion that other professional schools would follow its example. Both the school of veterinary medicine and the dental school, which conferred their first degrees in 1887 and 1879 respectively, were recognized by Slosson as leaders in their fields.[33]

William Pepper's opinion that a university should not only teach students but support scientific projects which could not be financed by individual investigators appears in a grant made to Eadweard Muybridge, the pioneer photographer whose pictures of moving animals gave technological impetus to the development of motion pictures. This somewhat eccentric investigator, who was born Edward Muggeridge in Kingston-on-Thames, set up his equipment—including an instrument which he called a "zoöpraxiscope"—in temporary buildings on Thirty-sixth and Spruce Streets. He had first photographed horses on the Leland Stanford ranch in California and, in addition to making pictures of animals, at the University of Pennsylvania, he went on to study normal and abnormal movement in human models. The funds for his early publication, *Animal Locomotion*, were provided by contributions from individual professors and administrators at the University.[34] The impact of his series of stills on realistic painting was immediate. More recently, individual studies by Muybridge have inspired some remarkable paintings by the English artist Francis Bacon.[35]

The most important change which took place during Pepper's administration, however, was in the area of graduate education. Thirty years after the debate initiated by Bishop Potter, William Pepper expressed current opinion when he remarked: "As the development of the American University system progresses, more and more importance attaches to the needs of advanced students." The University of Pennsylvania occupied an important place in satisfying these needs, for "advanced students and original investigators must still repair to the older seats of learning, whose rich collections and large corps of special teachers offer the needed facilities." For this reason, Pepper was pleased to note the direction recently taken by the Towne Scientific School as the offspring of Stillé's administration came to be called after an unexpected bequest from John

Nathan F. Mossell (1856–1946)
Drawing; artist unknown
Born in Canada, graduate of Lincoln University (M.A. 1877) and the University of Pennsylvania's school of medicine (M.D. 1882). Mossell worked as assistant to Dr. D. Hayes Agnew in the Out-patient Surgical Clinic of the University Hospital and was elected to the Philadelphia County Medical Society (1888) before pursuing postgraduate studies at St. Thomas' Hospital, London. He established the Frederick Douglass Memorial Hospital and Training School as a protest against racial segregation of nurses and interns. Founder of the Philadelphia branch of the National Association for the Advancement of Colored People and co-founder of the Philadelphia Academy of Medicine and Allied Sciences, for many years a thriving association of black physicians, dentists, and pharmacists.

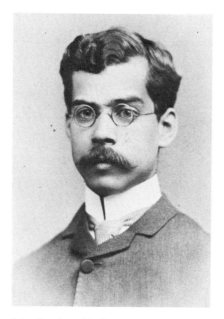

John Stephens Durham (1861–1919)
*Educated at the Institute for Colored
Youth before attending the Towne School
of the University of Pennsylvania (B.S.
1886; C.E. 1888). During his college
career, he supported himself by teaching
and as a reporter. He was associate editor
of the Pennsylvanian and, after graduation, worked as associate editor of the
Philadelphia Evening Bulletin. Appointed
United States consul to Santo Domingo
(1890), he followed Frederick Douglass
as minister to Haiti (1893). Admitted to
the bar (1895), he returned to Santo
Domingo to manage a sugar plantation
and practiced law there and in Cuba,
where he was appointed counsel for the
Spanish War Claims Commission by
President Theodore Roosevelt. A fellowship was established in his honor for
"the deserving young of various race
groups" (1910) a few years before he
died in London.*

Henry Towne in 1875. "It would seem destined," said Pepper, to develop
as "a strictly graduate school, with courses of practical training during two
years based on . . . scientific courses preparatory to the subsequent
advanced professional studies."[36]

Pepper made an early move to establish a faculty of philosophy where
advanced students could pursue a course leading to the degree of doctor of
philosophy. The same year, in 1882, recognizing the restrictions to further
study imposed on all but the prosperous, Pepper urged that scholarships
and fellowships should be provided. Before the year was up, he was able
to announce the endowment of three scholarships named in honor of
Benjamin Franklin. Higher standards in the department of philosophy
soon followed as it became more organized and encompassed a larger
variety of subjects. Although there was no provision for the admission of
female undergraduates in the older faculties of the University, women were
admitted to the Ph.D. program and they were also successful in gaining
access to certain non-degree courses. The first black students attended the
University in the 1880s, with Canadian-born Nathan F. Mossell graduating
from the department of medicine in 1882 and John Stephens Durham, who
succeeded Frederick Douglass as minister to Haiti, obtaining a B.S. from
the Towne School in 1886 and a degree in civil engineering two years later.
After postgraduate studies at St. Thomas' Hospital in London, Mossell
returned to Philadelphia where he founded the Frederick Douglass
Memorial Hospital at Sixteenth and Lombard Streets. He was a founder of
the Philadelphia branch of the NAACP along with W. E. B. DuBois who
served on the staff of the University in 1896–97. Mossell's brother, Aaron
A. Mossell, received the LL.B. from the Law School in 1887. Forty years
later his daughter, Sadie Tanner Mossell Alexander, already the first black
woman in the country to receive a Ph.D. (Wharton School, 1921), became
the first to receive a law degree at the University.

Pepper was deeply concerned with raising standards at the University.
Aspects of University policy urgently in need of reform were admissions
and the length of time that medical students were expected to attend courses
before qualifying for a degree. Pepper increased the requirements for
admission to the University in a step towards uniformity of policy with the
leading institutions in the country. His efforts were consistent with the
critical observations which he had made as early as 1877 when he delivered
an address on "Higher Medical Education" at the inaugural lecture of the
revised medical school course. On this occasion, he had compared the low
standards required for admission to medical school in America unfavorably
with those of all other lands—not merely the old aristocratic territories of
Europe, but even such places as Australia, Mexico, and the republics of
South America. He pointed out that, in all these countries, "a student of
medicine must, unless he has a degree from some literary college or
analogous institution, pass a preliminary examination."[37]

In the United States, a young man could enter the medical profession with the greatest of ease before the turn of the century. Small wonder, Pepper declared, that there was a glut of physicians. Even more of a disgrace, in his opinion, was the nominal period of required instruction. After he became provost, Pepper succeeded in extending the medical term from October to April, and later to a full year. But it was only in 1893 that he was able to announce a compulsory four-year curriculum for medical students, a reform he had urged since 1887. That year, at the opening of a medical complex in New York, he had commented scathingly on the perennial views currently being aired again on the relative merits of Greek and German in the ordinary college curriculum; meanwhile, precious little attention was being paid to "the minimum amount of instruction which may qualify us to take in charge the sacred lives of our fellow men."[38]

An immediate result of the greater stringency of entrance requirements was a falling off in the number of applicants at both the college and medical department. In 1884, fewer students applied to the department of arts because admission to courses leading to the degrees of bachelor of science or philosophy involved writing a sample of English and taking an examination in French and German.[39] The reduction in enrollments in the medical department had been fearfully anticipated all along by the professors who still drew their salaries from student fees. For this reason, they had been particularly adamant in opposing the measures needed to raise standards.

One consequence of raising the age of admission to the University was a lessening of the disciplinary problems which had plagued institutions of higher learning throughout the nineteenth century. Pepper believed that the

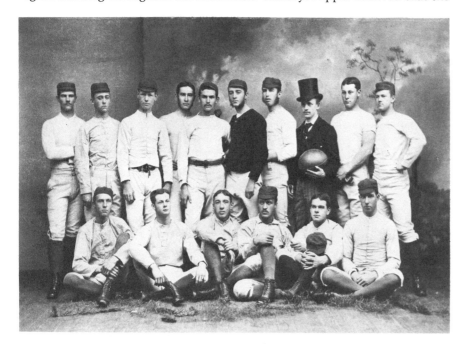

The University of Pennsylvania Football Team, 1878–79
Played under Rugby rules, intercollegiate football began at the University of Pennsylvania in 1876. The 1878–1879 team is shown in the first surviving photograph of the early years in a long tradition.

The Henley Regatta, 1901
Rowing, Penn's senior sport, traces its pedigree to 1854. The University's first Eight went to Henley in 1901, and is shown here defeating the London Rowing Club for the Grand Challenge Cup. A later Pennsylvania oarsman at Henley, John B. Kelly, Jr. (A.B. 1950), won the single sculls championship and participated in the Olympic Games of 1948, 1952, 1956, and 1960, a record never achieved by any other Pennsylvania athlete. In 1976, more graduates of the University participated in the Olympic Games than from any other university.

introduction of organized sports had also played a role in improving behavior. The first intercollegiate football game was played in 1869, and the sport was introduced at the University of Pennsylvania in 1876. The department of physical culture at the University was organized in 1883. The lingering prejudice against sport as "too frivolous to merit consideration" was finally overcome and measures were taken to give recognition to successful athletic exploits. It had taken institutions of learning in the United States many years to accept the classical adage: *mens sana in corpore sano.* Ever the physician, Pepper encouraged the development of organized sport with his remarks on the nefarious effects on the health of too much study with too little exercise. In a newspaper of 1887, he is reported to have congratulated a champion high-jumper and commented that the young man in question "has distinguished himself by his University career, while he has won the championship of the world in one branch of athletic work."[40]

In other developments as well, Pepper's administration fulfilled his expressed opinions on the extent and the quality of the offerings at an institution of higher learning. "The essence of a University," he said, "is a breadth of view embodied in its organization which makes it keep in touch with all the intellectual needs of the people, an atmosphere of freedom which encourages individuality and original thought; and a richness of equipment in library and museum and laboratory which stimulates research and investigation."[41] The University Library had been built to fulfill a need recognized by Pepper, although the project ran into opposition from former Provost Stillé. A full-time librarian came to the staff in 1892, a date by which, with the organization of the Wistar Institute of Anatomy and Biology, a total of fifteen new departments, schools, and divisions had been added along with two libraries, several laboratories, and plans for a University Museum.

On William Pepper's retirement as provost, Horace Furness drew a comparison between the University of 1894 and what had been there thirteen years earlier. Pepper had found a "sedate, conservative, respectable" University, "quiescent in the belief that the methods of education which were wholesome for the fathers must be wholesome and all-sufficient for the sons and grandsons."[42] Since then there had sprung up, in addition to the "modest quartette" of buildings which made up Stillé's new campus, a library, an electrical laboratory, a biological building, and a home for nurses. Again, according to Furness, "we see a Veterinary Building with its long row of pathetic hospital stalls." The Wistar Institute of Biology, the Hygienic Laboratory, and the Chemistry Laboratory, and, last but not least, Franklin Field (its stands to be built in the next century), attested to Pepper's achievement.

One further structure bearing witness to the advancing times deserves comment although the central light and heat station was only incidentally a product of the Pepper administration. In the description of Horatio C. Wood: "All of the lecture rooms and laboratories are heated by steam, and are thoroughly ventilated by currents of air forced into the rooms in such a way as to avoid drafts."[43] This must have been an improvement particularly pleasing to Pepper, who had suffered from the inadequacies in this respect in College Hall. On one occasion he writes: "At [Matthew] Arnold's lecture a good instance of retributive justice was seen: the room was very crowded, and there is absolutely no ventilation, the architect having been stupid enough to neglect it utterly. One woman fainted, and I learned afterwards it was the wife of the architect."[44] Even the provision for illuminating the library designed by architect Frank Furness had become obsolescent since, as Wood proudly goes on to note of the buildings, "they are also brilliantly illuminated by electricity."

If William Pepper regarded the creation at the University of many new departments, as well as libraries and laboratories, as only a partial fulfillment of a greater design, these projects are in themselves only a part of what he bequeathed to the City of Philadelphia. Much as he is identified with the University at this crucial stage of its development, he worked untiringly for civic improvements as well. The Commercial Museum and the University extension courses which occupied him after his retirement were a continuation of his idea of a university. He is also identified with the movement for the Free Library of Philadelphia for which the will of his uncle, George S. Pepper, had provided the impetus.

Pepper does not appear as an imitator of days past, but as a leader whose ambitions were attuned to his times. "He dreamed of a city greater than any Penn had planned, with nobler charities and vaster public works than Franklin had fancied—a city richer in hospitals, in schools, in institutions of learning, in libraries, in art, in commerce, and in public works. . . . Into the comprehensive schemes of foresighted men he entered with the ease of one accustomed to plans of magnitude."[45] In these words, Hampton L. Carson, a colleague and representative of the General Alumni Society, paid tribute to William Pepper at the time of his death. His contributions are summed up by his biographer Francis Newton Thorpe: "The University of Pennsylvania as it stands is his creation. The system of museums which ornament Philadelphia are his monument and the higher educational tone of the community is one of the results of his life. Art, science, and education, each for its own sake, was the principle which inspired his efforts."[46]

University Boat House
Standing among the houses of other clubs on the east bank of the Schuylkill River, the Boat House was built several years after the founding of the College Boat Club in 1872. The original Victorian frame structure, with its twentieth century addition, continues to serve new generations of oarsmen.

10

Sara Yorke Stevenson: The First Women at the University

Sara Yorke Stevenson (1847–1921)
by Leopold Seyffert
Founding member of the Archaeological Association of the University of Pennsylvania (1889), curator of the Egyptian and Mediterranean sections of the archaeological department (1890–1905), and prominently associated with raising funds to build the University Museum. Born in Paris, she lived in France and Mexico before settling in Philadelphia. Author of numerous articles on archaeology, she also wrote a book Maximilian in Mexico *(1899), and was literary editor of the* Public Ledger. *She was the first woman to be awarded an honorary degree at the University (Sc.D. 1894).*

In 1888, when Sara Yorke Stevenson was forty-one, William Pepper delivered a speech on the higher education of women. In concluding, he peered into a future which was still only obscurely perceived by most of his contemporaries:

> It were idle to speculate on the ultimate result of the constantly increasing share taken by American women in practical life. It does not concern us of this generation that at some distant day the franchise may be extended to them. This question cannot now be regarded as a practical one. . . . Nor does it concern us that at some distant day, when this continent is densely peopled, the struggle for existence may be all the more keen and severe because our women have been trained, as far as may prove possible, to be the intellectual peers of men.[1]

Six years later, in 1894, Sara Yorke Stevenson became the first woman to receive an honorary degree at the University of Pennsylvania. In recognition of her contributions to scholarship and her administration of the University's archaeological collections that led to the establishment of the University Museum, she was awarded the degree of Doctor of Science. Between her birth in 1847 and 1920—the year she became an officer of the Légion d'Honneur at the age of seventy-three—Stevenson created a life for herself that already illustrated what Pepper regarded only as a possible development of the future. For, in the course of these years, a dramatic change was already taking place in the status of American women.

The modest gains made during this time by women at the University provide an interesting background to Stevenson's life and the influence she had on the University. Prior to Pepper's inaugural, women had already gained access to certain courses of study at the University. If the ranks of those genuinely interested in promoting female education were thin at the time, a number of professors showed enlightened self-interest by their willingness to increase their income by accepting female students. When a clergyman who was an alumnus of the University proposed a faculty of music in 1874, the idea met with the approval of Provost Stillé and the trustees. A professor of music was elected the following year on the

condition that he provide for his own salary from the sale of tickets—
including tickets for women—to his course. He was also expected to pay
for alterations necessary to the room in College Hall allotted to him.
According to Pepper, there were still "potent reasons" in 1893 which made
it necessary to exclude female undergraduates as a policy described as
"quite definite."[2] Despite such strictures, it was almost twenty years since
the department of music had opened its courses to "such persons . . . male
or female as may desire systematic instruction in this subject."[3] According
to the University's historian writing in 1940, the reason for this departure
from custom was a "more adventurous spirit" which as it had led to the
creation of a new professorship, made it only natural for instruction in
music to be made available to both sexes.[4] The fact remains, however, that
degrees had been granted to only six women at the University by the time
that Sara Yorke Stevenson received her honorary Sc.D. in 1894.

Not stopping to rest on her laurels, Stevenson continued her active,
creative life, and on the occasion of her seventieth birthday celebration in
1917 she was described as "the best-known woman in Philadelphia."[5] Her
work as a scholar and as an administrator which had been acknowledged by
the University so many years before may have helped to modify Pepper's
initially ambivalent opinion on the education of women. It was certainly
through her efforts that he became an active supporter of the ambitious
project for a splendid new museum to house the University's archaeological
collections.

At a time when the University was expanding in many directions,
William Pepper had recognized the importance to higher education of
current archaeological discoveries. A strong program of Semitics was
established under Morris Jastrow, Jr., a graduate of the College who in 1886
became the first Jew to be a professor at the University in 1886.
Assyriology was introduced under Hermann V. Hilprecht in 1887, the year
that Pepper, along with other Philadelphians, subscribed funds to send an
archaeological expedition to Babylon. The conditions of the subscription
were that "all the collections secured shall be the property of the University
of Pennsylvania, provided suitable accommodation in a fire-proof building
is supplied."[6] The trustees accepted the proposal, and the expedition of
1889 to Nippur, headed by the Reverend John P. Peters, inaugurated the
first large-scale American archaeological excavation in the Near East.
Subsequent expeditions were led by John H. Hayes who "unflinchingly
faced the perils to which a cruel climate and turbulent, predatory tribes
daily exposed him."[7] In 1889, the Archaeological Association of the
University of Pennsylvania was founded, with Joseph Leidy as president
and Sara Yorke Stevenson as one of the founding members.

It is not clear when Stevenson first became interested in Egyptology,
which was to be her speciality as archaeology developed at the University.

Morris Jastrow, Jr. (1861–1921)
*Professor of Semitic languages (1892–
1921) and concurrently University
Librarian, Jastrow was educated at
Leipzig (Ph.D. 1884). Internationally
distinguished as a philologist, orientalist,
and Semitic scholar, and a prolific writer,
he received the LL.D. from the University
in 1914.*

Her cousin, Admiral Edward Yorke Macauley, had served in the Far East, and perhaps through him she became interested in the discoveries of William Flinders-Petrie, the English excavator, who had found remains of other cultures in the soil of Egypt. Her first article, entitled "Mr. Petrie's Discoveries at Telel-Amarna," appeared in 1880 when she was thirty-three, and she returned to the same subject sixteen years later in an address before the American Philosophical Society.[8] At the time of the earlier publication, she had been married for ten years to a Philadelphia attorney. But, until the age of twenty-one when she took up residence in the city at the home of an aunt and two elderly uncles, Sara Yorke had led a peripatetic existence. Her childhood was divided between France and America, and she also lived for five years in Mexico where she witnessed the brief, disastrous career of the Emperor Maximilian. She later related her Mexican experiences in a book.[9]

Stevenson's earliest contact with the artifacts of antiquity had been as a child in the home of a connoisseur and collector who became her guardian when she was sent from America to attend school in Paris, the city of her birth. By the time she left France for Mexico at the age of fifteen, she had acquired an interest in the priceless possessions belonging to her guardian as well as a command of French which affected the inflection of her English throughout her life. An enduring affection for France led her to organize relief for that country during World War I, a service for which she received decorations from France and America in 1920. "*Elle était brave, la citoyenne Stevenson,*" commented the novelist Owen Wister, when he succeeded her as president of the Alliance Française.[10]

On the death of her father, which followed shortly after the Mexican débacle, Sara Yorke at eighteen was faced with the alternatives of going to live with relatives or becoming a governess—a move at the time tantamount to a lowering of social status. She was personally acquainted, therefore, with the hardships endured by women of restricted means in a period when they had few sanctioned ways of supporting themselves. In later life, she became the president of the Philadelphia Exchange for Women's Work—an organization which enabled indigent women to earn a pittance by their labors without being exposed to social opprobrium. She herself had little choice in her decision to come to Philadelphia, but she seems to have fitted in very well with the life of her elderly relatives and their social circle. Sara Yorke made her entry in 1868, unannounced, on foot, and at midnight, after a number of fortuitous events had turned a journey from Brattleboro into something of an adventure. By this time, however, she was more than accustomed to strange voyages: in 1862, she and a chaperone had been the only women aboard the ship which sailed from St. Nazaire in France, bound for Mexico and French intervention there. Five years later, when the women of the family were advised to leave, they departed with the first

Joint Expedition to Mesopotamia (1922–1934)
The biblical city of Ur was excavated jointly by staff of the British Museum and the University of Pennsylvania Museum under C. Leonard Woolley, who was later knighted.

French army from Vera Cruz and spent three weeks at sea on the way to New Orleans because the captain of the ship was unfamiliar with the Gulf.[11]

After her marriage to Cornelius Stevenson—two years after her arrival in Philadelphia—she contributed to the exuberant life led by his large family in Chestnut Hill. In Paris, she had studied both voice and dancing. Now, she not only sang contralto in a musical group but, as a contribution to the Centennial celebrations, taught a large group of young Philadelphians the minuet. The dance was performed on a grand scale in eighteenth century costume. As her young family grew up, she became involved in philanthropic work, and her interest in antiquity was also revived at this time by a meeting with Francis C. Macauley, a collector related to her cousin the Admiral and a friend and supporter of Pepper's archaeological endeavors. A folklore society was formed which later developed into the Archaeological Society of the University of Pennsylvania and led directly to her involvement with the University's Museum.

When the new University Library was completed in 1890, the growing archaeological collection overseen by Pepper was moved from its cramped quarters in College Hall, and the exhibition of objects excavated in Babylon or donated by Philadelphia patrons was arranged on the upper floors of the Library. Here, it continued to grow, owing in large part to Pepper's encouragement and interest. The story is told of how an American woman warned a rich Mexican collector that the provost would be eager to obtain a certain priceless Moorish vase from him while on a visit to his country. The collector declared he would never part with it; some time later, the vase was nonetheless to be seen on display in the University Museum.[12]

Not surprisingly, the collection soon exceeded its bounds and started overflowing down the massive stairway of the Library. It became apparent that additional space would have to be found. Pepper was initially unwilling to add yet another large project to those for which he was already committed to raising contributions. Sara Yorke Stevenson had become honorary curator of the Egyptian section at the time that Pepper had raised money for establishing working relations with the Egyptian exploration fund. She now persuaded him that a museum was absolutely necessary to house the University's valuable and diversified collection which could no longer be adequately displayed—or even stored. Soon won around, he went on to contribute to the building fund with his customary generosity.

Pepper's unqualified respect for Stevenson contrasts strongly with his and his society's ambivalence toward the educated woman in general and her role in the professions. The early history of the incursions made by women into programs restricted to men at the University of Pennsylvania, as at other places of higher learning, often involved their ability to take

Gold Breastplate, Ecuador
Part of the Museum's treasure store of pre-Columbian gold, this breastplate was excavated in 1912. The human head in the center is surrounded by a design of alligators.

The First Women Students
Left to right, Gertrude K. Peirce (1859–1953), Anna L. Flanigen (1852–1928), and Mary T. Lewis (1854–1952). Admitted to classes in chemistry in the Towne Scientific School (1876), Gertrude Peirce and Anna Flanigen had both previously studied at Women's Medical College. Flanigen obtained her Ph.D. in 1906 and became associate professor of chemistry at Mount Holyoke. Peirce was the first female graduate to marry an alumnus of the University, Francis H. Easby (A.B. 1881). Lewis received her certificate in 1880, after being admitted as a special student in the chemistry laboratory (1878–1880). In addition to enumerating her activities in the University records as those of "a busy minister's wife & mother of a family with civic and philanthropic interests," she stated her interest in "the movement for granting equal political rights and duties to women," in which she worked with Susan B. Anthony. Together they brought about the establishment of a college for women at the University of Rochester.

advantage of the main chance—an ability which Stevenson's life might be said to exemplify in the best possible sense. It was the objection of the lecturers to the clicking knitting needles of chaperones obliged to accompany the first young women to attend lectures at Oxford which led to acceptance there of women as a normal part of the student body. At the University of Pennsylvania, the trustees' action in divesting themselves of the long-maintained charity schools for which they had been made responsible by the charter of 1749 seems to have benefited women. In 1876, at the very time that this action was being debated, the professor of chemistry, Frederick Genth, received an appeal from two graduates of Women's Medical College in Philadelphia who wished to study with him. He chose to present their petition to the trustees after a visit to the University by the Emperor and Empress of Brazil. Their presence at the opening of the Centennial celebration had put the board in a particularly affable frame of mind.[13]

Dental Hall, 1896
*Dental Hall was designed in 1896 by
Edgar M. Seeler for the school of dentistry
(organized 1878). In 1915, the school
moved to its present building on Fortieth
and Spruce Streets where, for many years,
it housed the Thomas W. Evans Museum
Collection, bequeathed by Empress
Eugénie's dentist whose generosity provided the building and equipment for the
school of dental medicine. An example
of the preservation and conversion of
existing buildings, Dental Hall was used
by the school of architecture, afterwards
the graduate school of fine arts (1915–
68), and has since been occupied by the
department of geology and renamed
Hayden Hall after United States geologist
Ferdinand V. Hayden (LL.D. 1887),
professor of mineralogy and geology
(1865–72).*

The board's agreement to allow Gertrude Klein Peirce and Anna
Lockhart Flanigen to start classes in the Towne Scientific School in the fall
of 1876 seems to have been influenced by the opportunity for some
advantageous trading with the city. Having admitted a number of "indigent
women" to classes at the University, the trustees felt better able to vote to
abolish the historic charity schools the following year. The income which
had supported them was immediately turned over to the newly named
Towne School. Soon afterwards, the trustees authorized the admission of
"such a number of female children in indigent circumstances, as they may
deem expedient to lectures on History and to the instruction by lecture and
in the laboratories in the Departments of Chemistry and Physics."[14] By this
time, Peirce and Flanigen were already enrolled in their courses as fee-
paying students. Clearly, if indigent female scholars were now acceptable
on campus, others willing and able to pay tuition could no longer be
neglected. The board went on to resolve, therefore, "that any other females
desiring to attend instruction in the aforesaid subjects may do so on payment of a fee to be settled by the committees."

On finishing their chemistry studies, Peirce and Flanigen were awarded,
not a degree, but the certificate of proficiency specified at the same trustees'
meeting. No disgrace to their class, these first alumnae placed second and
third in their final year. The first woman to earn a degree was another
graduate of Women's Medical College who entered the auxiliary faculty of
medicine when it was permitted to open its courses to women in 1878. For
a short period, that department awarded the Ph.D. to graduate physicians
after a further two-year medical program. When she completed her course-
work in 1880, Mary Alice Bennett thus became the first woman to receive a
doctorate at the University. The degree was subsequently reduced to a
Bachelor of Science. Because of this change in University policy, Emma
Virginia Boone, yet another graduate of Women's, was awarded a B.S. in
1891 for an identical course of study and became the first woman to
receive an undergraduate degree.

In the catalogue of 1888–89, the name of Emily L. Gregory, Ph.D., is
listed as the lone fellow in biology. She was also the first woman to teach
at the University of Pennsylvania—albeit without remuneration. Nothing
in the "Catalogue and Announcements" of that year indicates the nature of
her position. There is no other record at the University of the struggle of
this schoolteacher who decided to go back to college, received her B.A. at
the age of forty, and then went on to become one of the handful of women
to teach in the male-dominated universities of the East. In her own account:

> After fitting myself for doing advanced work in the science of
> botany, which I did by four years work in College at Cornell,
> followed up by four years work in universities abroad, I found
> to my surprise that there was little opportunity for me to teach
> in the grade for which I had prepared. There were places enough

for elementary work but this was not what I wished to do. Through my acquaintance with the botanists of Penn. University I went there to finish a piece of original work which required the advantages of a laboratory to accomplish. I went there in June and during the summer there were several applications from women students, the faculty of the bio. dept. decided to take these students provided I would be willing to remain through the year and give my course of lectures which I had prepared for the first year. As the class was small and my lectures were already prepared, I was very glad to accept this proposition, as I had spent just ten years of my mature life to prepare myself for a grade of teaching which my unfortunate sex prevented my obtaining in the regular way. During the year, a number of my friends made a strong effort to have my work recognized in some way by the authorities of the institution. They were not able to accomplish this, however, in any other way than to obtain a reluctant consent to my receiving the title of fellow. This was granted in some regular meeting of the Trustees but the only advantage arising from it was that it enabled the Faculty of the Biological Dept. to print my name on the list with the faculty of that dept.[15]

Gregory went on to teach at Columbia, at first without pay. She finally gained recognition in 1895 when she became professor of botany at Barnard College, but she died two years later at the age of fifty-six.

Another energetic pioneer in female education at the University of Pennsylvania was Caroline Burnham Kilgore, the first woman to graduate from the law school. She finally received her LL.B. in 1883, some twelve years after she had originally sought admission. On that occasion, her application had led the dean to threaten to resign if a woman was admitted. Orphaned at the age of twelve, Carrie Burnham had been put to work in the kitchen and the family factory by her guardians who considered that she "clearly had education enough for a woman."[16] She supported herself by teaching and domestic work while continuing her education, and in 1864 she became the first woman to earn the degree of Doctor of Medicine in the State of New York.

After arriving in Philadelphia where she took charge of a "French School for Young Ladies," she made application to the law school in 1871. Some time before, she had started to study privately with attorney Damon Y. Kilgore who was to become her husband. On the occasion of their marriage, the parties entered into an "ante-nuptial contract" in which it was stated that she should "not be subject to any of the legal disabilities imposed upon married women by the laws of this Commonwealth, or of any State or Territory of the United States."[17] Carrie Burnham Kilgore finally gained admission to the law school in 1881. The same year, she argued the case for admitting women to the legal profession before a joint session of the state legislature, and a bill forbidding exclusion to the bar on the basis of sex was subsequently passed. Kilgore became the

Emily Lovira Gregory (1841–1897)
Born in Portage, New York, Gregory taught school until, at the age of thirty-five, she entered Cornell University (B.A. 1881). After obtaining her doctorate in botany at Zurich, she took the position of teaching fellow in the department of biology at the University of Pennsylvania, thus becoming the first woman to teach on the faculty as well as one of the earliest to give instruction at any but a women's college. She was appointed lecturer at Barnard College the second year of its existence, and she played an active part in championing the cause of graduate students and encouraging laboratory assistants by paying them out of her own funds. She died only two years after becoming the first woman professor at Barnard College.

first woman admitted to practice before the Supreme Court of Pennsylvania.

In 1881 also, women sought admission to the medical department as well as to the College. They were equally unsuccessful in each case. The medical faculty supported a motion by Alfred Stillé, brother of the former provost, pronouncing it inexpedient to admit women. Policy against female undergraduates reflected a hesitancy on the part of the University to accept the responsibility of comporting itself *in loco parentis* in the case of young girls, while the decision of the medical department was certainly due in large part to a prudish contemporary reaction to the immodesty and embarrassment of conducting medical lectures and clinical studies before both sexes. Among its heirlooms, the Medical College of Pennsylvania (formerly Women's Medical College) preserves a cardboard mannequin formerly used for studying the male anatomy. During Philadelphia's Bicentennial celebrations, it was exhibited as a curiosity—so far has women's education come since the time of Pepper's speech on the subject in 1888.

Towards the end of his inaugural address seven years before, William Pepper had broached the question of higher education for women with the admission that "it seems impossible for any school which intends at the present time to exert its full influence in the intellectual life of the community to neglect the subject." The University was hampered, however, in making any marked contribution by the firm belief expressed in Pepper's following remarks: "I regard it as settled beyond dispute that the co-education of the sexes is inadmissible."[18] To some degree, he reflected the views of a century before, when the trustees had justified their attempt to renege on the charter provisions for educating girls at the Charity School in the following manner: "It is unbecoming and indecent to have Girls among our Students; it is a Reproach to our Institution, and were our Funds able to support them, as they are not, they should be removed to another Part of the City."[19]

In 1764, as in Pepper's time, financial considerations thus accompanied current prejudices against coeducation. The girls' school survived attempts to discontinue it in the eighteenth century, and, in his address, Pepper went on to express interest in any developments in female education as long as it was clear that the University could not "take the initiative" and would do no more than watch from the wings. As far as the cost of a program for women was concerned, it was obvious that University officials had no intention of exerting themselves to generate the funds for this particular purpose. Expense was the factor on which the question of facilities for female education ultimately hinged. For this reason, it was deemed "proper that further action should await the expression of some carefully matured wishes or plans on the part of those who may be assumed to represent the interests of women in this matter."[20] Both funds and initiative would have to come from outside the University.

Carrie Burnham Kilgore (1838–1909)
First woman to gain admission to the law school and to receive the LL.B. (1883). Born in Vermont, orphaned at twelve, she financed her own education by teaching and domestic work. Admitted to the Bellevue Hospital clinics, she became the first woman to receive a medical degree in the State of New York (1865). In Philadelphia she taught in a "French School for Young Ladies" and began studying law with Damon Kilgore, whom she married after entering into an "ante-nuptial contract" with him. After graduating from the law school she was admitted to the Orphans' Court of Philadelphia and to the state Supreme Court and all the lower courts after an act of the legislature (1885), whom she had addressed on the admission of women several years earlier. She was admitted to practice before the United States Supreme Court (1890). A year before her death she was the only woman passenger in the first balloon ascension of the Philadelphia Aeronautical Recreation Society.

Among those both interested and in a position to do something about it were various prominent people who contributed to funds for women at the University. In 1878, scholarships for women planning to be teachers were provided for by Mrs. Bloomfield Moore. A benefaction earmarked for women was made by Colonel Joseph M. Bennett—no relation of Mary Alice Bennett—who donated two buildings to "be occupied for the purpose of a College of Women." When no further funds were forthcoming, the premises became instead the administrative offices and social center for the graduate department of women, established in 1892. Its first director, Fanny R. M. Hitchcock, who had studied in Berlin before receiving her Ph.D. at the University of Pennsylvania, attempted to establish undergraduate courses for women in the arts and sciences. When her proposals were turned down, once more on the grounds of inadequate funds, she resigned. The graduate department did not long survive her departure. As for courses at the college level, despite its ever-growing body of alumnae, the University did not establish a true undergraduate course for women, as opposed to a curriculum designed for teachers, until 1933. Up until this time, the greatest changes in the policy towards women were those which occurred under the administrations of Stillé and Pepper.

However grudging early attempts to extend the privilege of higher education to women may appear in retrospect, they have to be viewed against the background of the times. Pepper's forceful opinion was undoubtedly conventional; nonetheless, he showed considerable insight into the implications of female education, while steadily opposing the admission of women undergraduates to the University of Pennsylvania. Indeed, the interest of rich women such as Mrs. Moore seems to have encouraged Pepper to give more thought to the subject. In his remarks on the higher education of women in 1888, he went out of his way to counter the popular opinion that education harms a woman's health—a claim which had caused Philadelphia's great medical authority, University trustee S. Weir Mitchell, to warn parents that girls could not hope to graduate from Bryn Mawr without becoming permanent invalids.[21]

Pepper's speech draws attention to the poor conditions under which the female usually received her education and the fact that ill health was equally prevalent among young women engaged in a number of occupations which no one thought to oppose. "Have you followed any large number of girls, drawn from the same class of society," he asks, "into occupations which do not tax the brain by study—into the shops, the mills, the factories—where, as a rule, the neglect of hygienic rules is no less striking? The ill-health may there assume other forms, but ill-health and stunted development there are in sad plenty." No efforts having been made to improve the deplorable surroundings in which girls are obliged to pursue their studies, Pepper suggests, "that judgment shall be suspended until for girls who are pursuing a higher education there are provided facilities as adequate as those which have been created for young men." As for women of his own social class who were traditionally prevented from pursuing higher studies, Pepper boldly asserts, "the amount of exertion connected with such lives as our young girls in society now lead is tenfold greater than all which can be charged against over-education."[22]

At that very moment, Sara Yorke Stevenson's life was illustrating the amount of energy possessed by a woman "in society" where there was a call for her to use it. Stevenson's unflagging enthusiasm for the University Museum collections resulted, in 1893, in an opportunity to gain attention for the University's archaeological ventures at the Columbian Exposition, the World's Fair in Chicago. The objects chosen for display testified to the vitality of the newly established department of archaeology and paleontology: far from being just artifacts from a collection, they had been acquired during the University's own expeditions to the Middle East. On the same occasion, Sara Yorke Stevenson was appointed to the Jury of Awards for Ethnology of the department of anthropology at the exposition. A special act of Congress was needed in order to permit women to serve on such juries, after which she was promptly elected vice-president. At its final meeting, the international jury approved a resolution recognizing "the wisdom of Congress in passing an act which has enabled scientific women to take their place on the highest planes of science, co-equal with men."[23]

The following year saw the opening of the University Museum; Stevenson, formerly secretary of the committee to establish the Free Museum of Science and Arts, became the secretary of the board of the department of archaeology and paleontology, a position she held for a decade before being elected president for one year in 1904. At this date, two other women were engaged in the unheard-of activity of archaeological exploration under the Museum's sponsorship. With funds provided by the Museum, Harriet Boyd was at work up the road from Sir Arthur Evans at Gournia on Crete. She was joined by Edith Hall, a Ph.D. from Bryn Mawr College, who later became curator of the Museum's Mediterranean section and who, in 1912, discovered the Minoan settlement of Vrokastro in the mountains of eastern Crete. A number of enterprising women were employed by the Museum from its foundation, with Stevenson the first whose talents were recognized. She attained a high point in her career in 1894, the year when she first took up her post at the museum and was awarded an honorary doctorate by the University. From this moment on, "no new enterprise appeared to be undertaken . . . without her sanction. No distinguished visitors could be entertained without her. Neither could national or international conventions or congresses take place without including her as a member of the reception committee."[24]

Among her numerous activities—scientific, civic, and philanthropic—she was invited to be the first president of Philadelphia's Civic Club,

Excavations at Gournia, Crete (1904)
Harriet Boyd, far right, Smith-educated archaeologist who was excavating in Crete at the same time as Sir Arthur Evans, with funds from the University Museum (1901). Her findings were published in the Transactions of the Museum. *With her and her Greek workforce is Edith Hall, who, after obtaining her Ph.D. at Bryn Mawr with a dissertation on Bronze Age Crete, returned to take charge of excavations under the auspices of the University Museum at Sphoungaras and Vrokastro (1910 and 1912). She was assistant curator at the Museum until her marriage to Joseph M. Dohan (LL.B. 1888) and again from 1920, becoming curator of the Mediterranean section before her death in 1943.*

established by a number of Philadelphia women to encourage municipal
reform. In this role, she even figured in satirical verses in *Punch* as
"Philadelphia's patriotic matron." Quoting the doggerel many years later,
Stevenson commented, "all these good-natured criticisms make for
publicity and publicity makes for interest."[25] In 1894, after delivering her
first public lecture at the University of Pennsylvania, she became the first
woman to lecture at Harvard's Peabody Museum. She was appointed as the
only woman to the board of trustees of Philadelphia's Commercial
Museum and, in subsequent years, she was the first woman to be called to
a position on a citizen's advisory committee by the mayor of Philadelphia.
The all-male Oriental Club of Philadelphia changed its laws to admit her
as a member, and she later became its president. In recognition of her great
contributions, she was elected a fellow of the American Association for
the Advancement of Science and a member of the American Philosophical
Society.

When the governor of Pennsylvania appointed her commissioner to the Paris Exposition, she refused on the grounds that it was a political assignment. In 1897, however, she went to Europe as the special representative of the University's department of archaeology and paleontology. On this occasion, she established cordial relations with English, French, and Italian archaeologists and secured treasures from a recent Egyptian excavation for the Museum. For the first and only time in her life, she actually traveled to Egypt in 1898 as a member of the American Exploration Society, a group she had founded the previous year. In Cairo she secured permission from the department of antiquities to explore Tanis and transport to Philadelphia sculptures found on the site.

After fifteen years of service to the University Museum, Stevenson resigned as president of the board in 1905. The following year, as a result of financial reverses, she launched upon an entirely new career as literary editor and columnist for the Philadelphia *Public Ledger*. Starting at the age of sixty-one, she contributed to a chronicle of events under the name of "Peggy Shippen" or, in a more serious vein, signing herself "Sally Wistar." Never before or since has Philadelphia had a society columnist who was also the president of the prestigious Acorn Club. While working as a journalist, she continued to exhibit the researcher's orderly mind. In a memorial speech at the University Museum in 1922, under the auspices of fourteen societies, schools, and organizations in which she had been active, the Honorable Hampton L. Carson gave an example of her quick intelligence: she had fully grasped the implications of a legal topic from a few hours spent among his own collection of papers. The result was a lucid Peggy Shippen letter on the growth of English law, of which he remarks: "Had she been specially interested in such matters she could not have done it more accurately, more intelligently or more thoroughly."[26]

An alumnus and professor of the law school and attorney general of the State of Pennsylvania, Carson was particularly interested in Stevenson's writings on legal questions. In an illuminating tale, he discloses the casual source of an odd title listed along with her archaeological publications: "Insurance and Business Venture in the Days of Shakespeare and Those of William Penn." It seems that an old insurance contract belonging to one of her uncles had awakened her interest in the terms of such documents, and she had proceeded to study those prepared in England and America and on the Continent. With her discovery that marine insurance was far from unknown in Italy in the days of Shakespeare, she added to what was generally regarded as the most comprehensive English authority on insurance law. To Carson, who speaks of Portia's eloquence in *The Merchant of Venice* as "a strained literal interpretation, which a modern lawyer would not approve," Stevenson's contribution was of particular interest since it tended to refute the assumption that Antonio did not have the option of insuring his ships—a premise crucial for the entire plot of Shakespeare's play. Her article was published in a British legal journal and translated into more than a dozen languages—no small accomplishment for a person with only an incidental interest in the law.

In addition to her many intellectual accomplishments, Sara Yorke Stevenson was, as her contemporaries were eager to insist, well versed in the domestic arts. Not only did she entertain frequently in her house, but she sometimes supplemented the efforts of her cook. She seems to have been an innovator of recipes, serving, at one repast, a dish combining "larded and browned sweetbreads, with broiled oysters and truffles—all together."[27] She was also a needlewoman, and crewelwork in the style of the Royal School of Needlework in South Kensington, designed and executed in the early days of her marriage, adorned her drawing room at 237 South Twenty-first Street. In addition to being the first president of the Equal Franchise Society of Pennsylvania and head of numerous intellectual and cultural organizations she was, during the last eleven years of her life, honorary president of the Philadelphia Branch Needlework Guild of America. For all her academic accomplishment, it was important, in those days, for her contemporaries, both men and women, to uphold her as a model of accomplished Victorian womanhood. In the last year of her life, when she was seventy-three, there was a ceremonial unveiling of her likeness in a bas-relief by R. Tait McKenzie, whose statues of the young Franklin, the Reverend George Whitefield, and ideal athletes adorn the campus. At the ceremony, Stevenson was lauded by her contemporary, the essayist Agnes Repplier, who declared: "She has been in her day president of almost everything except the United States and the Women's Christian Temperance Union."[28] Most of all, she was the first of many talented women to contribute extensively to life at the University of Pennsylvania as students, teachers, trustees, alumnae, and friends.

The Twentieth Century

*This is the university that added to its traditional
curriculum such subjects as applied mathematics,
foreign languages, political science and economics—
all very new at the time. This is the university that
introduced multidisciplinary education well before
the term was even invented. This is the university
that established the country's first school of
medicine, then realized that theory could not be
separated from practice and consequently developed
the system of the teaching hospital now in general
use. For all these reasons the University of
Pennsylvania has been a true pioneer, and as we
look back today, it is virtually impossible for us to
estimate the contribution this institution has made
to free intellectual development.*

M. Valéry Giscard d'Estaing,
President of the French Republic
on receiving an honorary doctorate
from the University of Pennsylvania
May 19, 1976

11

Alfred Newton Richards:
Biomedical Research

The Agnew Clinic
David Hayes Agnew (M.D. 1838), professor of surgery (1871–1889). When his clinic at the University Hospital was photographed in 1886, perhaps by Eadweard Muybridge, then working on campus, neither teacher nor assistants wore surgical garb. In Thomas Eakins' great group portrait, based on this photograph, which hangs in the school of medicine, the celebrated surgeon, who attended President Garfield at the time of his assassination, is shown wearing a white gown while operating for cancer of the breast.

The change in "the art and science of medicine" between 1875 and 1889 is depicted in two paintings by Thomas Eakins: "The Gross Clinic" at Thomas Jefferson University's medical college and "The Agnew Clinic" of the University of Pennsylvania.[1] In the decade and a half which separate these two paintings, surgical procedure had radically altered. By the time the Pennsylvania professor was portrayed at work with his associates, white gowns had replaced the black frock coat and gold watch-chain of both the earlier work and the photograph on which "the Agnew Clinic" had been based. An awareness of antisepsis is at least suggested in the later composition despite the lack of surgical gloves. Other improvements in medical practice and teaching had come about since the days midway through the nineteenth century when Leidy's associate, William Hunt, had described the state of the school as one of "innocuous desuetude" and "medical dotage or senility."[2]

The many reforms which had been instituted led, however, to a problem of a different sort. In the words of Charles Harrison Frazier, who was dean in 1910, the atmosphere had become one of "self-satisfied complacency and scientific stagnation."[3] A few years earlier, Provost Charles Custis Harrison, Frazier's uncle and namesake, had expressed the fear that the University's school of medicine was not keeping up with the rapid advances being made in basic science. "A modern medical school," he wrote in a report to the trustees, "should be a centre of research in the science of Medicine. Nor should research be fostered solely in the spirit of advancement, but also because it insures activity on the part of the instructor, while stirring up increased interest on the part of the student."[4] Although both Frazier and Harrison had progressive views, their own close relationship was an example of the inbreeding at the University in those days, particularly in the faculty of medicine, which contributed to the conservatism of America's oldest medical school.[5]

The practice of looking only to a narrow circle of alumni to fill chairs had been breached in 1884 when the brilliant, informal Canadian physician William Osler was appointed to the professorship in clinical medicine. Although he did not stay in Philadelphia long, five years were enough for him to have an effect on the teaching of medicine, for "Osler breezes were felt everywhere in the old conservative medical center."[6] It was almost the first time in more than a century that a man who was not an alumnus of either the College or the school of medicine had been offered a medical chair. Osler even suspected a friend in Montreal of playing a practical joke on him and delayed responding, "fearing that Dr. Shepard had perhaps surreptitiously taken a sheet of University of Pennsylvania note-paper to make the joke more certain." Even so, there were doubts about the suitability of an outsider, and trustee S. Weir Mitchell was com-missioned to examine the prospective candidate in London. In Osler's account, great importance was attached to his table manners, particularly his method of disposing of the pits while eating cherry pie.[7] The professor, who arrived by streetcar rather than carriage and, far from having a polished delivery, "sat on the edge of the table swinging his feet and twisting his ear instead of behaving like an orator," was something of an oddity. During his brief tenure, however, he left an indelible mark on the school of medicine. Refusing to practice, he enthusiastically gathered students for pathological studies in the "half-way house" between the Blockley Hospital in West Philadelphia and the burial ground of Potter's Field.[8]

Osler's use of the microscope for clinical studies and his emphasis on the autopsy as a mean of furthering medical knowledge was an object lesson for the students in more ways than one. Much could be learned from the distinguished physician who gleefully pointed out to his students the evidence of a mistaken diagnosis which had come to light at the post mortem. The diagnosis in question had been made by Osler. On another occasion, he is reported to have expressed regret that he would not be present at his own autopsy, as it was the case he knew better than any other. Although he saluted the school of medicine as the "premier school of America" and Philadelphia as the *Civitas Hippocratica*," he departed in 1889 for Johns Hopkins whose medical school, when it opened, immediately set standards superior to those elsewhere in America. Osler later moved from Johns Hopkins to become Regius Professor of medicine at Oxford.

When Provost Harrison addressed the trustees in the first years of the twentieth century on the subject of research, he was influenced by Simon Flexner, the brilliant young professor of pathology who had come to the University from Johns Hopkins in 1899. In those days, few of the medical faculty had any interest in Harrison's hope of "stirring up interest" through research. During the four years Flexner remained at the University, pathology became the most scientific of the preclinical departments. Even while he was successful convincing Harrison of the necessity for scientific investigation at a university, Flexner was debating whether to leave for New York to head a risky new venture—the recently

Joseph Leidy in His Anatomy Class, 1888
The last of the great natural philosophers of his age, Leidy was also of the genera-tion that taught anatomy by didactic demonstration. Hundreds of students listened to him as he lectured from the "bull pit."

chartered Rockefeller Institute for Medical Research. To his former chief, William H. Welch, he wrote of his "agreeable position" at the University of Pennsylvania, although he was aware of tacit and continuing opposition to his ideas. He felt the entrenched position of the older Philadelphia physicians, along with the school's lack of endowment, as cause for concern.[9] Taking up the challenge at the Rockefeller Institute in 1903, Flexner was responsible for overseeing the development of one of the major research organizations in America. Exactly half a century later, the founder of biophysics at the University of Pennsylvania, Detlev Bronk, professor for twenty years, first director of the Johnson Foundation, and trustee of the University, became the third head of the Rockefeller Institute for Medical Research (now the Rockefeller University), after having served as president of Johns Hopkins.

Three years after Simon Flexner joined the Rockefeller Institute, his brother, Abraham, began to look into the nation's medical schools as part of an examination of professional education in the United States supported by the Carnegie Foundation for the Advancement of Teaching. What came to be known as "The Flexner Report" was the single most influential study of American medical education of this century and its influence continues to be felt after seventy years. The evaluation of the University of Pennsylvania's school of medicine pinpointed not so much sins of commission as those of omission. Its limitations became apparent in comparison with the most forward-looking school of the time, Johns Hopkins. Despite the national stir the report had created, the complacency with which it was received at Pennsylvania is reflected in the fact that no mention of the report's findings appears in the Minute Book of the trustees.[10] One reason for such indifference was undoubtedly the security engendered by the unrivaled position the school had occupied right up to the twentieth century, when the need for research was recognized. A recent statistical survey of leaders in the first three centuries of American history concludes with the statement that, over this period, the University of Pennsylvania "at the professional level trained more than twice as many 'noteworthy' doctors as Harvard. Indeed," the comparative study goes on, "Pennsylvania contributed more noteworthy physicians than all the medical colleges and hospitals of New York, and almost as many individuals as Harvard, Yale and Princeton put together "[11]

Even before the Flexner report was published in 1910, Provost Harrison had been preparing for reforms in the school of medicine. He hoped to replace older department heads with younger, scientifically oriented faculty. With support from trustees, principally physician and novelist S. Weir Mitchell, rather than with medical school faculty approval, he recruited new professors from Chicago, Harvard, California, and Northwestern. Selected for their scientific reputation, these men were probably the choice of David Edsall, the dynamic young researcher and alumnus of the medical school already occupying the chair of therapeutics and pharmacology. When he agreed to accept the position as the new head of medicine, Edsall became the central figure in the attempted reforms. But the progressive movement backfired: of the new appointees one alone stayed on at the University. This was Alfred Newton Richards, "the youngest and most inconspicuous of the group and the only one without medical training in an institution that prided itself on clinical excellence."[12] In the face of opposition within the medical school and the reaction which followed the resignation of Provost Harrison, Edsall departed for Washington University, later becoming dean of medicine at Harvard. Having reached his eighties, trustee S. Weir Mitchell also resigned at this time, tired as he wrote to his friend Sir William Osler of the "constant hot water in the faculty."[13]

Although the reformers accomplished little at the time, the young pharmacologist they brought to Philadelphia was to become one of the giants of biomedical science of the twentieth century. During the course of his long life, Richards attracted to his laboratory some of the brightest young physicians and scientists of the time and was active in the administration of medicine at the University as well as of national medical programs. In 1931, when the office of vice-president for medical affairs was created, Newton Richards and T. Grier Miller conducted a *Survey of Medical Affairs*. In the twenty years since Richard's arrival, the situation in the school had changed along the lines projected by the earlier reformers, not through coercion but largely as a result of his own example as a dedicated teacher and leader in research. Over the same period, the attitude to outside grants for scientific investigation had undergone an equally significant change. Fifteen years earlier, the medical school had missed an opportunity for financial aid at a time when Abraham Flexner was presiding over Rockefeller funds for the support and development of medical schools, in part because of reluctance to risk outside interference.

The problems inherent in a dependence on outside funding were only too well known to Richards, who at eighty-two addressed himself to this very question in a speech on the fiftieth anniversary of the John Morgan Society.[14] Nonetheless, after World War II, when the United States government was most favorable to funding medical research, in large part owing to the wartime success of programs directed by medical administrators such as Richards, the University's school of medicine was this time in a position to benefit from federal support. In the words of one of Richards's earliest associates, Isaac Starr, first professor of therapeutic research at the medical school:

> When such funds became available, in amounts undreamed of, the Medical School of the University of Pennsylvania which he loved so much and for which he worked so hard was out of the doldrums; research was the order of the day, and it was of a

Hugh Wynne Free Quaker (1897 edition) by S. Weir Mitchell; frontispiece illustration by Howard Pyle *Physician-novelist S. Weir Mitchell (1829–1914) was educated at the University Grammar School (the old Academy), and had studied but not graduated with the College class of 1848. He was awarded the A.B. in 1906 long after being elected a University trustee (1875). A Civil War surgeon and a Foreign Member of the Royal Society, widely acclaimed for his treatment in private practice of nervous disorders, he is also known as a writer of poetry and prose. Two of his best-known novels are Hugh Wynne Free Quaker (1896) and The Red City (1907).*

"IN THE PRESENCE OF WASHINGTON."

quality that quickly attracted liberal support. So the school was in readiness for the expansion in medical education and research that shows no signs of abating, and he had done more than any other to bring this about.[15]

In 1967, the Kober medal was presented to Starr by Joseph Stokes, Jr., who at the time he became chairman of pediatrics had made it the first full-time position in one of the oldest strongholds of part-time clinical teaching.[16] Playing on the name of the colleague he was honoring, Stokes described Starr as "part of a planetary system with its central sun . . . Dr. A. N. Richards." A photograph of 1928 shows Richards, like another Pennsylvania professor, Alexander Dallas Bache, appropriately known as "The Chief," surrounded by his planets, all of whom later became professors and deans in medical schools around the country, "while still responding to the . . . gravitational or magnetic pull at the center so warmly acknowledged."[17] A future vice-president for medical affairs and a Nobel laureate appear in the photo; two among his entourage were knighted and one ennobled.[18] Richards attracted this brilliant group by the interest and excitment of his personality and work at a time when little money could be paid to those who entered his laboratory.

If Newton Richards was eminently capable of attracting good young scientists to the University of Pennsylvania, he himself had benefited from the scientific and humanitarian example of his professor at Yale. Science and learning had been brought alive for him there by Russell H. Chittenden, who taught physiological chemistry to future medical students. When Richards was unable to come up with the needed tuition for medical school, Chittenden offered him a fellowship for further research and study. After receiving his M.A. from Yale, Richards went to Columbia for his Ph.D. and, the same year, became the first Rockefeller Institute Scholar. His treatment of his associates reflected his own experience with the man he described as "the personification" of physiological chemistry, whose laboratory was the "American fountain head." Chittenden believed in letting his students work out their problems alone, and Richards maintained: "That, I think, was the beginning of any independence of thought or action which I have since developed."[19] He observed the same pedagogical principle with the people who later worked in his own laboratory. They learned a simple procedure for experimental research and one which Richards followed himself. "In planning your approach to a problem," he would say, "ask yourself the question to which you want the answer. Make the question so specific that you can devise an experiment to answer it."[20]

It was in 1910 that Richards was called to the University of Pennsylvania on the advice of David Edsall, who had heard him give a paper some years earlier. Although associated with men such as Chittenden, Christian A. Herter, and John Howland, Richards at thirty-

HUGH WYNNE

FREE QUAKER

SOMETIME BREVET LIEUTENANT-COLONEL ON
THE STAFF OF HIS EXCELLENCY
GENERAL WASHINGTON

BY

S. WEIR MITCHELL, M. D.

LL. D. HARVARD AND EDINBURGH

VOL. I

NEW YORK
THE CENTURY CO.
1897

William Osler (1849–1919)
by William Merritt Chase
*Professor of clinical medicine at the
University of Pennsylvania (1884–1889).
Born in Canada, he received his M.D.
from McGill, where he was professor
before coming to the University. He later
organized the medical service at Johns
Hopkins Hospital, before it opened
(1889), and became physician-in-chief
there (1893). Appointed Regius Professor
at Oxford (1905), he was created a
baronet in 1911. Although he published
numerous articles—over 300 while at the
University—and many books, including
The Principles and Practice of Medicine
(1892), he wished to be remembered
principally as one who "taught clinical
medicine on the wards."*

four had principally exemplified himself by the methods he had devised for teaching the area of basic science which was only beginning to be known as pharmacology. The traditional subject—materia medica—had been steadily decreasing in importance and, after much neglect, the subject had fallen into disrepute. "Is your son so stupid that he can't do anything better than waste his life on Pharmacology?" was the question asked of Carl Schmidt's father when the man who followed Richards as chairman of pharmacology joined the department in 1919.[21] Having learned little about teaching the subject from Oswald Schmiedeberg, the recognized "Grand Master of Pharmacology" whose methods for organizing a laboratory course in the new discipline he had observed in Strasbourg in 1903, Richards was forced to start from scratch when he returned from Germany to create an elective course in pharmacology at Columbia. Before coming to Philadelphia, he had also set up a teaching department in the subject at Northwestern medical school. During his first year at the University of Pennsylvania, his concern with teaching as well as his editorship of the recently established *Journal of Biological Chemistry* left him precious little time for research.

As a matter of fact, Richards's investigative projects, including the experiment which brought him international fame, frequently grew out of his efforts to improve his teaching. Gifted young collaborators soon presented themselves, and some of the University's brightest medical students were so impressed by Richards as teacher, scientist, and person that they took time out to work in his laboratory.[27] The first student to do this was Cecil Drinker, afterwards dean of Harvard's school of public health. With his cooperation, Richards created an improved perfusion pump for pumping liquids through tissues and kept a mammalian brain alive by this means. He next decided to perfuse the kidney in an attempt to determine the function of this organ. In teaching renal physiology to medical students a problem arose because there were conflicting theories concerning the formation of urine. There were no experimental data to show whether urine was formed by selective secretion in the kidney of only those constituents found in the bladder, or by nonspecific filtration of the blood followed by selective reabsorption of the valuable constituents leaving only waste products behind.

A first round of experiments in Richards' laboratory had been interrupted by World War I when Richards was invited to London to collaborate with Sir Henry Dale, "the Pope of Pharmacology," with whom he produced, among other things, a classic study on the action of histamines—compounds which occur in all mammalian tissues. After demobilization, Richards's laboratory started up again in earnest. With Joseph Wearn, a postdoctoral fellow from one of Harvard's teaching hospitals, the Peter Bent Brigham, who was sent to him by Drinker, Richards set up "one of those simple, direct, unambiguous experiments that re-

Alfred Newton Richards (1876–1966)
by J. C. Johansen
Professor of pharmacology at the University of Pennsylvania (1910–1946). Educated at Yale (A.B. 1897, M.A. 1899), and Columbia (Ph.D. 1901), where he taught physiological chemistry and pharmacology at the College of Physicians and Surgeons, he was brought to the University as a promising young research scientist by David Edsall. In addition to his discoveries concerning the action of chloroform and histamine, his most notable contribution resulted from his famous experiments on the kidney. Chairman of the Committee on Medical Research of the Office of Scientific Research and Development during World War II, he took the action necessary to make penicillin commercially available as well as supervising important work on malaria. He was vice-president in charge of medical affairs at the University (1939–1948) and president of the National Academy of Sciences.

searchers dream of but seldom attain."[23] The question asked on this occasion was: "Does glomerular filtrate contain substances that are not present in bladder urine?" The experiment to answer it which Joseph Wearn and he dreamed up over a bottle of beer involved micropuncturing the renal tubule. Not only did this permit substances to be injected directly into the encapsulated network of capillaries called the glomerulus but, by the same procedure, the fluid contained in a glomerulus could be withdrawn for chemical comparison with bladder urine.

Without the aid of sophisticated modern micro-manipulators or radioactive isotopes, pipettes were placed in functionally different regions of the kidney and a "vanishingly small" volume of fluid was analyzed. Since the minutest vibration disturbed fluid collection, Wearn describes working at night when the only visitors to the laboratory were a friendly mouse and an occasional cockroach. Richards frequently joined him in his vigil.[24] Their discovery in glomerular fluid of chemicals not found in bladder urine constituted conclusive evidence in favor of the filtration-reabsorption theory. In their own published account: "Direct testing of the fluid eliminated by the frog's glomerulus proves the assumption which was made by the earliest of the modern students of renal physiology, that a protein-free, watery fluid is separated from the blood-stream as it passes through the glomerular capillaries."[25] This finding was modified when they later showed that small protein molecules were filtered by the glomerulus but were subsequently reabsorbed by the tubules.

When the results of the investigations were reported at the meetings of the American Physiological Society in 1922, they shared the limelight with another vital discovery: the isolation of insulin by Banting and Best. An expert in the field has described the Richards-Wearn experiment as "the most significant single original contribution in the field of renal physiology," and the research was crucial for modern nephrology. Without it, advances in medicine such as the development of the artificial kidney could not have come about. "After again reviewing the accomplishments of Dr. Richards and his colleagues," concludes this commentator, "I wonder once again, as I am sure have others, why Dr. Richards was never honored by the award of a Nobel prize."[26]

If this award was never made for the field of renal physiology in which he worked, Richards's other degrees and decorations have led to the comment that "we know of no other American medical scientist who has been so greatly honored both here and abroad."[27] On the occasion of his honorary Doctor of Science from the University of Pennsylvania, he posed for a photograph with a frog in one hand and a caduceus of live snakes awaiting glomerular puncture in the other. One of his "boys" composed a limerick to celebrate the occasion:

> There once was a Richards named Newton
> Who collected degrees high fallutin'
> A.B., Ph.D.
> M.D., Sc.D.
> And there's more yet to come, you're damn tootin'.[28]

Arthur Walker, to whom the verse is attributed, could only have suspected in 1925 the numerous awards and rewards which would follow. The scientist who had been prevented from studying medicine for financial reasons received the M.D. from the University of Louvain and honorary degrees from many universities. In 1947 he became president of the National Academy of Sciences, of which he had been a member since 1927. Invited to give the Croonian Lecture before the Royal Society in 1938, he was elected a Fellow in 1942, the fourth Philadelphian to become a Foreign Member after Benjamin Franklin, David Rittenhouse, and S. Weir Mitchell.

When Richards departed for England in 1938 to give the Croonian Lecture, he and his family were accompanied by Detlev Bronk. During the journey, Bronk recalls, Richards fretted about the additional experiments which ought to have been done and the literary quality of his paper which he feared was "not good enough for a British audience." And every day aboard a slow ship crossing the Atlantic, he revised his manuscript. When he presented his material in the crowded lecture hall of the Royal Society in Burlington House, he spoke with humility and, following the Quintilian dictum, "not so much that his audience could understand, but so that they could not misunderstand." At last, looking up at a final slide of a chart which summarized the experiments, he was heard to whisper: "My God, what a lot of work." The response was thunderous applause, and the man sitting next to Detlev Bronk remarked: "If he does not get a Nobel prize, the Prize will never again be worth getting."[29]

One result of Richards's international scientific fame was his tardy election to the American Philosophical Society in Philadelphia. "He has been a member for years," was the response when the vice-president was asked why Richards had not been elected and, on being assured that this was not the case, "incredible, he is one of the great American scientists; the greatest Philadelphia scientist since Franklin."[30] The omission was immediately rectified, and Richards later became vice-president himself, although he declined nomination for president. In addition to these academic accolades, Richards received many awards and medals, including the Philadelphia Bok Award in 1937 for the greatest contribution made by a local resident. Among the decorations which his wife gave to the University is the Medal of Merit presented to him by President Truman and the insignia of an Honorary Commander of the Order of the British Empire which he received from King George VI.

These last awards were made in recognition of his contribution to a wholly different area of research and administration during World War II. In 1941, Roosevelt wrote: "I hereby appoint you as Chairman of Medical Research created by Executive order establishing the Office of Scientific Research and Development. In this capacity you shall receive no salary. . . . Cordially yours."[31] Many years later, the director of the Office of Scientific Research and Development, Vannevar Bush, who had informed Richards of his new assignment, recalled that "even under this mild provocation he became profane." Detlev Bronk, who was in his office when Richards received the call from Bush, remembers only that Richards' brief acceptance was followed by the modest hope that he merited the confidence placed in him.[32] It appears that infractions of the prohibition against profane language—and tobacco—at the seminary in Stamford, New York, where Richards had started his education, were among his few faults. In view of the hardship he is said to have endured as a result of the wartime restrictions on cigarettes, it seems unlikely that he should have been a fire hazard in Washington, as reported by one associate, because of his habit of trying to keep four or five cigarettes burning at the same time.[33] Nonetheless, among the original apparatus used to collect fluid from

Simon Flexner (1863–1946)
by Adele Herter
Professor of pathology and morbid anatomy at the University of Pennsylvania (1899–1903), and member of a famous family of scientists and educators. Born in Louisville, Kentucky, graduated in medicine at the University of Louisville (1889), he taught pathology at Johns Hopkins before coming to the University. Resigned to become the first director of the Rockefeller Institute for Medical Research which, under him, became one of the most active institutions in the world. His discoveries include a dysentery bacillus which bears his name, and he made important contributions to the treatment of meningitis and poliomyelitis, as well as to the area of toxicology. Among numerous honors he received an honorary Sc.D. from the University (1929).

Detlev W. Bronk (1897–1975)
Professor of medical physics at the University of Pennsylvania (1929–1949), director of the Institute of Neurology (1936–1940), and trustee of the University of Pennsylvania (1954–1975). The first director of the Johnson Foundation at the University of Pennsylvania, he left to become president of Johns Hopkins (1949–1953) and was afterwards president of the Rockefeller Institute for Medical Research, which he helped rename the Rockefeller University (1953–1968).

the glomeruli and tubules of frogs, snakes, salamanders, guinea pigs, rats, and opossums is an ingenious device for holding experimental material carefully constructed in a Lucky Strike tin.[34]

Richards is remembered for his courage, integrity, both of the "scientific and the garden variety," as well as his great modesty.[35] This last quality is evident in the final article he wrote on the subject of penicillin production in the United States. Little is made of his own important role in getting the drug into production, and he does not mention that Sir Howard Florey, who first obtained the antibiotic in relatively pure form, had spent a year in his laboratory. As early as 1944, however, the importance of Richards' contribution was fully recognized in an editorial of the *British Medical Journal*. Without his efforts, Sir Alexander Fleming's discovery, as well as Florey's signal victory, would have remained ineffectual at the time of greatest need. The fact that, when the allies invaded Normandy, penicillin was available in sufficient quantities to save the lives of the wounded was the direct result of Richards' decision, as chairman of medical research, to promote production by natural fermentation. The editorial points out that, as director of government research programs, Richards need not have involved himself in problems of production. Furthermore, the decision to go ahead with the natural fermentation process when at any moment a synthetic process could make the plant for growing the mold obsolete, rested entirely with A. N. Richards.[36]

Even Florey, who visited the States in the summer of 1941 in the hope of persuading American manufacturers to start mass production of the drug, was confident that synthesis was at hand. That Richards should have stood almost alone in making the far-reaching decision to proceed with natural fermentation was predictable in view of his lifelong adherence to the principle of going from the known to the unknown one step at a time.[37] Within eight months, the drug had been tested on some ten cases. Its experimental application to chronic war wounds is described in Richards's own laconic report:

> Treatment of military casualties by penicillin began on April 1, 1943, when Dr. Champ Lyons, a member of the Chemotherapy Committee of the National Research Council, was authorized by Surgeon-General James Magee of the U.S. Army to inaugurate at the Bushnell General Hospital, Brigham City, Utah, a programme of treatment of patients from the Pacific area.[38]

Behind this flat statement of fact lies the whole touchy question of permission for civilians to carry out experimental treatment on soldiers. As a result of Richards' ability to listen carefully and to take decisive action, the necessary sanction was speedily obtained. Dr. Lyons actually arrived in Utah with a plan and a program before the commanding general had been fully informed.[39] Consequently, the *British Medical Journal* could well claim in the last stages of the war that "Dr. Richards has the reward of knowing that as the result of his efforts the lives of very many American and British wounded are being saved every day."[40] By D-Day, allocation of penicillin had been made to 1,000 civilian hospitals, and by the end of the war the use of the drug had increased sharply to 650 billion units per month. "By this time—but not before," writes an observer, "British and American chemists had finally synthesized minute amounts of penicillin, but the cost of producing 100,000 units by natural fermentation had become less than the cost of putting it into an ampule, and there was— and is—no prospect of economic advantage from synthesis."[41]

During World War I, Richards had spent some time setting up a field laboratory in France. At that time, Base Hospital 20 at Châtel Guyon was staffed entirely by University of Pennsylvania-trained doctors and nurses. When Richards was summoned to Washington during World War II, the Pennsylvania contingent was also reactivated under the command of I. S. Ravdin, Harrison professor of surgery. After preliminary training in Louisiana, U.S. General Hospital No. 20, as it was now called, with its 73 commissioned officers all recruited from faculty and alumni, departed for notheastern Assam. Here, "a few shacks in a muddy and malarious valley" were rapidly transformed into a 2,000-bed hospital delivering superior medical care. As described in a contemporary report, "by its intelligence and skill it reduced the mortality of our troops to a record unequaled by any nation in the annals of war."[42]

The physicians who returned to the University of Pennsylvania at the end of the war were to become international leaders in such fields as ophthalmology, radiology, dermatology, and surgery. Now nearly seventy, Newton Richards himself reassumed the post he had held since 1939 of vice-president of the University in charge of medical affairs. Even after his retirement, he remained active as emeritus professor, was made a trustee of Merck & Co., and served as a member of the first Hoover Commission on the Organization of the Executive Branch of Government. In the late fifties, he could still be described as "a man who has been living at least three full lives for more years than he wants to remember."[43] In 1960, the most important work of modern architecture on campus, designed by Louis I. Kahn, was dedicated in his honor. The Alfred Newton Richards Medical Research Building has become one of the architectural attractions of Philadelphia and the United States, and it is a fitting memorial to a great scientist who died a few days after his ninetieth birthday, having devoted more than two-thirds of his long life to medical science and administration at the University of Pennsylvania. A note penned by Carl Schmidt on a copy of the memoir he wrote for the Royal Society sums up the feeling of a generation of scholars and physicians who came under the influence of Newton Richards: "There will never be another like him and we were extremely fortunate to have been where and when we were."

12

Simon Nelson Patten: Economics and Social Thought in the Wharton School

Two years after the Wharton School came into being in 1881, Edmund Janes James was appointed professor of public finance and economy. Within three years, he had become its first director and, although the school did not separate from the college department of the University until 1912, under James the project for a business school connected with an academic institution was expanded to include the social sciences. Although in general James's economic theories were shared by the business community, he also showed interest in improving the conditions of the industrial worker, which led to his defense of labor unions. In his opinion, "all the Johann Mosts of the world could make no impression on the American working man if conditions made him contented with his lot."[1] Reform was thus an important way to preempt the appeal of socialism or anarchism.

James's interest in social issues was shared by a generation of economists many of whom had, like him, received their advanced education in Germany. In the 1870s, the social sciences were developing in such universities as Berlin, Heidelberg, and Halle. In addition to the intellectual environment and the inspiration of professors like Johannes Conrad, the experience of an old-established society based on different social premises from that of the New World was a revelation to the young Americans who went to Germany to study. Among those who were most impressed by the Germans and their use of limited resources, as well as by the teachers they encountered, was Simon Nelson Patten, who first met James while they were studying at Halle. It was James who was responsible for bringing Patten to the University of Pennsylvania in 1888. If James, its first director, was responsible for laying the foundation upon which the Wharton School has been built, Patten was the first original thinker, whose teachings and writings were to bring wide reputation—or notoriety—to himself, the University of Pennsylvania, and its Wharton School.[2]

Although James himself departed from the University of Pennsylvania in 1896 to become president first of Northwestern University and then of the University of Illinois, in Patten he bequeathed to the University a man who could be described by the president of the American Economic

Association he had helped to found, as "the most original and suggestive economist America has yet produced."[3] Patten was soon identified with a new school of political economy in revolt against classical economics, and he was one of the men responsible for bringing the United States to the forefront of the social sciences. He was also in a line of economists going back to Adam Smith and earlier who treated economics as a part of moral philosophy—albeit, for Patten, the most significant part, since he considered economics as "the fiber and essence of all knowledge."

True to this tradition, Patten wrote on the subject with verve and charm, unlike the economists who succeeded him and who have been described as "a great deal less charming and a great deal more exact."[4] If Patten's philosophical roots were in the past, however, his interests and methods were all oriented to the future. At a time when Thorstein Veblen believed that men would most likely fail to close the gap between their nature and the machine process, Patten with unwavering optimism and in the face of continual criticism ranged himself on the side of the new social order he foresaw, poles apart from the view his Yale colleague, William Graham Sumner, summarized in the title of his essay: "The Absurd Effort To Make the World Over." During a lifetime of writing and lecturing, Patten addressed himself to a wide diversity of topics in addition to economics. Mental defects, personal traits, prohibition, and evolution received his attention, along with aspects of the family and the church, heredity and education. What interested him most was "the application of economic reasoning to the practical rules for conduct for the individual, and for society, to social organization and group activity. He was quite as much a sociologist as an economist."[5]

Patten and James shared a common background and upbringing, having each been raised on a farm in Illinois. Patten's theories were strongly influenced by the perceived contrast between his experience of the riches yielded by his paternal homestead in return for hard work and technological improvements, and the theory of scarcity of classical economics—Thomas Carlyle's "dismal science"—in which nature was viewed as niggardly, a hostile force, unsusceptible of mastery by man. As a child Patten had witnessed the effect of the transition from manual labor to farm machinery. "The wonder is not that one could see these changes and forever after believe in the unlimited power of man over nature," writes his former student, Rexford G. Tugwell, "but that there could be a generation growing up in the same knowledge who could follow blindly into the cul-de-sacs of classical English economics." As Tugwell comments: "Nature in these years had poured out her largesse in growing rivers of grain that flooded the markets of the world and Simon Patten, looking on, formulated a new philosophy to be substituted for the old philosophies of misery."[6]

The observations Patten made on his father's farm in Sandwich,

Illinois, where he had been taken soon after his birth in 1851, were reinforced by the theories which he heard expounded by another farmer's son, Johannes Conrad, who taught at the University of Halle. Rejecting the notion that the increase of population and its obverse—the limited fertility of the land—were immutable natural phenomena, Conrad considered that each could be controlled by man. His predictions for the future were predicated on the implementation of population control and improved techniques in the science of agronomy. Although Conrad later claimed that he had learned more about economic theory from Simon Patten than from the work of any other writer on the subject, Conrad's optimism was responsible for sparking the views of the young American who had witnessed the transition from scarcity to abundance on his father's prairie farm in Illinois. It was Conrad who drew him from the general field of philosophy into economics for, "in Conrad's seminar, Patten found a rational explanation for his father's commitment to agricultural experimentation, to education, and to the restraints of the Protestant ethic."[7]

On his return to America, after receiving his doctorate from Halle, the new convert to economics did not find any employment in his chosen profession. Both he and James became schoolteachers, a not uncommon employment for followers of a discipline more often pursued by amateurs than by professional academicians in most countries apart from Germany. Moreover, Patten's German orthodoxy was heresy in America, and he noted a pervasive atmosphere of narrow-mindedness in the United States which made for a harsh return to reality after his experiences abroad. There followed a time of frustration which, even in the case of one of the most aggressive German-trained economists, Richard Ely of Johns Hopkins, Wisconsin, and Northwestern, led to thoughts of suicide.[8] Despite a period of protracted illness, Patten nonetheless devoted seemingly idle hours on the farm to the occupation of his life—the formulation of a corpus of original economic theory. Rexford Tugwell writes: "The story of his life is the story of a mind."[9] Even at this stage, according to Scott Nearing: "He lived on ideas."[10] Long before he finally found himself in a suitable academic environment, Patten had started to work out his general principles of economic and social change.

His first book was completed after Herculean labors and extensive revision on the part of Joseph F. Johnson, who had found work as a reporter on the *Chicago Tribune*. Johnson, the friend most responsible for Patten's decision to study in Germany, described the manuscript Patten sent him as "unbelievably awful in grammar, spelling, and general construction" with an opening sentence fifteen pages long.[11] When it was finally published, however, *The Premises of Political Economy* represented a break with theories of the past, a reworking of the very assumptions on which they were based. It also brought Patten an appointment, at the age of thirty-seven, to a professorship in political economy at the University of Pennsylvania.

A few years later, Johnson, who later became dean of the school of commerce at New York University, received an appointment at the University of Pennsylvania as professor of journalism. Before his departure, Edmund James also brought in, as professors, historians John Bach McMaster, the first holder of a professorship in American history in the United States, and Edward Potts Cheyney, as well as the statistician Roland P. Falkner and Samuel M. Lindsay the sociologist. "The history of the Wharton School," comments an observer "reflected the history of social science in America in the late nineteenth century."[12] Immediately after Patten's appointment, James and he started the *University of Pennsylvania Publications in Political and Social Science*, and in 1889 they founded the American Academy of Political and Social Science with its publication, the *Annals*. Under the influence of a handful of men trained in Germany, the United States, at one bound, joined the mainstream of the developing social sciences, with the University of Pennsylvania a focal point in America.[13]

In the course of his 30 years at the University, Simon Patten produced in all some 20 books and over 150 articles. A large variety of subjects, from philosophy to psychology, from economic theory to industrial and social programs, were treated in a manner often so brief as to give the impression of having been condensed from longer works. Despite his productivity, many of Patten's articles reflect a general impatience with the necessity for writing in a life concerned with action. "The place of the economist is on the firing line of civilization," he proclaimed.[14] For him, being on the forefront involved the activity of the mind. It was up to the men and women he influenced to implement his theories in a changing world. In the same presidential address on "The Making of Economic Literature" which Patten delivered in 1908 before the American Economic Association, he noted that a three-hundred-page thesis by a young doctor advanced neither the science nor the nation, unconsciously echoing arguments against the literature of science advanced earlier by both the reforming Lazzaroni in the natural sciences and progressive faculty in the medical school. In Patten's account: "Book-making has become an art of collection and restatement that substitutes clippings and card catalogs for clear thought." His observations of this danger besetting academic endeavors throws light on the nature of his own writing. Patten's practice reflects his opinion, "the better the economist, the clearer, shorter and more precise are his utterances." The diversity and sometimes contradictory nature of his work is further illuminated by his evaluation: "A book is merely the trail along which its author has gone in his search for clear expression and sharp analysis. This is of great importance to the author but of little consequence to the reader."[15]

Simon Nelson Patten (1851–1922)
*Professor of political economy at the
University of Pennsylvania (1888–1916).
Born in Illinois, educated at the University of Halle, where he was influenced by
the ideas of the German economist
Johannes Conrad. Starting with* The
Premises of Political Economy *(1885),
which antedated his academic appointment, he wrote numerous books and
articles on a wide variety of subjects,
including* The New Basis of Civilization
*(1907–1921), his most popular work
aimed at a general audience. His economic theories were in revolt against
classical doctrine and heralded Keynesian
economics. Influential as a teacher, he
included among his protégés at the
University of Pennsylvania Rexford Guy
Tugwell, member of Franklin D. Roosevelt's "brainstrust," and Frances Perkins,
the first woman member of a U.S.
Cabinet.*

The central thesis of Patten's economic theory was the replacement of traditional assumptions of scarcity with the assumption of potential abundance. Not restricted resources, but rather their unintelligent use, constituted the principal limitation upon human welfare. Even the problem of an increasing population would be solved by technological developments and new standards of consumption, and these would revise upwards the point of diminishing returns. Unlike other economists who had paid scant attention to consumption or, like John Stuart Mill, had denied that it could have much effect on production, Patten believed that, in the dynamic society which he envisaged, consumption would obey a law of increasing utility. Habits of consumption, he claimed, are subject to the law of "survival of the fittest," and those which do not stand the test of social utility must necessarily be discarded:

> The environment formed by this group of economic objects surrounding and supporting a given race changes with the several objects in which the interests of the race are centered. With the new objects come new activities and new requisites for survival. To meet these new conditions, the new motives, instincts and habits of the race are modified; new modes of thought are formed; and thus by the modification of institutions, ideals, and customs all of the characteristics of the civilization are reconstructed. These changes take place in a regular order; the series repeats itself in each environment. In its amplification and illustration lies the economic interpretation of history.[16]

Faults in consumption exist at all levels of society. The consumption of luxuries by high-income groups—the "conspicuous consumption" of Thorstein Veblen—is objectionable, as is the rigidity of the general populace when they insist on food which is not necessarily produced in their region, rather than adapting their diet to the commodities readily available to them. Although he thought that generous and wise consumption would do more to reduce economic inequalities than would a more direct redistribution of wealth, Patten was alive to the advantages of cooperative economic action.

He had great influence on students and colleagues alike, but his deductive habit of mind addressed itself "not so much [to] statistical evidence as the evidence he could absorb—as it seemed to less brilliant minds—from the atmosphere."[17] In defense of this method which he shared with the classicists whom he nonetheless criticized for their lack of realism, Patten asserted that "to show that a mass of facts do not correspond to the conclusions which may be drawn from a given theory does not disprove the theory. It merely indicates that some other cause is working which prevents the effects of a given theory from being shown by all the facts."[18] This independence of facts or statistical evidence stems in part from the dearth of economic and social data available for analysis at the time; but, in any case, Patten was better suited temperamentally to the role of the prophet, the pioneer in uncharted territory, than to that of the quantifier. "Beyond the mountains and the snow," he wrote, "is a land that we may see from afar, even if we cannot enter. Better be a Moses seeing what others can enjoy than a worshipper of idols that once were gods, but now are merely crumbling clay. Any food is better than the pickled remnants of ancient creeds."[19]

The apparent lack of system which prevails among his theories is one reason that there is no clearly defined area in which Patten's ideas predominate. The views disseminated in the many articles he wrote remain separate and incomplete, and he was repeatedly unsuccessful in his effort to create a synthesis. In the opinion of his contemporaries, help was needed to bring "into a systematic whole his various thoughts."[20] At the same time, one effect of his modesty, which his students found an admirable quality of his teaching, was his readiness to admit to error and to change his opinion in the face of a convincing argument against one of his tenets.[21] Whatever the reason, it is all too easy to distill contradictory views from the extensive body of his expressed opinion. He advocated governmental welfare provisions, yet his proposals for the care of the destitute in some ways hark back to the English Poor Law of 1834. He believed in the development of resources to the optimum extent for the welfare of society, but favored a protective tariff. In general, his conviction that economic principles were relative, without meaning except with reference to particular societies and situations, impeded his ability to develop his ideas into a logical system of economics.

Perhaps one reason that Patten is remembered as a great teacher is precisely because no rigid or facile statement of doctrine could be adopted by his students, and they were therefore constrained to search out the truth for themselves. When he was asked his opinion of his instructors, sociologist Samuel McCune Lindsay described James as "more like the Prussian drill master," while, in his view, Simon Patten was "by all odds, the greatest teacher I have ever known, and [he] had something that no school of pedagogy has yet been able to reproduce—a gift of sympathetic understanding of his pupils and ability to make them think."[22] Contrary to the usual methods of the time, Patten "welcomed a question as a thirsty traveler welcomes water." In contrast, one of his colleagues, when interrupted by a question, "looked about with the terror one sees in a wild rabbit who has heard a twig snap in the thicket."[23] The fact was that Patten never actually lectured, but proceeded rather by the Socratic method: "His remarks were intended to evoke a reply. His aim was to arouse mental activity." Once his students had formulated their opinion on paper, Patten would readily have consigned the written examination to the wastebasket had there not been the necessity for providing grades. For students raised in the belief that "the perfect parrot was the perfect pupil," contact with Patten at the University of Pennsylvania could not fail to have a lasting impact. His inspiration was such that a large number of his

students were won over from business to the social sciences. At the turn
of the century those who "liked their professors to stay on the
campus, and were uneasy when they crossed the Schuylkill, and came
down into the city" were disconcerted to see the Wharton School "taking
boys who might grow into good businessmen, and converting them instead
into social experts and engineers . . . of a new order."[24]

Patten's teaching method involving a dialogue with students, a sharing
with them in a mutual quest for knowledge, may have appeared
idiosyncratic in those days. In the classroom, Patten simply ignored current
practice: he had no time for formal discipline, or even the notion that the
function of the lecturer might be to impart information. He seldom
presented systems of thought other than his own.[25] By inviting attention
through a discussion of whatever was of particular concern to himself at
any given moment, he demonstrated the capital importance in intellectual
training of stimulating the student's interest through contact with a mind
in action rather than merely communicating a known body of facts to him.
If Patten was ahead of his time, the effectiveness of his teaching was soon
recognized by the students who sat at his feet and returned to him for
counsel after graduation. His presence contributed to the way the
University of Pennsylvania and its Wharton School developed in the early
years of the century, fulfilling the expressed hope of Joseph Wharton, on
whose generosity the school was founded, that it would be concerned with
social and moral as well as business issues. At the same time, the school's
programs of management and political economy were emulated by "scores
if not hundreds of other colleges and universities throughout the country."[26]

One of the causes which Patten championed, for personal reasons as
much as because it was consistent with his other policy positions, was equal
suffrage.[27] In reply to a journalist's inquiry about his attitude to "the
woman suffrage question," he smilingly denied being a convert to the
cause. As far as he could remember, he had believed in it since the
days when he was a little boy in Sandwich, Illinois.[28] Indeed, he recalled
having made a statement to that effect to his mother after hearing Anna
Dickinson speak at the close of the Civil War. He was conspicuous in his
advocacy of female rights, appearing in parades under the banner of "Votes
for Women" and responding to all the ridicule and reproach he encountered
with the calm conviction that time would demonstrate the justice of this
cause.

It was frequently for their connection with women that Patten's
economic and social theories made headlines in the popular press. His
notion that women should contribute to the economy of the family by
working and, in another connection, that women wage-earners should be
encouraged as consumers led to outraged or sarcastic responses. "Man for
breadwinner and woman for the homeworker is the true relation of life,"
responded a local Pennsylvania newspaper, and Patten was criticized both

for suggesting that married women constituted the new leisured class and for wishing them to be household drudges; for encouraging girls to be spendthrifts and proposing that they should support their husbands.[29] In his obituary in the Philadelphia *Bulletin* in 1922 he was even held responsible for "the first faint beginnings . . . that have brought the flapper of today."[30]

One response to Patten's view that women should take their place in the labor force was the observation: "It is as natural for a real man to wish to support his wife as it is for water to flow down hill." This, along with other statements of a woman's right not to work, was attributed to none other than Charlotte Kimball Patten. When his pretty wife, twenty years his junior, divorced Patten after five years of marriage, the press gleefully recorded the failure of the professor's attempts to implement his economic theories in his own home. Readers were again reminded of his personal record some years later when he claimed that divorce was a direct result of the dependent status of women. Later still, a Midwestern journalist dismissed his opinions as those of a celibate professor and indeed, after his divorce in 1909, Patten lived a solitary existence which led Tugwell, to call him "one among the lonely souls of earth."[31] But with his earlier students, Samuel McCune Lindsay recalls, there existed a bond of friendship and intimacy which persisted "in the case of an ever-widening circle of students from every succeeding class" until his retirement in 1917.[32]

Patten's last years were clouded by another incident which was also reported with eager interest and a measure of *Schadenfreude* by the press. The optimistic doctrines which he had propounded did not take into consideration the possibility of a return to warfare which, according to some reformers earlier in the century, would no longer plague a society advancing towards a future of economic reform and social justice. With the outbreak of World War I, Patten refused to join the ranks of those who considered the Germans as barbarians when, for him, they were the inhabitants of the land of enlightenment where the professor, not the Kaiser, controlled the thought—a thought which had recognized the implications of the transition from scarcity to abundance.

Even after events had made American neutrality—strongly advocated by Patten—an impossibility he continued to point out the dangers of suppressing the civilized intellectualism which existed side by side with the element of brutality in Germany. In a speech before the Philomathean Society, the University's student literary society, in March of 1917, he emphasized the existence of "two Germanies"; meanwhile the economic considerations, never far removed from his social theory, made a brief appearance when he attributed Teutonic independence to the introduction of the sturdy potato into the diet of Northern Prussia. In his speech, he compared America to Rome at the time of Carthage and declared: "We should take heed from the result of that struggle and of many similar ones that to overcome people by force means not only their demoralization, but also that of the conquerors."[33] A month after this address had been delivered at the University, Patten was associated with a pacifist rally which was canceled by the Philadelphia authorities. A few days later, he received a letter from the trustees of the University of Pennsylvania informing him that, since he had reached the statutory age of retirement, his contract would not be renewed the following year. Patten had no doubt that his unpopular attitude was responsible for this action which was not then common practice. Amid such headlines as: "Pacifist Professor Forced To Resign," the trustees continued to deny any cause other than Patten's having reached his sixty-fifth birthday, a position from which they never departed thereafter.

On this occasion, Patten did not bring his case before the newly formed American Association of University Professors as he had two years earlier in championing the cause of his colleague Scott Nearing. The dismissal of the young assistant professor because of his public stand against established interests had led to a bitter conflict at the University. Patten's attempt to enlist the support of the Association on the grounds of academic freedom had been unsuccessful at the time. Patten's own logic was commonly held to be "the fount and origin of the doctrines against vested interests . . . said to be rife in the faculty of the Wharton School." In the view attributed to the trustees by the press: " 'The young fellows are the cubs; Patten is the old lion. You cannot deal with the Nearings until you have reckoned with the teacher of the Nearings.' " According to this report, Patten's public statements on the war provided the perfect opportunity to "put him down."[34] The ensuing faculty revolt against the ousting of a scholar and teacher of Patten's reputation went unnoticed; by an ironical twist of fortune, "the protest was submerged in the excitement over American entry into the war, which occurred on the day it was published."[35] In 1973, William L. Day, as chairman of the trustees, on behalf of the board and on the recommendation of the president and the faculty, reinstated Scott Nearing as a member of the faculty.

Simon Patten, according to Scott Nearing, was a man who "had few followers and no disciples; but of loving students and of friends, a host."[36] Even Rexford Tugwell, who considered the theories of the professor with whom he had studied at the University of Pennsylvania as the greatest single influence on his thought, never felt that Patten was cut out to lead a group or found a school. "The Patten method," he writes, "was a way of genius and so highly individualized that only by the remotest chance could the permutations or juxtaposition have thrown together a group who could have functioned in his way."[37] What Patten did succeed in doing was to direct the interest of his students to areas which they might not otherwise have known or considered. While he was at the Wharton School, Tugwell was exposed to the idea that planning and management could and should be applied as much to public activities as to the private sector. One of the lessons he learned before he went on to become an imaginative adviser and distinguished administrator under President Franklin D. Roosevelt was that public investment can compensate for gaps in levels of private investment where the aim is to stabilize the national economy. The first academic after Woodrow Wilson to play a central policy role in the government of the United States, Tugwell demonstrated a pragmatism which reflected his mentor's view that men could make an efficient adjustment to their environment through planning. The reforms which he proposed as necessary and feasible also reflect the optimism which was a necessary part of Patten's economic theory and which caused Tugwell to appear to some contemporaries as a typical product of an ivory tower.[38]

If Patten was instrumental in directing Tugwell towards service through government, in the course of which he held among other posts the governorship of Puerto Rico, there was another professional field in which his influence was particularly strongly felt. True to his practice of finding things that needed doing and passing them on to those he considered best suited to perform the tasks, he had already brought the field of social welfare to the attention of others among his students before the turn of the century.[39] "Patten's central theme, that the goal of social action was adjustment to the economy of abundance, has become so basic to modern social work that details about his influence are no longer known," writes an observer, and the fact that he seems to have coined the term "social work," or, at the least, to have played a part in its adoption in preference to others, has been forgotten.[40] With the development of this field, graduates associated with Patten went on to hold positions of major influence. Samuel M. Lindsay became professor of social welfare at Columbia, and Edward T. Devine's first position at the New York Charity Organization Society, obtained with the help of Patten, led to a quarter of a century as the leading philanthropic executive in America. It was also through his assistance that Frances Perkins, who did graduate work with Patten at the University, started her outstanding career. She was later to become Secretary of Labor under Roosevelt and the first woman ever to be a member of the cabinet.

Patten's own articles on the philosophy of social action and on economics were primarily directed towards specialists. But he came to realize that it was necessary to reach a larger audience, and at fifty he set himself the task of making his economic and social theories readable.[41] A series of lectures given in 1905 was published in what became his most popular work, *The New Basis of Civilization*.[42] Although eight editions of the book made his views familiar to an ever-widening public, he nonetheless remained the prophet rather than the leader of the movement he had supported with such energy. In 1912, when the Progressive party included in its platform some of the social ideals so earnestly advocated by Patten, he preferred to remain loyal to the party of Lincoln. He cast his vote for Taft even though his most intimate friends and disciples were supporting Theodore Roosevelt. When one of the "Patten men" complained to him of his inconsistency, Patten justified his preference with the words: "When the torchlights pass by and the band plays, I'm one of the boys of '61."[43]

In general, Patten was read but misunderstood during his lifetime. His economic theories were in advance of his time, and the implications of those theories were frequently obscured by the variety of means he proposed in the hope of realizing an economy of abundance more rapidly. It has taken more time than Patten had at his disposal for his economic tenets to become respected. In the generation after his death, Lord Keynes and an increasing number of economists and social scientists proclaimed ideas similar to those of Patten, the pioneer, who, during his lifetime, trod alone where few had been and few would consciously follow. His thought nonetheless provides a bridge between the world of John Stuart Mill and the age of John Maynard Keynes: born in time to experience Lincoln's America and Bismarck's Germany, he heralded the economic and social developments of the New Deal.[44]

Owen J. Roberts (1875–1955)
Seated second from left,
Supreme Court of the United States, 1941
*Alumnus of the college (1895) and law
school (1898), lecturer and professor of
law (1898–1918) and dean of the law
school (1948–1951). After a successful
career as an advocate in Philadelphia,
Roberts was appointed special prosecutor
in the Teapot Dome scandals (1924) and
became an associate justice of the
Supreme Court (1930–1945). Life trustee
of the University.*

13

Justice Owen J. Roberts: The Law School

One of Simon Nelson Patten's most gifted students was to leave his mark on the University as dean of the law school. Like many students of the time, William Draper Lewis did not limit his interests to a single subject. While writing a dissertation in economics entitled "Our Sheep and the Tariff," he was also studying law, with the result that he received both his Ph.D. and his LL.B. degrees in 1891. In 1893, he was appointed instructor in legal institutions at the University's Wharton School, a post he held for only three years before being elected professor of law and dean of the law school, at the age of twenty-nine.

Only a year before Lewis became dean, a young Pennsylvanian of Welsh ancestry entered the law school at a moment in its history when it was housed in historic Congress Hall, the structure on the west side of Independence Hall. Owen Josephus Roberts was a member of one of two classes who had the opportunity to spend the entire period of their legal studies in these memorable surroundings. Valedictorian of his class at the College, Roberts graduated from the law school *summa cum laude* in 1898. After graduation, he received the law school fellowship, following in the footsteps of another alumnus, George Wharton Pepper, who later became United States Senator from Pennsylvania. Although neither Pepper nor Roberts was then full time, each continued to be a faculty member in the department of law. When the family of Professor A. Sidney Biddle endowed a chair in law in 1893, Pepper was appointed to fill it; Roberts, who was eight years Pepper's junior, became a professor in 1907. Just over forty years later in 1948 Roberts returned to the law school as dean. The intervening decades had seen him, in turn, the most successful advocate in Philadelphia and a skilled special prosecutor for the United States government, and had brought him finally to the Supreme Court. In the same period, the law school Roberts had attended had been transformed under men such as Lewis, Goodrich, and Harrison into one of the most promising schools in the land.

In 1914, when William Draper Lewis entered the race for governor of Pennsylvania on the Progressive ticket, he showed himself to be an adherent of the social philosophy of Patten. At the time of his resignation from the law school in order to enter politics, Lewis had been dean for seventeen years, a tenure equaled only by George Sharswood, first dean of the reorganized school, and Jefferson Fordham whose energy and persistence have more recently shaped the law center of the present. After resigning as dean, Lewis continued to teach at the law school which, by the end of World War I, had been transformed from a modest law department, in no way different from those existing elsewhere in 1850, into a professional school of the highest academic order with regard to faculty, facilities, and students.

Despite two short-lived attempts early on to integrate law courses into the program of studies, the University remained without a full-fledged law school long after James Wilson's lectures in law had been delivered before so eminent an audience in 1790. An initiative in 1817 by Charles Willing Hare was ill-fated since the poor health of the lecturer caused him to give up teaching after the first season. The principal association for Philadelphia students of law continued to be at meetings and moot courts held for their benefit by the Law Academy of Philadelphia. Indeed, in 1832, this respected professional organization petitioned the University "soliciting the appointment of a Professor to the Chair of Legal Science in that institution" in recognition of the fact that many young men from Philadelphia were seeking instruction in Cambridge, New Haven, and Charlottesville and then sometimes settling in those regions. As in earlier generations, members of Philadelphia's prominent families continued occasionally to be sent to London to study at the Inns of Court. For prospective students of law who remained at home, however, there was no alternative but to study in private or with a preceptor while working as a clerk in the office of an established attorney.

Even after the law school was reestablished in 1850, the Commonwealth courts continued to require candidates for the bar to register with a preceptor, and, in their regulations for admission to practice, the Court of Common Pleas for the county of Philadelphia, the United States District Court, and the State Supreme Court only grudgingly recognized the LL.B. from the law school as a substitute for the usual two years of practice in an attorney's office. No law school of the time required a college degree of its students, and the faculty continued their private practice in addition to lecturing at the university. The first professors in Philadelphia are characterized as "active practitioners" who happened to have a flair for teaching and whose nonteaching colleagues affected to despise them for their title of professor.[1] It was only at the turn of the century that the teaching of law came to be regarded as separable from the practice of the legal profession. Although "the men who gathered in the court rooms of Philadelphia were the acknowledged leaders of the legal world of the day, they were inclined to undervalue the merits of a system of training which they had not undergone."[2]

George Sharswood (1810–1883)
Artist unknown
Professor of law and first dean of the
reorganized law school (1852–1868) and
trustee of the University (1872–83).
Three years after graduating from the
College (1828) he was admitted to the
bar, becoming associate judge of the
District Court of Philadelphia (1845–
1848) and president judge (1848–68).
Among numerous legal works, he edited
Sharswood's Blackstone's Commentaries,
published popular lectures on common
law and commercial law, and wrote books
on professional ethics.

Originally, law and medicine had both been learned through apprenticeship to a respected practitioner in the field; the legal preceptorship, however, outlived its medical counterpart by many years. As late as the 1880s, George Wharton Pepper registered in a law firm at the same time that he was attending the courses at the law school. In his autobiography, he takes us back another generation. Drawing on his mother's recollections, he describes how as many as twelve students would assemble for the semi-weekly quiz in his grandfather Wharton's ground-floor office. After being examined, they would go upstairs to the drawing room to dance and partake of wine and cake with the wife and daughters of the head of the office. "Whatever may have been the educational shortcomings of this process," Pepper observes, "it at least had a civilizing influence on the students." Although, when it came into being, the department of law at the University might provide a sounder training than the apprenticeship system, it offered no such entertainment as dancing parties with Wharton's six daughters each of whom had been promptly nicknamed after one of *Wharton's Reports of Pennsylvania Decisions*—in six volumes.[3]

At centennial celebrations in honor of the organization of the University's board of trustees in 1749, alumnus William B. Reed, a former attorney general of Pennsylvania, made allusion to a familiar scene when he complained of the way young students of law were obliged to waste their time running errands and copying papers. This had been the manner of things ever since the first lawyers were trained in colonial America. As it happened, the picture painted by Reed of the inconveniences of studying law "in the din and distraction of a practicing lawyer's office" came at an opportune moment. The trustees had just appointed a committee to consider new courses and, acting on its recommendation which followed closely after Reed's exhortation, it was finally decided that the law professorship of 1790 should be reestablished the following year.[4] The Honorable George Sharswood, a member of the class of 1828, was elected professor of law in April 1850 and delivered his first lectures in September that year. Belonging to a prominent Philadelphia family, Sharswood had himself studied law in the office of trustee Joseph R. Ingersoll after taking highest honors at the University of Pennsylvania.

The two-year course of study Sharswood drew up embraced "international law, constitutional law, personal rights and relations, corporations, real estate law, mercantile law, practice pleading and evidence at law and in equity, and jurisprudence." The new course met only two evenings a week and was "adapted principally to those who have already devoted one or more years to the study of law "although the aim was also "to render it as purely elementary and useful to others as possible."[5] An indication of Sharswood's success in appealing to undergraduates as well as to the men already engaged in practice who mingled with them at his lectures appears in resolutions of appreciation and thanks which the first class presented to the trustees.[6] As a result, the board was finally convinced of the propriety and practicability of a law school, and in 1852 the faculty was expanded to three and Sharswood became dean. Nonetheless, as has been seen, the students who enrolled in the University's newly reorganized law school were still obliged to register in a law office. Their professors, meanwhile, taught part time and continued their private practice. Sharswood himself served concurrently as presiding judge of the District Court of Philadelphia and only resigned his professorship on being elected to the Supreme Court of Pennsylvania eighteen years later.

The first thing that William Draper Lewis did on becoming the sixth dean in 1896 was to give up his private practice and initiate the movement towards a full-time faculty. By the time he resigned in 1914, there were five full-time professors and the total faculty had been enlarged from eleven to twenty-six. The time allotted to teaching was increased, and it became possible to cover a broader range of material. Lewis succeeded in instituting the requirement that law school applicants must hold a college degree. When it became compulsory in 1915, this standard for entrance was shared by only two other law schools in the country, and, a few years later, the University of Pennsylvania and Yale were alone in introducing a selective admissions policy with the aim of limiting class size. For some years, the *American Law Register* had been in the hands of Pepper and Lewis, who had undertaken the editorship in 1891. Soon after Lewis became dean, this professional journal was adopted as the regular publication of the law school and renamed the *University of Pennsylvania Law Review*. During Lewis's tenure, the Biddle Law Library grew from 9,000 volumes in 1895 to 35,000 in 1914. More than 600 of these were acquired abroad in 1910 by Margaret Center Klingelsmith who was Biddle law librarian for 34 years.

There appears to have been something of a race early in the century as American librarians pursued ancient law books to the cellars and attics of Europe. Klingelsmith later reported on her acquisitions as well as her adventures which included a visit to "the historic institution on the bank of the Thames"—Scotland Yard—to retrieve a lost manuscript. Rejoicing in being "first on the ground" and beating Mr. Crossley of Chicago into the damp dungeons of a London bookseller, Klingelsmith describes this treasure-room of titles:

> By the aid of some dim gas jets, and a dangerous candle, which fell over at critical times, and some steps from which I came into contact with the gas jets and did not know I was on fire until I found myself inhaling the fumes of burning millinery, and then proceeded to put myself out, I searched through the stock of old books, selecting the best copies and the older editions of the books on my list.

Before the end of her tour of bookshops in England and on the Continent, she even found time to have some of her purchases rebound in English buckram, not wishing "to import so much English dust into our already too dusty library."[7]

One of Dean Lewis' earliest moves was to convince Provost Harrison of the need for a more permanent home than historic Congress Hall. At the time of its dedication in 1900, the new law building at Thirty-fourth and Chestnut Streets was acclaimed as the most complete educational building in the country. In the course of its existence, the law school had already been housed in a number of different places, including a brief period on the third floor of College Hall after the University moved to West Philadelphia. When he graduated in 1887, George Wharton Pepper recognized that "the process of legal education had become a somewhat haphazard combination of office work and law-school education."[8] Although the move to a downtown location was somewhat at odds with Provost William Pepper's usual interest in building up the West Philadelphia campus, on this occasion he agreed with his nephew's view that law students should be closer to their preceptors' chambers. In 1887, the law school therefore moved first to the sixth floor of the new Girard Bank building at the corner of Broad and Chestnut, and later to temporary quarters in Congress Hall on Independence Square. Thus it was that, for a time, the large room on the first floor of Congress Hall, which had witnessed the deliberations of the first Congress of the United States as well as the second inaugural of Washington and of the first Adams along with Vice-president Jefferson, served as a lecture hall for the University's law department. It was in these august surroundings that William Draper Lewis, the first dean to devote himself fully to the law school, began his work. Here, too, Owen J. Roberts completed his law studies.

When he majored in Greek at the College of the University of Pennsylvania, Owen J. Roberts was considering becoming a teacher. His interests at the time appear in the subject of his graduation essay on the Agamemnon myth and the Attic dramatists. Describing himself later as a "reactionary in education," Roberts continued to consider the classics as a vital subject of study, regardless of a student's intended vocation, since "there are no subjects in the college curriculum which tend more to bring about accurate thinking, the accurate use of language, and the concentration of mental powers."[9] All these qualities stood him in good stead during his subsequent career although, according to his father, "Ownie" had needed to be persuaded that he was really cut out for the law. When Roberts expressed the opinion to a master at Germantown Academy that lawyers were not honest, he had been reassured with the words: "Owen, you can be honest at anything."[10] Roberts continued to be regarded as the image of integrity throughout his subsequent legal career in private practice, as a public investigator, and as justice of the Supreme Court on which he took his place in 1930 at the age of fifty-five.

Dean E. Coppée Mitchell Lecturing to Law Students in College Hall
by Mary Franklin, 1879
Courtesy of Hirschl and Adler Galleries
George Sharswood's successor as dean of the law school (1872–1877) graduated from the University (A.B. 1855). An expert in the law of real property, he became a commissioner of Fairmount Park. This painting by a young woman student of the Pennsylvania Academy of the Fine Arts is the only known painting of a College Hall interior in the nineteenth century.

Six years earlier, in 1924, Roberts had gained national prominence over-
night when President Coolidge selected him as special counsel to investigate
the Teapot Dome scandals of the Harding administration. Until that time
his reputation had been mainly limited to Philadelphia where he was
known as an outstanding attorney who worked long hours and expected
similar dedication from those around him. He was viewed as "a lawyer's
lawyer," an advocate who represented both plaintiffs and defendants in
negligence cases, who was "a lawyer for corporations without being a
corporation lawyer."[11] While his partnership in a prominent law firm
prospered, Roberts was counsel for the Pennsylvania Railroad, and a
director of insurance companies and of the American Telephone and
Telegraph Company. It was at this point in his career as an attorney that
President Coolidge, acting on the advice of Senator George Wharton Pepper,
appointed Roberts to prosecute the parties in the oil scandals of the
previous administration.

The prosecution lasted six years and involved "an impressive display of
shrewd detective work."[12] In the course of a long and tortuous investigation
which included numerous dead-ends and continuous setbacks, it was finally
established that payoffs had been made to the former Secretary of the
Interior to procure the lease of Teapot Dome for Harry F. Sinclair's
Mammoth Oil Company. The fact that Secretary Albert B. Fall was
financing improvements to his New Mexico ranch by the sale of Liberty
Bonds led counsel to trace the bonds through numerous resales from the
original wartime owners. In the course of the investigation, it was further
discovered that Liberty Bonds were being used to conceal secret profits
made by a small ring of American oil executives through a company
organized for the purpose.

Reporters of the time compared Roberts' patient pursuit of the case
with his favorite pastime: stalking big game in Maine. There was, however,
a notable difference in the outcome. On one occasion, after tramping
through the woods, Roberts had come in plain sight and within easy shot
of a large moose. After watching it for a while, he reportedly turned
round and went back to his cabin, well satisfied with the activities of the
day but to the puzzled dismay of his guide. In the Teapot Dome case,
however, Roberts pressed for convictions, making his Democratic
colleague, Senator Atlee Pomerene of Ohio, "appear as useful as a one-
armed strap-hanger in a New York subway" in the description of
journalist Drew Pearson, usually no friend to Roberts's judicial standpoint.[13] Roberts successfully prosecuted the wrongdoers, and both Fall and
Sinclair were eventually sentenced to jail terms. The Pennsylvanian's lead
in the proceedings is confirmed by a remark attributed to Sinclair himself:
on hearing Roberts referred to as "one of the government's prosecutors,"
he reputedly replied, "Hell, that's all of them."[14]

In 1928, his government assignment completed, Roberts returned to

George Wharton Pepper (1867–1961)
Center, in *The Acharnians* of
Aristophanes, 1886
*First teaching fellow at the law school
and first Algernon Sydney Biddle professor of law (1893). Born in Philadelphia,
Pepper attended the University of Pennsylvania, from which he graduated (A.B.
1887), received his law degree (LL.B.
1889), and which he served as a trustee
1911–1961). United States Senator from
Pennsylvania (1922–1927), he organized
the Pennsylvania Bar Association, serving
as president (1928–29). His autobiography,* Philadelphia Lawyer *(1945), was
an informal history of four decades of
life in the United States and Pennsylvania. Performances of* The Acharnians
*were given in Philadelphia at the
Academy of Music, and in New York,
and were entirely in Greek. In the role
of Dikaiopolis, "an exacting part . . .
quite two-thirds of the whole play,"
Pepper's "remarkably powerful voice . . .
never failed him during his long
performance."*

private practice. Only eighteen months later, he was appointed to the
Supreme Court after the Senate, in a most unusual move, turned down
Hoover appointee Judge John Parker of North Carolina. It became imperative to nominate a man of stature who would be acceptable to all parties.
As a lifelong Republican who had successfully prosecuted the scandals of a
Republican administration, Roberts appeared an ideal choice. The strongest
objection was "Mr. Roberts' allegedly 'wet' attitude" and his statement
that prohibition had no place in the Constitution. There would be a fight,
it appeared, if "either an extreme wet or a pronounced dry were to be
nominated."[15] Six years earlier, Roberts had decried the eighteenth
amendment as a policy regulation which, if introduced into the Constitution, would reduce it to the status of a city ordinance. Somehow, Roberts
managed to allay the fears of the most ardent supporters of prohibition,
and the Senate confirmed his appointment without a single negative vote.

The initially reluctant nominee took his place on the highest court in
the land as the critical "swing man" in the ideological division between
four justices who espoused a laissez-faire philosophy, and Louis D.
Brandeis and Oliver Wendell Holmes, Jr., who, for fifteen years, had
dissented from many of the majority opinions. In addition to these two
justices, Chief Justice Hughes and Justice Stone frequently aligned
themselves with a more liberal interpretation of the Constitution. For this
reason, it was generally recognized that "Justice Roberts had something
very close to a controlling vote on the Supreme Court in many types of
cases . . . from 1930 until after there were several changes in the membership of the court beginning in 1937. This was a crucial period in American
constitutional history and Justice Roberts played a more central part in it
than could have been anticipated and more than he relished."[16]

During his first years on the bench Roberts moved freely between the
opposing judicial camps. On the one hand, he cast the deciding vote to rule
the first Agricultural Adjustment Act unconstitutional. Later on, however,
he confirmed much of Roosevelt's legislative program, and his vote was
decisive in upholding the constitutionality of the Wagner Act and the
unemployment compensation provisions of the Social Security Act. He also
made important contributions to the Court in cases involving freedom of
speech. One of the most assiduous workers on the Court, Roberts was
noted for the clarity of his opinions, which were delivered orally from the
bench without the aid of written notes. His mastery of the process
appeared in his ability to summarize the substance of a case clearly and
concisely without any hesitation or fumbling. It became impossible for his
listeners to remain in any doubt as to the decision which had been made or
why it had been made.[17]

Whether or not Roberts' own mastery of language was the product of
his training in the classics, it seems to have reinforced his reliance on the
soundness of "common parlance." In a tax decision written early in his

judicial tenure, the ruling turned on the meaning implicit in the word *interest*. Roberts insisted that Congress had used the word in a generally comprehensible lay sense in the statute in question and that the word should therefore not be forced into the less familiar technical definition. Since the statute had not been written by Congress in "refined" language, he saw no reason to search for a "refined" result behind its simple words.[18]

An opinion of 1934 upholding the validity of the New York Milk Control Law was taken as a sign that Roberts would side with the liberal group on the court.[19] George Wharton Pepper cautioned those tempted to put a label on the justice: "Roberts ought not to be classified as a liberal or a conservative. By that I mean that, while all groups in the country will find him friendly, none will ever be able to claim him simultaneously an ally."[20] Although the majority opinion in the milk price-fixing case might be in the spirit of the New Deal, "he has disclosed detachment which would have qualified him for an umpire any day." Before he resigned his chair at the law school, Pepper himself had adopted what he termed "the laboratory method of stimulating the self-development of the students."[21] He further considered that Roberts exemplified the pursuit of law as an "exact science." If the trustees of the University could describe Pepper as "the first man in this community to demonstrate the possibilities of modern scientific methods of law teaching," he in turn attributed to Roberts' findings all the validity of a carefully controlled experiment in a laboratory of physics. A similar observation was made in the classroom where Roberts gave his pupils no idea of his personal opinion on any given legal problem, appearing "as detached as a physicist in his laboratory." He displayed the same objectivity in his judicial opinions and, for this reason, he was "probably closer to the fulcrum of Supreme Court rulings than even Chief Justice Hughes."[22] Political labels were therefore particularly inappropriate. "None of us," Senator Pepper is reported as saying, "would have thought of trying to identify him as to right or left tendencies."

One result of the impossibility of anticipating the stand Roberts would take was that he came in for criticism from all sides. After the Agricultural Adjustment Act opinion, it was quickly recalled that he had belonged to a conservative Philadelphia law firm with a big business point of view. Yet, at the identical period, he was described as the "Fighting Welshman" who "saved the New Deal twice."[23] The labeling dilemma appears at its most pronounced in a characterization of Roberts as a " 'conservative liberal' whose unpredictable vote had the balance of power for several years."[24] Naturally enough, his record soon led to accusations of inconsistency. The principal evidence cited in attributing his vacillating position to political motives was the change of heart he was said to have experienced between two opinions on minimum wage legislation. In June 1936, Roberts had voted with the majority to invalidate the New York Minimum Wage Law because no appeal had been made to overrule the Court's decision of 1923 against a similar law. Less than a year later, he again sided with the majority, this time overruling the precedent and sustaining minimum wage legislation.[25]

In the intervening time, Roosevelt had won a landslide victory and was threatening to pack or enlarge the Court if it did not better accommodate itself to his New Deal program. Roberts' change of heart might therefore be attributed to political considerations although, among others, Felix Frankfurter defends Roberts against the charge "that a mercurial Justice had switched in time to save nine."[26] In a memorandum which Frankfurter later persuaded him to write on the subject, Roberts indicated that the different results of the two cases was a simple legal consideration centering on the earlier Supreme Court decision. It was only in the second case that contention had been made for the earlier precedent to be overruled. Wherever his sympathies lay, his opinion had been guided by the differing legal aspect of the two cases. Frankfurter later published the memorandum in order to counter the accusation that Roberts had been brought to heel through political pressure. Such a hypothesis impugned the integrity of a justice of whom Frankfurter writes: "Only one who had the good fortune to work for years beside him, day by day, is enabled to say that no one ever served on the Supreme Court with more scrupulous regard for its moral demands than Mr. Justice Roberts."[27]

A later commentator, David Burner, writes of being "wary of public men who seek in retrospect to set the record right."[28] But, when he published the memorandum, Frankfurter laid before the public an inside account of secret proceedings by a man who, far from setting out to justify himself, is represented as being almost totally indifferent to misrepresentation. This favorable interpretation receives backing from a parallel account by Erwin N. Griswold, dean and professor at Harvard University law school. Although ignorant of the memorandum, he reached the very conclusion which Frankfurter had declared available to anyone willing to delve into the "interstices of the United States Report," rather than idly repeating the assertions of uncritical, political talk.[29]

Whatever its motivation, Roberts's *volte-face* was a cause of some consternation at the time to the conservative justices on the Court. Roberts himself reports: "I heard one of the brethren ask another, 'What is the matter with Roberts?' " With the emergence of a "new Court" in the forties, Roberts no longer had the power to surprise his colleagues or the nation, and he felt progressively less at home than in the old one. In 1930 he had been far and away the youngest justice on the Court. His wife, whose sister was the wife of the first president of the University, Thomas S. Gates, and helped raise her nephew, Tom Gates, later to be the United States envoy to China, and a University trustee, would jokingly remind him: "You're just an old man! One of the Nine Old Men."[30] The age and makeup of the Court, now comprising seven Roosevelt

**Celebrating the Bicentennial
of the University, 1940**
*Three alumni of both college and law
school and recipients of honorary
degrees: U.S. Supreme Court Justice
Owen J. Roberts, later dean of law,
U.S. Senator George Wharton Pepper,
faculty member and trustee, and University president Thomas Sovereign Gates.
They were leading figures in the celebrations and convocations which marked
the University's two centuries of
existence.*

appointees, changed radically: Roberts became the elder in a body
which, for the first time in its history, was totally lacking in whiskers.
Towards the end of his tenure, Roberts cast dissenting votes with
ever-increasing frequency, and in 1945, just after his seventieth birthday,
he resigned "to make room for younger men."[31]

Speaking before the New York Bar Association on the relation between
the Supreme Court and the rest of the government some time later,
Roberts opposed interference from the executive branch and expressed
the view that former justices should not seek further office.[32] In actual fact,
Roberts had at one time been widely considered as a possible Republican
candidate for the presidency since it was well known that he had "more
friends in both parties . . . and fewer powerful enemies than any other
prominent Republican."[33] Had a current journalistic prediction come
about in a ticket composed of "Roberts of Pennsylvania, Warren of
California," the views of the former justice on holding office would have
been in need of adjustment. The later history of the Court might also have
been very different with the elimination of Eisenhower's appointee Earl
Warren. In his speech before the New York Bar Association, Roberts had
even gone so far as to regret having undertaken *extra curiam* activities
which had necessitated his absence from the work of the Court. One such
appointment had been his assignment to investigate the Pearl Harbor
attack.

On an earlier occasion Roberts had been selected as umpire of the
Mixed Claims Commission after World War I because of his reputation as
"a fearless independent and thorough finder of facts."[34] In this charge,
Roberts presided over what came to be known as the *Black Tom* cases in
which the United States was suing the German government for damage to
munitions on Black Tom Island in New York Harbor before the country
had entered the war. At the time, Roberts showed no hesitation in over-
turning earlier decisions in the light of new evidence in spite of the
international embarrassment which resulted. Roberts was not only above
partisan maneuvers; he could remain equally objective in international
affairs as well. Appointed to another wartime investigation in 1941, he
conducted it with his customary energy and integrity: the findings of the
Roberts Commission on Pearl Harbor were made public under the signature
of every participant and without a single change to the document. Although
little of what had actually happened was disclosed in the report, it became
apparent that much had been suppressed for security reasons.[35] The facts
themselves had mostly been unearthed by Roberts, who, by avoiding the
politics in which subsequent investigations indulged, "made an invaluable
contribution to the stability and security of the nation at a very critical
period in its history."[36]

Roberts was thus very much involved in accounting for the events
which led up to Pearl Harbor. The United States entered the war on

December 8, 1941. Two months later Executive Order 9066 led to
the internment of thousands of United States citizens and residents of
Japanese ancestry on the West Coast. In one of the last cases on which he
sat before resigning from the Supreme Court, Roberts offered the following dissent on the legality of this internment program against the majority
opinion written by Justice Black with Justice Frankfurter concurring and
Justice Douglas voting with the majority:

> I dissent because I think the indisputable facts exhibit a clear
> violation of Constitutional rights . . . it is a case of convicting a
> citizen as a punishment for not submitting to imprisonment in a
> concentration camp, based on his ancestry, and solely because of
> his ancestry, without evidence or inquiry concerning his loyalty
> and good disposition toward the United States.[37]

This strong language, coupled with Roberts' independent stance on the
issue, lends forceful support to a colleague's characterization of him in
regard to another case. In the words of Justice Frankfurter: "Long before it
became popular to regard every so-called civil liberties question as
constitutionally self-answering, Roberts gave powerful utterance to his
sensitiveness for those procedural safeguards which are protective of
human rights in a civilized society."[38]

In 1946 Earl G. Harrison, then dean and vice-president of the University
of Pennsylvania for law, presented Roberts with the Philadelphia Bok
Award, the city's highest civic honor. "This man," he declared, "realized
in 1945 that he had something more important to do than sitting on the
highest tribunal of the land. And he came back to Philadelphia as president
of the United Nations Council, to lend his mind, time, energy, and strong
voice toward the establishment of world government."[39] One of the reasons
that Roberts resigned rather than retiring from the Supreme Court was
because he wished to be able to contribute more freely to the cause of
Atlantic Union to which he gave both moral and financial support throughout the last decade of his life. It was a subject very close to his heart and
one on which he spoke in an address to the Law School Forum in 1954, a
few months before his death. Even though much of his time was devoted
to this cause, the former justice did not flinch from assuming a variety of
other responsibilities. He was cited as a perfect example of the "truism that
many men retire in their late sixties from their lives' work—and then
proceed to work harder than ever before."[40]

Like so many Pennsylvanians who have achieved prominence in other
fields, Roberts was remembered as an inspiring teacher. A student who had
heard him during his earlier years as a professor of law later wrote: "It is
hard to see how the doctrine of dependent relative revocation or the
distinction between a specific and a demonstrative legacy could inspire a
group, even of second year law students, at four o'clock in the afternoon.
But somehow, under Professor Roberts, they did. There was something

electric about that class of his, something vital and invigorating. Undoubtedly it was the personality of the man. He was a born teacher."[41] In his last years, Roberts once again combined his earliest ambition of becoming a teacher with his father's more far-reaching view that he was even better suited for the law: in the seventh decade of his life, as an act of loyalty to the law school, he accepted the invitation to become dean.

In his straightforward account of how he came to be carving out a new career at the age of seventy-three, Roberts remarked: "They said they wanted a dean and asked me if I would try the job. I said I would."[42] During his tenure, which took the school into the fifties, Roberts succeeded in obtaining substantial increases in faculty salaries and additional funds for student scholarships. Although he had not expected to do any teaching, and methods of instruction had radically altered since his earlier days as law professor, his interest in legal education induced him to give a seminar on constitutional law and to instruct a section of the class in torts. In addition, his connection with the Supreme Court resulted in an increased number of graduates appointed to clerkships. During his last year as dean, Justice Roberts delivered the Holmes Lectures at Harvard law school. As soon as he retired as dean, he was elected the twenty-fourth president of the American Philosophical Society, and throughout the last years of his life he continued as a trustee of the University of Pennsylvania.

Against the name of Owen J. Roberts in the University of Pennsylvania *Record of the Class of '95* is the motto: "Fain would I climb." In the course of his career, the imposing founder of "The Six-Foot Club" reached the pinnacle in every enterprise which engaged his energies. "If Roberts is properly described as character in action, it was the power of his personality which made him effective in whatever he undertook."[43] After achieving the personal success and rewards attending the most prominent lawyer in Philadelphia, he went on to serve the country as counsel to the government and Supreme Court justice. He was further honored for the powerful support he lent to a wide number of civic causes and to the furtherance of world peace. In the words of John J. McCloy: "A man capable of error but incapable of persisting in it—a powerful, effective, eloquent advocate; a firm and honest judge and upright citizen of the nation and the world—this was his profile."[44] At his University, his contribution is memorialized by the line of distinguished scholars who deliver the annual Owen J. Roberts Lectures, inaugurated in 1957.

14

Paul Philippe Cret and Louis I. Kahn: Architecture and Design

Perspective Drawing of the Richards Building
by Louis I. Kahn (1960)
Collection, The Museum of Modern Art, New York
Glazed tiers of laboratories alternate with soaring brick service stacks in this view from the west of the Medical Research Building and Biology Building designed for the University by professor of architecture Louis I. Kahn.

The building dedicated to Alfred Newton Richards in 1961 was the work of the first Paul P. Cret professor of architecture, Louis I. Kahn. Together, Cret and Kahn span the existence of instruction in architecture almost from its origins as a branch of engineering in the Towne Scientific School to its present-day status as the largest constituency in the Graduate School of Fine Arts. Both men were recipients of the gold medal of the American Institute of Architects and, as teachers of architecture, each marks a distinctive high point in the career of the school: as the premier Beaux-Arts institution of the twenties and, again, the spawning ground of notable architects at the time when Louis Kahn was coming into his own as America's most original architect.

Before he designed the University's new buildings on the campus in West Philadelphia, Thomas W. Richards had given instruction in drawing there—an accomplishment recommended immediately after the ability "to write a *fair Hand* and swift" by none other than Franklin. Not only had the founder considered drawing "a kind of Universal Language understood by all Nations," but he saw it as a skill "no less useful to a *Mechanic* than to a Gentleman."[1] In 1874, Richards' title was changed to professor of drawing and architecture. Since, in classical times, architecture had been considered an indispensable branch of education, Richards was eager to see this most ancient of the arts restored to its former eminence through recognition by the University. His hopes were fulfilled in 1890 when the school of architecture opened with stimulation from the Philadelphia chapter of the American Institute of Architects, whose president, Theophilus Parsons Chandler, became its first dean.[2] When the school was permanently organized at the end of the academic year, he was succeeded by Warren Powers Laird, whose greatest accomplishment for the school was to bring over Paul P. Cret, *diplomé* of the Ecole des Beaux-Arts and already a winner of several of the most coveted prizes of the French school.[3]

After taking up residence at the University of Pennsylvania in 1903, Cret returned to France almost immediately to marry a French wife. A decade later, he left the United States again, this time to join the French

Paul Philippe Cret (1876–1945)
*Assistant professor and then professor
of design at the University of Pennsylvania (1903–1916, 1918–1924, 1929–
1937). Born in Lyons, he studied at the
Ecole des Beaux-Arts in Lyons and Paris
and designed the prize-winning Pan
American Union in Washington soon
after arriving in the States. In addition
to buildings, he designed war memorials
and the Valley Forge Arch; also several
major bridges in the Philadelphia area
where, with Jacques Greber, he laid
out the Parkway. One of the most
influential of the French teachers who
brought the Beaux-Arts tradition to
America, he inspired a generation of
architects and made the department of
architecture at the University of Pennsylvania the most important school in
America of the time. He received an
honorary Sc.D. (1913), was appointed
architect to the University (1930), and,
upon his retirement, was named associate
trustee. Received the gold medal of the
American Institute of Architects (1938).*

army in which he served as a cartographer. He had been awarded an
honorary degree of Doctor of Science at the University just before the war
broke out, and he was described in the press as "Penn's fighting professor."
In 1916, the papers printed his obituary, accompanied by a statement that
Provost Edgar Fahs Smith refused to believe the report that he had died in
action.[4] The provost's optimism proved well founded, and in 1919 Cret duly
returned as an officer of the Légion d'Honneur. There was a reunion at the
T-Square Club of Philadelphia to which he had also given his time in
prewar days and where he was now "enthroned as a 'King' in the presence
of hundreds of loyal and affectionate former students."[5] Cret had been
wounded at Arras and remained partially deaf from the noise of bursting
shells. He described the war as a terrific waste: "waste of time, energy and
young men, waste of architecture and homes."[6] Having designed the
Washington Memorial Arch in Valley Forge before the war, he was now
appointed consulting architect to the American Battle Monuments
Commission. Cret designed a chapel at Waregem in Belgium and
memorials in Gibraltar as well as at Fismes, Varennes, Bellicourt, and
Château Thierry in France and, at home, the Frankford War Memorial and
the Gettysburg Memorial.

After settling in the United States Cret seems to have found no difficulty
in reconciling his own training in the most respected architectural tradition
of the time with a sympathetic awareness of the diverse requirements of
this continent and the need to develop a system of teaching based on
American educational methods. Cret's great influence as a teacher and
practitioner during his years at the University of Pennsylvania carried over
into papers discussing instruction in architecture, which he always viewed
against a larger canvas of the philosophy of education and general culture.
Perhaps in part because of his deafness, Cret developed the art of communicating eloquently as a design critic by means of a few strokes of his
pencil. A similar skill permitted him to pass swiftly to the essentials in
arguments on the nature of the architect and the best method of training.

Cret opposed the notion of importing the French system, which involved
a longer, more specialized training for architects, because, as he pointed
out, it overlooked the different situations and needs of the American
student.[7] Nonetheless, he remained faithful to many of the tenets of the
Beaux-Arts tradition of instruction. Cret believed in the efficacy of a
preliminary sketch or *esquisse* by students, "done within a specified limit
of time without reference to documents or criticism by an instructor." The
main features had to be maintained throughout the solution of the
assigned problem.[8] By this means, Cret aimed at showing that there was no
such thing as one ideal solution, but only a number of different ways, of
varying merit, of approaching any architectural problem.

> In the beginning of any work of composition, the finding of the
> scheme may seem a sort of chance game in which some are

luckier than others. . . . There is, however, a corrective to the
chance which seems to treat indifferently good or bad designers.
If the bad designer starts with a poor idea, he is unable to better
it. . . . A good designer, on the other hand, if he does not find
the best solution of a problem at first, has enough training to find
many approximate solutions, seeing immediately the possibility
of retaining some parts of them, and by the end, and after a
good deal of work, if he has not produced a masterpiece, he will
certainly have at least designed a building fitting the conditions
of the programme, well studied and of good proportions. . . .
We see at once that superiority in design is mostly knowing
how to study, that is to say, to give form to an idea to make it
constructible, and to improve it by good proportions.[9]

Similarly, architects trained at the Ecole started out with an abstraction,
called the *parti*, which involved making "an initial, philosophical decision
as to what the building should be."[10] This was given progressive architectural form by the *marche* of the composition consisting of a series of
consecutive sections. Cret's own method reflected his training in design,
and he is described as visualizing his buildings as though he were able to
see through the walls.[11]

In his emphasis on the need for "study," Cret lucidly detracted from
the popular myth "that designers are born, not made." For the same reason,
when the pendulum of taste in architecture, of which he often spoke, was
swinging far away from classical to modern values—values whose revolutionary tenets, as he pointed out, nonetheless all had a historical precedent
—Cret noted at what sacrifice of sound educational principles the dubious
spark of individual "originality" was nurtured. Proposals for educational
reform are merely one consequence of the "old conflict" against tradition
although, he suggests, "there is probably no more justification for it than
for revising the teaching of piano scales when Debussy instead of Mozart
is to be played."[12] On an earlier occasion, Cret drew an analogy with
literature rather than music to illustrate the lack of foundation for
fashionable—and recurrent—architectural prejudices which obscure the
fundamentals of architectural knowledge:

The words of a modern language . . . are themselves trans-
formations or deformations of radicals whose origin is lost in the
darkness of philology. One does not cast away in a day the
patrimony acquired by centuries of labor. . . . Architectural
forms, which are like the words of our language, are transformed very slowly and without much regard for the rules
which we should like to establish. But what remains in our
power is to use these forms in giving expression to our own
ideas and not to those of our fathers. The vocabulary of
Stevenson or Carlyle is not very different from the one of Sterne
or even Milton. Nobody, however, fails to recognize differences
between these men.[13]

If the battle between the moderns and the traditionalists ended with the defeat of the latter, the revolution in style and taste which has taken place over the years is particularly marked with regard to Cret's own buildings. Cret had started his career in the United States, by winning in association with Albert Kelsey the competition for the International Bureau of American Republics. Chosen from among eighty-seven entries, the Pan American Union, as the prize-winning building came to be known, originally called for stucco to be used. So highly acclaimed was the building, however, that Andrew Carnegie gave an additional $500,000 permitting the use of marble for the 1907–8 construction. Even as late as 1948, according to the poll of architectural opinion taken that year by the American Institute of Architects, Cret's Folger Library in Washington was voted the most admired building of the time. In the sampling of their tastes taken in 1976, the views of architects were very different. Although Cret's student, Louis Kahn, was one of the few to have two buildings cited by six or more of the architects and critics who responded to the survey, not a single work by Cret himself was mentioned.

The training of the Ecole centered on the principle of competition, and Paul Cret, nurtured in this tradition, won first place in seven such competitions and saw all his winning designs become a reality. He left his mark on the Philadelphia area with his designs for Rittenhouse Square, as well as the Benjamin Franklin Parkway, started by Cret and finished by Jacques Greber, with whom he also collaborated on the Rodin Museum. Another important local commission was a private residence in Merion designed to house the collection now known as the Barnes Foundation. On a much larger scale, the Benjamin Franklin Bridge—formerly the Delaware River Bridge—resulted from a collaboration with engineer Ralph Modjeski. This mighty structure in unmasked steel was followed by the construction of the Henry Avenue Bridge spanning the Wissahickon Drive and the University Avenue Bridge as well as the graceful Calvert Street Bridge over Washington's Rock Creek Park.

The Benjamin Franklin Bridge
Drawing by Paul Philippe Cret, 1922
*Commissioned as the Delaware River
Bridge, Cret's design for a structure in
naked steel was approved by engineer
Ralph Modjeski with whom he collaborated on many projects. It was the
longest suspension bridge in the world
at the time of construction. Appearing
light and graceful in this drawing, the
bridge has massive anchorages in
rusticated granite at either end for the
cables.*

Quite atypical of his usual style is the chemistry building at the University.
Designed in a gesture towards modernism and under the urging of his
students, this late building was immediately denominated "Battle Ship
Corner" by the residents of the wartime campus.[15] In a more far-reaching
contribution, the French architect also devoted considerable attention to
the first major attempt at planning for the future growth of the
University of Pennsylvania.[16]

With the triumph of the modern movement, Cret's buildings have
suffered an eclipse shared by those of other architects whose work
stemmed from the Beaux-Arts tradition or reflected the eclecticism of the
last, and the early part of this, century. Renewed interest in the Ecole,
however, resulted in a major exhibition at the Museum of Modern Art
in New York at the end of 1975. It is increasingly recognized that "the
theoretical basis of modern architecture is as much a collection of received
opinions as were the doctrines it overthrew."[17] Furthermore, "the majority
of the architects who reached professional maturity by the end of the
1940s had received at least an American version of Beaux-Arts training."[18]
One of the main reasons for its reputation was the highly sophisticated
teaching method of the Paris Ecole. Now, in addition, the Ecole has come
to receive credit for influencing imaginative American architects of recent
times:

> During the last few years there has taken place a reappraisal of
> the relative importance of certain American architectural schools
> after the arrival of the International Style. Gropius' Harvard
> and Rudolph's Yale have been challenged, in retrospect, by the
> University of Pennsylvania and Princeton. The reason for this
> reappraisal has been the quality of the work of certain men
> trained at the latter two institutions—Louis Kahn at the former,
> Robert Venturi, Charles Moore and Donlyn Lyndon at the
> latter—and because of the credit these men give to their
> teachers—Paul Philippe Cret at Pennsylvania and Jean Labatut
> at Princeton. Cret and Labatut were Frenchmen, products of the
> Ecole and faithful to their tradition.[19]

Louis I. Kahn (1901–1974)
Professor of architecture at the University of Pennsylvania (1956–1974), Kahn received his degree at the University (B.Arch. 1924) and later the honorary D.F.A. (1971). He was chief of design for the Sesquicentennial Exposition in Philadelphia (1925–1926) and organized the Architectural Research Group of thirty unemployed architects during the Depression. Taught at Yale before returning to the University of Pennsylvania where he designed the Richards Medical Research Building, a commission which was followed by a great demand for his work both at home and abroad. Among many awards, he received the gold medal of the American Institute of Architects (1971) and of the Royal Institute of British Architects (1972).

Among the aspects of the Parisian *ateliers* which Cret did not import to the University was the attitude of the *patron:* "Where the Patron of an atelier in the Paris Ecole would arrive in the atelier in a swallowtail coat, complete with top hat, a stick, and gloves, and the students never knew when to expect him, Paul Cret would walk into the great drafting room at the University of Pennsylvania in his shirt sleeves promptly at two in the afternoon every week day and, toward the end of a problem, on Sundays."[20] The students, who did not arrive in Cret's atelier until their senior year, would listen—and watch—attentively as he passed among them. The highest praise from Cret was his utterance of the terse gallicism: "It can go," while the reverse was comprised in his most famous observation: "You do not know what you are doing," or the equally devastating query: " 'Ave you a sponge?"[21] In the twenties the alumni attributed the high reputation of the school of architecture almost entirely to the "master," Paul Philippe Cret.[22] Under his guidance students from the University of Pennsylvania won the Paris prize three years in a row. One of these, Harry Sternfeld, who was later a professor at the school, speaks movingly of the influence of Cret on himself and others:

> . . . As one who personally had experienced the revelation and inspiration which emanated from that incomparable guiding tutelary of architectonic beauty and perfection—Paul Philippe Cret—it is my considered opinion that he was the brightest luminary among the other French masters (in the country). . . . My judgment, so personal, is equally shared by thousands of his other devoted students—from all over the world—whose perceptions and powers burgeoned and expanded through the magic and mystique of his ethereal potency.[23]

In *The Book of the School* put out in 1934 by the department of architecture there are illustrations of both the Pan American Union and the Folger Library designed by Cret. In the same book, Louis I. Kahn is listed as an alumnus of 1924 with nothing more beside his name than his current address. He had started his architectural studies at the University in 1920, the year the department of architecture became the principal unit of the newly created school of fine arts. A pamphlet on architecture, which the school brought out soon afterwards, includes a prize-winning "Esquisse for a monumental fountain" by Kahn. The stated purpose of the publication was to show that the "study of design is a vital element in architecture."[24] It is clear that the underlying academic theory of his education made a lasting impression on Kahn, particularly in its stress on a masonry architecture of palpable mass and weight with clearly defined spaces formed and characterized by the structural solids themselves.[25] Long after the Beaux-Arts tradition had fallen into disfavor, Kahn remarked: "I don't know it as a tradition. I know it as an introduction to the spirit of architecture which has very little to do with the realistic solving of problems."[26]

As a student, Louis Kahn had initially been torn between architecture and music. In fact, faced with insufficient space in his room for a bed and a piano, he claims to have slept on the piano. He had been told by the director of the Philadelphia School of Industrial Art for drawing, carving and modeling, from which he graduated: "No music. Nothing but art" and he went on to win first prize in drawing in a city-wide competition sponsored by the Pennsylvania Academy of the Fine Arts in both his junior and senior years at Central High School. To support himself during his student days at the University of Pennsylvania, however, he earned money as relief pianist in two movie houses.

The parallel between the work of the architect and the world of music is a recurring theme of his poetic pronouncements on art and architecture. In 1955, he wrote:

> Is the auditorium a Stradivarius
> or is it an ear
> Is the auditorium a creative instrument
> keyed to Bach or Bartok
> played by the conductor
> or is it a convention hall.[27]

A decade and a half later, Kahn returned to the same image:

> The auditorium wants to be a violin. Its lobby is the violin
> case. . . . Open before us is the architect's plan. Next to it is a
> sheet of music. The architect fleetingly reads his composition as
> a structure of elements and spaces in their light. The musician
> reads, with the same overallness, his composition as a structure
> of inseparable elements and spaces in sound.[28]

The implicit synesthesia in this description appears again more forcefully in the statement: "To the musician a sheet of music is seeing from what he hears. A plan of a building should read like a harmony of spaces in light."[29]

In 1966, Louis I. Kahn became the first Paul P. Cret professor of architecture at the University of Pennsylvania, to which he had returned as professor ten years before. Kahn once remarked: "A city is a place where a small boy, as he walks through it, may see what he wants to do his whole life." Philadelphia was the city where he himself had walked and grown and in which he claimed to have been educated at the Free Library, the Museum, and the University of Pennsylvania.[30] Kahn's return in 1956 to the University at which he had studied coincided with the end of what, in view of his achievements after the age of fifty, appears something like a protracted apprenticeship in the theory—and philosophy —of architecture. His friend and client Jonas Salk wrote:

> For five decades he prepared himself
> and did in two
> what others wish they could do in five.[31]

The Museum Rotunda
Drawing by Louis I. Kahn, 1924
This drawing of the Romanesque rotunda of the University Museum, finished in 1914, was made by Kahn in his senior year in the school of architecture. Although his own career would carry him in a very different direction, Kahn acknowledged a debt to the instruction in the Beaux-Arts tradition which he had received at the University.

It was not merely the war and the depression but something in Kahn's own creative genius which held him in check and made the impact of his work, with its far-reaching intellectual and emotional content, all the greater when it came. Through the brilliance of Kahn, the University of Pennsylvania acquired "one of the greatest buildings of modern times."[32] With its treatment of space, its structural techniques, and its solutions to the special problem of creating a functional laboratory complex, his design for the Alfred Newton Richards Medical Research Building and the Biology Building next to it marked a turning point in the career of its architect. His other work for the University of Pennsylvania was the renovation of the president's house on Spruce Street which he undertook fifteen years later.

Because of Kahn's predilection for visible structure, the Richards Building "remains a record of how it is put together."[33] In this, Kahn's

The Duomo, Florence
Drawing by Louis I. Kahn, 1950
During a visit to Europe, Kahn sketched the dome of the Renaissance cathedral in Florence, along with its campanile.

practice had much in common with the theory underlying his architectural training. It was perhaps a result of this natural bent, too, that Kahn found it difficult to adapt his own design to the fluidity and lightness of the so-called International Style. The form taken by the buildings of his maturity was one which aimed at revealing inherent problems of structure and function. In describing his conception of a skyscraper Kahn writes: "The tower is an experimental exercise in triangulation of structural members rising upward to form themselves into a vertical truss against the forces of the wind."[34] The solutions he proposed are very different from those put forward by Mies van der Rohe in his Seagram Building, of which Kahn wrote: "Take the beautiful tower made of bronze that was erected in New York. It is a bronze lady, incomparable in beauty, but you know she has corsets for fifteen stories because the wind bracing is not seen."[35]

For many years, Kahn's influence was mainly as a teacher and theoretician. Some of his projects, together with the poetic evocations of the problems to which he addressed himself, were published in *Perspecta*, the architectural journal founded in the fifties at Yale. He possessed the "magic ability to communicate with the young."[36] In part this was a result of his striking use of recurrent images and pronouncements on the theory of architecture which have been compared to zen koans: "Q: What does a brick like? A: An arch."[37] Much of his theory takes on the rhythm of blank verse, with individual thoughts expressed in sentences not dissimilar to Japanese haiku. This is particularly true of his much-quoted statement, "Order and Design," in which he gives paradoxical expression to his deeply seated belief in the existence of something resembling the Platonic "form" in the mind or imagination, precedent to the tangible Form which belongs to the realm of design and action:

> Order is
> Design is form-making in order
> Form emerges out of a system of construction
> A Form emerges from the structural elements inherent in the form.
> A dome is not conceived when questions arise how to build it.[38]

One of his basic tenets is the "will to be" of the spaces themselves which his colleague and collaborator, engineer August E. Komendant, attributes to Schopenhauer.[39] Kahn endows the disparate elements with animistic vitality: "A street wants to be a building."[40] The building itself takes on life as an individual:

> A building being built is not yet in servitude. It is so anxious to be that no grass can grow under its feet. . . . When it is in service and finished, the building wants to say, "Look, I want to tell you about the way I was made." Nobody listens. Everybody is busy going from room to room. But when the building is a ruin and free of servitude, the spirit emerges telling of the marvel that a building was made.[41]

For Kahn, "a column should be regarded as a great event in the making of space," not a post or a prop; "a stair is a very important event in a building." In distinction from mere decoration, "the joint is the beginning of ornament. . . . Ornament is the adoration of the joint."[42]

Kahn's philosophy of architecture comes together with his feelings as a teacher and his general view of knowledge when he discusses "what School *wants to be.*" His conception involves the nature of the place and its translation into space: "I think of school as an environment of spaces where it is good to learn. School began with a man under a tree who did not know he was a teacher discussing his realization with a few who did not know they were students." This observation reflects the Socratic aspect of his own manner of instruction with its emphasis on dialogue, and this, in turn, was based on Kahn's firm belief that a good question is greater than the most brilliant answer. This is the way he speaks of buildings which do not give the correct answer to the architectural questions: "The schools are good to look at but are shallow in architecture because they do not respect the spirit of the man under the tree."[43] One reason that Kahn built very little before the age of fifty appears to be his own struggle with the right question. His uncompromising attitude is revealed in the statement that "the right thing badly done is always greater than the wrong thing well done."

Kahn was known and respected by other architects at the time of his return to the University of Pennsylvania; but he had relatively few buildings to his name, despite the fact that "his students generally felt with some uneasiness that he should have been, even might have been," great.[44] His most important design up until that time had been for the Yale University Art Gallery, the first contemporary building on the campus near where the new Yale Center for British Art, the last building designed by Kahn, was opened in 1977. The years of theorizing were necessary to Kahn, almost as though his unrealized projects were in themselves what he called "an offering to the spirit Architecture."[45] In the last years of the fifties, Kahn burst on the scene still dominated by the giants of earlier in the century—Gropius, Le Corbusier, Mies van der Rohe, Wright—with his Richards Medical Research Building. In ten years, he more than made up for any previous leanness in tangible constructions. In the late forties, he had drawn up a "Plan for mid-town Philadelphia" which was lovingly presented a few years later in *Perspecta 2.* Then, in the sixth decade of the century and of his life, Kahn received the commission to design the regional capital of Pakistan at Dacca, since become the capital of Bangladesh.

At the time of its construction, the Alfred Newton Richards Medical Research Building was the subject of an exhibition at the Museum of Modern Art in New York. In the bulletin accompanying this display devoted to a single work of architecture, the Richards Building is described as "probably the single most consequential building constructed in the United States since the war." It is, the account goes on, "simultaneously a building and a manifesto. Its impact is derived from its inventive and rigorous integration of form, function, space and structural technique. More than any other building recently constructed in America it is principled, vigorous, fundamental and exhilarating; it states, teaches, and questions."[46]

Newton Richards, the scientist, believed in asking the quintessential question and designing an experiment which might answer it. The building which was dedicated to him in his last years was designed by an architect

Medical Research Building
by Louis I. Kahn
Perspective drawing, preliminary version, 1957
Collection, The Museum of Modern Art, New York
Gift of the architect
In its final form, the building looks very different from the intermediate version seen in this sketch by the architect.

whose stated concern was also with asking "good questions" architecturally and functionally. Kahn describes some of the answers he devised to those posed by the medical research laboratories:

> The laboratories may be characterized as the architecture of air cleanliness and area adjustability. . . . The Medical Research Building at the University of Pennsylvania is conceived in recognition of the realizations that science laboratories are studios and that the air to breathe should be away from the air to throw away. . . . I designed three studio towers for the University where a man may work in his bailiwick and each studio has its own *escape sub tower* and *exhaust sub tower* for isotope air, germ-infected air and noxious gas.[47]

As usual, "Kahn explains the structural interaction in the anthropomorphic terms he favors. For him, buildings feel, think and act."

Responses to the building are described as suggesting "old-fashioned terms of morality: honesty, integrity, truth, a dedicated search for the best artistic means of expression to the best functional end."[48] In some cases, the answers at which Kahn arrived in this his first major project may not have been altogether satisfactory. With his view of knowledge in terms of dialogue and an overarching humanism, he overlooked such elemental considerations as the scientist's need for a controlled environment. But if the "scientist occupants" have set up divisions felt as "visually confusing" in terms of the architect's conception of inner spaces, the soaring towers with their ingenious solution to the relation of served to service spaces, and the engineering feat which permits of a great cantilevered porch, "one of the most heraldic entrances in modern architecture," have set a landmark on the campus which is also a milestone in contemporary architecture in America.[49]

Kahn describes Jonas Salk's reaction to the Richards Building before he gave the architect the commission to design the Salk Institute in La Jolla: "How nice, a beautiful building. I didn't know a building that went up in the air could be so nice."[50] The question of size was the first consideration; but Salk soon expressed another objective:

> He said: "There is one thing which I would like to be able to accomplish.
> I would like to invite Picasso to the Laboratory!"

In Kahn's haiku-like extrapolation:

> Science finds what is already there,
> but the artist makes that which is not there.

He goes on to say: "This consideration changed the Salk Institute from a plain building like the one at the University of Pennsylvania."[51] The measured lines of print interpret the cadences of Kahn's utterance made on this occasion before an audience of architecture students at Rice

University. In the accompanying photographs, his listeners are sitting outside on the grass with Kahn in their midst—the man under the tree.

Even after commissions crowded in on him in larger numbers than he could handle, Kahn continued to teach the students who loved to hear him. "Teaching is essential to me," he said. "I think it is my chapel."[52] It was on his way to teach a class at the University of Pennsylvania, traveling home from Ahmedabad where he had designed the Indian Institute of Management, that he died in March, 1974. Only a few weeks before, the president of the University had persuaded him to serve as an advisor on the physical development of the campus and its surroundings. In his tribute to Kahn, Jonas Salk expressed the regret: "It will never be known how much, nor what more, would have been expressed had life lingered until the capacity to create began to ebb." Years before, Kahn had given his own poetic expression to the consolation which belongs in so unique a way to the creative artist: "It's what a man makes, what he writes, his painting, his music, that remains indestructible. The circumstances of their making is but the mould for casting. . . . Whatever happens in the circumstantial course of man's life, he leaves as the most valuable, a golden dust which is the essence of nature."[53] Louis Kahn left such a legacy in the students he taught, in the ideas he expressed, and in the buildings he designed.

15

Roy F. Nichols:
Historian and Scholar

A Library within A Library
The Henry Charles Lea Library is an outstanding collection of works on the subjects of the Inquisition, church history, canon law, and other medieval and early renaissance areas. The majority of its 400 manuscripts and 17,000 volumes were assembled by Lea, a businessman and medieval historian, in the tradition of the amateur and scholar, who used to walk to the University Library every night from his home at Twentieth and Walnut Streets. The collection, formerly installed in the Furness Building (1925), is now on the top floor of the Van Pelt Library, housed in the room of black walnut paneling and cabinetry which was originally part of the Lea house. The centerpiece here is a portrait of lawyer-historian Joseph George Rosengarten (A.B. 1852, LL.D. 1906), trustee and benefactor.

Like prominent figures elsewhere, those associated with the University of Pennsylvania have not merely left their mark on their own time but have continued to influence the world of learning and the professions. While molding the future from his vantage point in the present in this way, the historical scholar provides an additional temporal dimension since his own work and interests are directed towards the past. Roy F. Nichols, one of the most respected students of American history of the twentieth century, continually brought his historical perspective to issues of scholarship, education, and life. A historian of international reputation, Nichols nonetheless underscored the importance of local history, and after he joined the Pennsylvania faculty at the age of twenty-nine, much of his attention was directed to the history of his new city and state. In his last years, Nichols continued the work of Edward Potts Cheyney as historian to the University of Pennsylvania.

The period of American history which Nichols studied and wrote of most comprehensively in the course of practically half a century at the University is that of the 1850s, the decade which culminated in the Civil War. In his doctoral dissertation, published as *The Democratic Machine, 1850–1854,* he wrote of the structure and function of the political party at a moment in American history when its organization had failed to prevent differences from being settled by war instead of through deliberation. According to his fellow historian Professor David M. Potter of Yale University, "During the succeeding forty-four years, Nichols produced a series of volumes which ranged forward and backward over his context, in a progression that moved through the tensions of the fifties, to the Civil War and into the Reconstruction period, and then turned back to examine political origins from the time of Alfred the Great, through English political history and the history of the colonies, to the study of the political organizations of Federalists, Jeffersonians, Jacksonians, and Whigs which preceded the party organizations of the eighteen fifties."[1]

In his autobiography Roy Nichols describes how in 1925, two years after he and Jeannette Paddock Nichols had received their Ph.D. degrees from Columbia University, "a call from the University of Pennsylvania

185

brought us to live in Philadelphia, at the other end of the Pennsylvania
Railroad."[2] Here the Nicholses were to remain. Though other universities
were eager to have Nichols on their faculty, the history department
"obstructed three pre-depression efforts to get him to move his base of
operations."[3] He swiftly became identified with the department, and it was
to Nichols that Ezra Pound addressed himself from Italy to express regret
at the death of historian Herman Ames. For Pound's former teacher
was thus deprived of "the minor entertainment of knowing that his
paitiences [*sic*] and indulgences of 30 years ago hadn't been wholly wasted
on one of his most cantankerous pupils."[4]

During his years at the University of Pennsylvania, which he entered
at the age of fifteen, Pound struck up a friendship which would last a
lifetime with medical student William Carlos Williams, who after
graduation devoted his energies to "the art of medicine and the medicine
of art." After receiving an A.M. in Romanic languages, Pound had
enrolled in all the courses offered by the English department and he
writes: "In 1907 I achieved the distinction of being the only student
flunked in J[osiah] P[enniman]'s course in the history of literary criticism."[5]
At the time Pound was studying with the dean who later became provost,
he considered himself to be the only student with the slightest interest in
literary criticism; indeed, his purpose on entering the University had been
to study the comparative values of literature "unbeknown to the faculty."
He had accomplished much in this area by the time he wrote, in a letter
addressed to "Doc. Nichols," of the "Time Lag, between real culture and
that TAUGHT."[6]

During his first years at the University, Nichols was engaged in
research on Franklin Pierce, publishing his study of this president in 1931.
Intent on the "reconstruction" of the state capital of former times in order
"to place Pierce in his habitat," he spent time studying government records
not only in Washington but also in Concord, New Hampshire.[7] This
technique of steeping himself in the physical environment in which his
subjects had lived was one which Nichols applied constantly in order to
visualize that life to the fullest possible extent. Nichols' understanding of
the nuances of the Civil War period resulted from this familiarity with all
aspects of its milieu as well as the fact that he knew "the hangers-on and
the back-benchers as well as the leading actors in the drama."[8] During a
year as Pitt professor at Cambridge, he commented on his personal
experience of the influence of environment. In the opening words of his
inaugural lecture there, he evoked the "American historian passing
through the Great Gate of Trinity or walking in the courts of Emmanuel"
and observed: "These Cambridge surroundings recall to him the fact that
the University was the birthplace of much of significance in American
culture."[9]

The place of biography in the teaching of history was a question much debated at the time. In the face of evident shortcomings in traditional teaching, Nichols took the position that, so long as biography is not allowed to disintegrate into gossip and anecdote, it serves a major function by drawing attention to one of the fundamental intellectual problems of analyzing history: the complexities of human motivation. The subjects for a biographical approach to history need not be limited to great men even though there is a tendency for political biography to concentrate on the leaders at the expense of the led.[10] Although his book was the biography of a president, Pierce was an example of "the historical outcast or scapegoat [who] seems as necessary to teachers and writers of history as does the hero."[11] In order to point up the historical significance of even obscure members of the human race, Nichols proposed that students should be encouraged to study the lives of their own relatives or of other people close to them as an antidote to the purely formal tendencies of historical study: "In other words," he notes, "history without biography is like faith without works; it is dead."[12]

Nichols was deeply interested in the process involved in studying and writing history as well as in actual events and personalities. Much later, in an article entitled "The Genealogy of Historical Generalizations," he analyzed the way historical "truth" evolves.[13] The point of departure is provided by eyewitness accounts, unabashedly tinged with emotion, favorable or otherwise. Nichols takes as his example the progress of Civil War historiography with a vivid sample of the earliest stage of generalization from a contemporary account which declared: "Never since the revolt of Lucifer has there been a more causeless rebellion against a justly constituted and beneficent government."[14] A countervailing position written by Alexander H. Stephens, the vice-president of the Confederacy, and entitled *A Constitutional View of the Late War between the States*, reflected Nichols' point that, in the primary phase, the slant from which the generalization is to be made often appears in the title.

Only then, according to Nichols, do more precise evaluations start to appear. These, though depending on the historian's particular point of view, pave the way for "definitive" accounts. At this stage, "some sacred cows are slaughtered and what is known as 'debunking' appears." Last of all, concepts borrowed from the social sciences and psychiatry contribute to produce a new body of generalizations and provide a theoretical framework for the events. In the case of the Civil War, additional insights are gained through reference to similar wars fought in widely different areas, and a more universal interpretation is reached. This "progress" in historical thinking which Nichols illustrates from his own period of interest does not follow a simple linear direction. It is therefore incumbent on each successive generation of historians not only to reinterpret the events but also to reevaluate the conclusions of earlier scholars, according to what Nichols describes as "rigorous 'genealogical' thinking."[15]

Roy F. Nichols (1896–1973)
Jeannette Paddock Nichols
Professor of history (1925–66), dean of the graduate school of arts and sciences (1952–66), and vice-provost for graduate affairs. Author of numerous historical books, some written in collaboration with Jeannette P. Nichols, who received her Ph.D. from Columbia the same year he did (1923). A specialist in the American Civil War period, he won the Pulitzer Prize for his biography of Franklin Pierce in 1931. His last years were devoted to the history of the University, work continued by Jeannette Nichols.

For his own analysis of the events and circumstances which led to the Civil War, Nichols won the Pulitzer prize for history in 1949, the year that Arthur Miller's *Death of a Salesman* also received an award. Looking over this work, *The Disruption of American Democracy*, Nichols later remarked: "I can now discover a model which emerged and can describe it 'after the fact.' " Among the most important factors resulting from his copious researches which ranged over 117 manuscript collections from 48 depositories in 26 different states, he pointed to the destabilizing effect of the almost constant elections conducted on the state level. At the same time, the national parties were "but loose federations of state machines" whose differing interests could be variously exploited. Even as he described the insecure political federation among the states, Nichols also dealt with what he terms " 'cultural' federalism" or the association of people and communities exhibiting various contrasting attitudes which make it necessary for political leaders to find "ways and means to hold citizens dominated by a variety of attitudes in one body politic."[16]

In answer to the criticism that Nichols placed insufficient emphasis on the question of slavery, traditionally regarded as the largest obstacle to peaceful settlement, he underlined the political nature of his model: "One anomaly of the slavery issue is that, while the two sections disagreed deeply about slavery, the two political parties disagreed only marginally in what they were prepared to do about slavery—they had different proposals for the territories, where the issue was perhaps fictitious, but they were both pledged to leave slavery unmolested in the states, where the issue was real." More important than the degree of perfection of the model which Nichols was developing—without being aware of it at the time—was the effect his writing was to have on political history. According to Potter: "When he left it, it had been revitalized by the recognition that political history must be analyzed as a process involving fundamental interactions between various factors in the society, and that, as the medium for the functional use of power, politics is as crucial as any process in the society."[17]

Towards the end of Nichols' four-decade tenure at the University of Pennsylvania, a radical challenge began to be mounted to the methods of traditional American historiography. Rejecting what has been described as the doctrine of "implicit importance," the so-called new historians turned from a study of prominent figures and great public events to focus upon neglected groups in the general population—the poor, women, and children—for what the basic conditions of their lives could reveal about underlying processes of economic, social, political, and cultural change. That Nichols applauded these developments is suggested by remarks he made just after World War II. Employing a timely analogy, the Pennsylvania historian wrote: "Just as the natural scientists turned from galaxies to atoms, so should historians turn from their nationalistic macrocosms to

William Carlos Williams and Ezra Pound
Photograph by Richard Avedon, 1958
Published with his permission
Although Williams (M.D. 1906, Litt.D.
1952) thought of himself as a physician
first and a poet second, he gained wide-
spread literary recognition with his
poetic saga Paterson *and* Make Light of
It, *a collection of short stories. Works by*
Williams and memorabilia were pre-
sented to the library by his wife in 1965.
After World War I he lived in France in
the circle of expatriates which included
Gertrude Stein and James Joyce. Among
his close friends at college was H.D.
(Hilda Doolittle, College Course for
Teachers 1908–9), the daughter of the
director of the Flower Astronomical
Observatory at the University. A lifelong
friend was Ezra Pound (a member of
the College class of 1905, A.M. 1906), a
leading force in modern literature in the
twentieth century whom Carl Sandburg
hailed as "the greatest single influence
on American poetry."

the microcosms of community behavior. For the community can be dubbed the historical atom; in villages, towns, cities, counties and the like are found the basic units of human behavior."[18] In just such locales, in fact, a younger generation of historians was to search out census data and parish registers, eschewing the memories of the famous for these humbler sources of information which lent themselves to quantification and had previously been ignored or underutilized.

Roy Nichols seems to have anticipated the new history which was only beginning to appear in print towards the end of his life. The "atomic" or local history he proposed was, however, very different from nationalism reduced to mere *Lokalpatriotismus*—"those glorifications of the unique virtue of various towns and cities inspired by chambers of commerce and publicity writers on the occasion of centennials and the like."[19] The important contribution which could be made by improving research into the history of urban communities had been recognized by Nichols long before, on the occasion of just such an anniversary celebration. Newly arrived in Philadelphia at the time of the Sesquicentennial of the Declaration of Independence in 1926, he had been surprised to find no historical society representing the Commonwealth as a whole. Whatever their names might seem to indicate, the Historical Society of Pennsylvania and that of Western Pennsylvania were closely linked with the urban centers of Philadelphia and Pittsburgh.[20] Soon after he made the move to Philadelphia, Nichols read a paper before the American Historical Association detailing suggestions for the study of local and state history. He was promptly invited by the president of the Pennsylvania Federation of Historical Societies which met annually in Harrisburg to chair a committee whose purpose was to investigate further these suggestions. As a result, a few years later, in 1932, the Pennsylvania Historical Association was inaugurated with Nichols the first vice-president and the second president.

One of Nichols' papers on Pennsylvania history dealt with a local occurrence in 1866, the year that the Union party failed to be founded at a convention at Twentieth Street and Girard Avenue in Philadelphia. As a result, no bronze tablet was needed to mark the spot where a great party was almost born.[21] In contrast, those events which actually came about within the state's boundaries came to be publicized in the 1940s with "blue and gold aluminum markers . . . set up literally by the hundreds along the highway."[22] An important aim which Nichols had expressed in his paper on state and community history before the American Historical Association was "the use of local history as a convenient and efficient way to get historians who were not in a position to work on a larger scale to do much-needed research in local history from sources nearby."[23] The suggestion was put into effect through work carried out under his aegis at the University of Pennsylvania, where an extensive study was made of Pennsylvania politics from 1740 to 1877 through a series of doctoral dissertations completed during several decades.

When he spoke of local history in terms of atoms, Nichols was reflecting the influence that work in the natural sciences was having on other branches of thought. As a result of general interest in changing theories and knowledge about the structure of the natural world, attempts were being made to apply the principles concerned with the indestructibility of matter, indeterminacy, and relativity to social questions. By applying the second law of thermodynamics to human behavior and thought, Henry Adams had come to the pessimistic view that the world necessarily had to be running down. Nichols, in turn, was intrigued by the implications of relativity, an idea which he used for striking effect in one of his addresses in 1933. Disposing of analogies based on Newtonian physical law as too simple to guide historians any longer, he described an "intellectual crisis"

Unveiling the Nichols Portrait
Photograph by Frank Ross
A portrait was dedicated to Roy F. Nichols on his retirement in 1966, thirteen years after President Harold E. Stassen appointed him dean of the graduate school of arts and sciences. He is seen at unveiling ceremonies with the chairman of the trustees, the late Wilfred D. Gillen, and President Gaylord P. Harnwell (immediately to the left of the portrait). Professor Harnwell, a nationally known physicist, served as president from 1953 to 1970.

resulting from new scientific perceptions. For example, "time is no longer a sequence of events, it is the fourth dimension which is necessary in physics because of the fact of relativity."[24]

Much of Nichols' stimulation for thinking along these lines came from discussions with colleagues at the University of Pennsylvania, particularly with Detlev Bronk, the biophysicist, who was himself concerned with applying the principles of dynamics in physics to the life sciences.[25] Whether or not Nichols saw the implications for history as very profound, he made the most of an opportunity to question Albert Einstein on the value of such extrapolations from the natural sciences. In their discussion, he recalls, "Dr. Einstein disposed very quickly of the second law of thermodynamics," and, expressing disapproval of the way precise scientific terms came to be loosely applied by philosophers, he convinced Nichols that historians might do well to restrict their use of them to analogies. They should certainly stop short of seeking to apply laws which could only be valid for a closed system to philosophical constructs, since these rules were not applicable to human behavior.[26]

Nichols often made use of these analogies from the natural and, in particular, the physical sciences. In his 1933 address dealing with the "intellectual crisis," he surveys briefly the social developments which have accompanied man's changing conception of himself as a result of past scientific discoveries. When he arrives at the present, Nichols writes: "We must break up the atoms of facts in each epoch and chase the electrons to find these data which are not the height, breadth, width and weight of the electron but the direction of its motion—the force which the fact represents and the speed and general direction. This we might call the historical fourth dimension." When he describes the curricular changes which must accompany the new material of history, Nichols develops the analogy: "This new synthesis will in great measure make use of a principle roughly akin to relativity. It will have as its core a theory of relative values—the complexity of life can be resolved only by sorting out some of the threads and analyzing and comparing them."[27]

With his historian's fascination with time, Nichols envisions many changes which might result from a move away from defining the past through a chronological succession of dates and periods. In one instance, he speculates on the possibility of teaching history backwards. In addition, he foresees a new regard for the discipline itself, with historians no longer considered, as he once put it, as "reasonably satisfactory handmaidens worthy of Thursday afternoons and alternate Sundays on which to do what they really wish," but leaders in a field which will be respected as the linchpin of a curriculum for the future which might, Nichols suggests, be called "Society, past, present and improved."[29] Here, as well as in his choice of title for his autobiography—*A Historian's Progress*—Nichols shows himself "unblushingly 'progressive'" in his vision of history and the objects of its study.[30]

The most important influence on Nichols' thought from outside history itself undoubtedly came from the behavioral sciences. The formation of two interdisciplinary groups in the twenties—the Social Science Research Council and the American Council of Learned Societies—had led the American Historical Association, which was represented in each, to conduct an investigation of new areas and approaches to historical research. In Nichols' account, the report of a conference arranged for the purpose of discussing the findings of the investigation had "a decidedly 'behavioral' flavor." Among the approaches recommended because they revealed social and behavioral trends was one on which he had already reflected intensively: that of biography. Nichols contributed to this report and was afterwards chosen as a delegate of the American Historical Association to the Social Science Research Council in 1934, along with Guy Stanton Ford and the elder Arthur M. Schlesinger.[31]

He remained on the board for twenty-two years, and the influence of the developing behavioral sciences is visible in his works, particularly in his emphasis on recurring patterns of behavior. As a result of his familiarity with the leading social scientists of his day, he applied their general outlook, rather than their particular concepts, to history.[32] Under his influence, the Social Science Research Council produced two bulletins entitled *Theory and Practice in Historical Study* (1946) and *Social Sciences in Historical Study* (1954).

Among the problems encountered by the contemporary historian is one to which Nichols frequently returns. "Historians suffer from one of the most distressing of the mental ills of this complex life of ours," he remarks; "they are not sure of their identity or of their functions." Allegiance to past affiliations is in conflict with the company which the historian now finds himself keeping: "Once the historian had been confident of his place as a humanist. Now he was referred to as a social scientist. What was he?"[33] The historian's link with the humanities has to do both with man's position in regard to time and also the recurring question of the uses of time. "From the study of literature and history, from a keen sense of the process and development which comes from science and history, can be gained a sense of the long and slow growth of anything worthwhile. We are creatures of the moment in the universal sense of time.

> Time goes, you say? Ah no
> Alas! Time stays, we go."[34]

While examining the role of this dimension in the study of history, Nichols also envisaged the possibility that future reductions in labor requirements might result in a thirty-hour week with the consequent need for instructing people on how to use their leisure. This necessity would strike a blow for the liberal arts, continually under pressure from considerations of "practical" education: "Knowledge of art and letters, their history and achievements, will become a very definite part of the systems we are to construct."[35]

Continued support for the humanities appeared to Nichols to involve more than the preservation of disciplines which have in the past been regarded as valuable: their perpetuation is, additionally, "a demonstration . . . of faith in history, in the need for a realistic and comprehensive understanding of the past. The whole corpus of history, if adequately studied and interpreted, would yield much of past experience by which this day might profit." It is because of what has been done to compress the sense of time in the modern world that a historical perspective takes on added importance. The fundamental processes of the mind change slowly and do not keep up with the tempo of modern life; deeply rooted concerns are therefore set aside in favor of more immediate, practical considerations, and the mind loses its freedom to probe the basic nature of problems.[36] This freedom is itself the etymological source of the branch of learning comprising the "liberal" arts; its preservation depends on man's sense of history.

In his discussion of "the social uses and functions of written history"

ENIAC
The circumstances of the Second World War and the support by the University of Pennsylvania brought together John William Mauchly (assistant professor in engineering, LL.D. 1974) and alumnus J. Presper Eckert, Jr. (B.S. 1941, M.S. 1943, Sc.D. 1964). Together with John Brainerd (B.S. 1925, Ph.D. 1934, professor of electrical engineering), this design team at the University's Moore School developed the outsize ancestor of all modern computers. The first all-electrical digital computer, known as ENIAC (Electronic Numerical Integrator and Computer), was dedicated in 1946. It weighed over thirty tons, occupied 1,500 square feet of floor space and employed 18,000 vacuum tubes, 70,000 resistors, and 10,000 capacitors. Able to make computations 1,000 times faster than any existing machine, ENIAC was the point of departure for the computer technology which has transformed the modern world.

Henry Hope Reed (1808–1854)
Attributed to Thomas Sully
*Assistant professor of English literature
and moral philosophy, later professor of
English literature and rhetoric (1831–
1854) and vice-provost (1845). Born in
Philadelphia of a family with many
connections with the University, he
studied for the bar, practicing law for a
few years after graduation (A.B. 1825).
Reed brought out the first complete
American edition of Wordsworth's
poetical works (1837) and published
articles on the poet by himself and by
Christopher Wordsworth. Returning
from a visit to England which had
included a stay at Wordsworth's home,
Rydal Mount, Reed was lost at sea in
a major steamship disaster. His lectures
were published after his death by his
brother, William B. Reed, and his manuscripts and memorabilia were presented
to the library in 1913.*

and the "practical" aspects of knowledge as contrasted with the materials of traditional humanistic study, Nichols looks ahead to the much-touted question of "relevance."[37] The subject is in a direct line of descent from the educational principles propounded by Benjamin Franklin at a time when the classics dominated higher learning. It was a result of Franklin's influence, seconded by the inclination of the first provost and vice-provost of the college, that "in a day of classical absorption these two Scots, with Franklin behind them, set up a curriculum, forty per cent of which was devoted to science."[38] With this tradition reinforced by the strength of the medical school, the scientific bias has sometimes overshadowed the considerable contribution of able professors in the arts at the University of Pennsylvania. In the mid-nineteenth century, while Alexander Dallas Bache was professor of natural sciences, Henry Vethake, a professor of mathematics, was introducing political economy as a separate course of study at the University. An example rare at the time of a teacher who shared with his students the results of his own investigations, Vethake published his widely read *Principles of Political Economy* based on his courses, a book which became a standard work.

Another eminent nineteenth century professor in the department of arts who, like Vethake and Nichols, had also served as vice-provost was Henry Hope Reed. As both assistant professor of moral philosophy and professor of belles-lettres, Reed found no difficulty in reconciling these two disciplines for he believed in literature as a means of bringing men together. "We live too much in ignorance of the hidden feelings which connect us together," he wrote. "Whatever awakens the common principles of human nature or creates a fellowship among men, adds to the stock of moral power." He befriended Wordsworth, both editing his works and guiding his financial investments, and, at Reed's suggestion, the poet wrote sonnets on American subjects. It was on his return from a visit to the poet's widow in 1854 that Reed went down in the sinking of the *Arctic*. Professor Reed's brother, the lawyer William Bradford Reed, encouraged the reestablishment of the law school and was also responsible, according to Nichols, for stimulating interest in history at the University. Reed gave an address on the subject to the Philomathean Society in 1839, and eleven years later he gave the first lectures in American history at the University. In Nichols' opinion, Philomathean, the oldest undergraduate literary society in the United States, had initially provided a parallel road to the goals of "self-discovery, self-identification, and finally, self-realization," which must be the aim of all teachers of "the arts and sciences as humanities," in their search to promote "the humane way of life."[39]

Nichols' interest in education as well as the liberal arts led him to accept the deanship of the graduate school of arts and sciences in 1952. The tremendous boost given to science had served to unbalance universities in the postwar period, and Nichols used his position to mediate between the growing sciences and the needs of the humanities. Graduate education was also in a period of rapid expansion, and Nichols became vice-provost for graduate affairs in 1953, holding the post concurrently with that of dean. With rapid growth of the graduate student body in the fifties, Nichols set about providing the graduate school with more effective and more diversified services. The needs of individual students were supplied through the creation of new graduate groups, often interdisciplinary, as well as the introduction of the "Independent Study and Research" course which permitted any part of the requirements for an advanced degree to be satisfied by informal reading and study. At the same time, the semester credit system was abandoned in favor of the course unit and the foreign language requirement was relaxed to allow each graduate group to set its own requirements for the tools most necessary to a given discipline.

With the Educational Survey of the University conducted over several years by Joseph H. Willits, alumnus, former dean of the Wharton School, and longtime director of the social science branch of the Rockefeller Foundation, Nichols was in large part responsible for facilitating the external examination of the graduate school of arts and sciences. Nichols himself became president of the Association of Graduate Schools in 1964 and chairman of the Council of Graduate Schools of the United States the following year. In expressing his admiration and gratitude for Nichols' service as dean and vice-provost, former Provost Jonathan Rhoads remarked: "It is no small achievement to preside successfully over a citizenry of intellectual aristocrats and this Roy F. Nichols did superbly and I believe in so sympathetic a way that he was appreciated by everybody concerned."[40]

In the view of Rhoads and many others, the Pennsylvania historian was a superlative speaker as well as a great presiding officer. Certainly, he will be remembered by thousands for his humor and his histrionic talents which appeared so often, whether he was addressing a gathering of alumni, a learned society, or a class in history. In his early days at the University of Pennsylvania, Nichols had lectured before very large classes. His *forte* was the dramatic presentation of certain events from the history of the Civil War, and it became a custom for his "Webster's Reply to Hayne" presentation to be greeted at the climax of the debate with "The Stars and Stripes Forever" played on a trumpet from the back row.[41]

His "performances" enlivened the graduate courses which he continued to give after becoming dean. Despite the many claims on his time which caused the Nicholses to move nearer to the University, he did not cease his prolific writing, and he went on to complete four more scholarly books before his retirement. Some of his articles now had to do with the problems of universities and graduate education, in the same way as his publications had formerly included reflections on the philosophy and the teaching of

British Thouron Scholars in the Sixties
Established in 1960 to promote understanding between the people of Great Britain and the United States, the unique Thouron–University of Pennsylvania Fund is the largest British-American fellowship exchange program operated by an American university. It was founded and is supported by Philadelphians, Sir John and Lady Thouron. Sir John, born in England, belongs to a family whose University affiliation dates back to 1835, while that of his wife, the du Pont family, began its Pennsylvania connection in 1831. With a total of 359 students having participated in the program by the academic year 1977–78, numerous British students have spent a year or more studying at the University of Pennsylvania, and an equivalent number of University students have studied in the United Kingdom.

history along with books and articles on scholarly questions pertaining to the Civil War. After his retirement from the University in 1966, Nichols served as president of the American Historical Association, and he proceeded to carry out important work as chairman of the joint Administrative Board of the Benjamin Franklin Papers Project for the American Philosophical Society. In 1969 he was also made Honorary Consultant in American History to the Library of Congress. His ability to do all this and much more is explained by a remark of his to the effect that academic work was not only a duty but a hobby and a recreation.[42]

In 1962, while speaking on the subject, "What a Century Has Done to the Civil War," Nichols remarked: "Birthdays and other anniversaries present many opportunities. One of these is the opportunity to assess the results of growth, to discover whether there has been an increase in wisdom accompanying intervening experience."[43] Occasions for humanistic observations of this kind were abundantly associated with Nichols' period of scholarly interest, and Potter describes him as one of the few professional historians who took spontaneous pleasure in the four long years of the Civil War Centennial.[44] Referring to the part he played in the national observances, Nichols remarked: "There have been times when I have felt that I had commemorated almost every engagement in the conflict," an illusion which he hastened to ascribe to "battle fatigue."[45] Nichols further noted the way history, politics, and the human yen for cyclical celebration are all united in that most American of perennial pursuits—the election of a president: "Every four years, in leap year by strange chance, the American people enjoy, and I literally mean enjoy a spectacular contest for the presidency."[46]

Perhaps a key to Nichols' achievements is to be found in the way his own various interests and activities seem to have been coordinated throughout a life from which history was never absent. The hill on which his Newark, New Jersey, family home stood overlooked the Essex Country Courthouse, and from it he could sometimes see the cogs of the notorious local Democratic machine which did not omit "the temple of justice" from its sphere of influence and was a reality to him from an early age.[47] Moreover, by the time he left high school he apparently knew more of the facts of American history than the average doctoral candidate.[48] This achievement only seems to have convinced him, however, of the need to improve on the instruction in history, which traditionally involved "a long, an interminably long, series of dates and petty chronicles with no suggestion of great forces of destiny or of vital relationships of phenomena in cause and effect sequence."[49] But perhaps the most important catalyst in the developing interests of the young historian came between the years of 1909–15, in the shape of the centennial of Lincoln's birth and the semicentennial of the Civil War. Celebrated by the Lincoln penny and journalistic accounts which could be cut out and assembled in binders, these momentous events encouraged a youthful commitment to history and the Civil War period which was to last Roy Nichols a lifetime.[50]

It is human nature to wish to celebrate birthdays and a no less human historical instinct to enjoy surveying neatly divided periods—such as centuries—of time past. Nichols himself could never resist alluding to the neatly rounded historical perspective which allowed him, on one occasion, in the context of a historian's report on social science, to recall that the essay in social analysis, *Leviathan*, had been published exactly three hundred years earlier—an essay in which Hobbes used the biblical image to which Nichols also alluded in the title of his last historical work.[51] Another reference encompassing two distant centuries, appears in the opening paragraph of a paper on the Civil War published about the same time: "On March 4, 1461, Edward IV assumed power as King of England. On March 4, 1861, Abraham Lincoln was inaugurated President of the United States."[52]

The two hundredth birthday of the nation—a leap year, and time once more for a presidential election—would also have been the eightieth birthday of Roy F. Nichols, who died in 1973. He had looked forward to the nation's celebration of 1976 with mixed feelings, on one occasion remarking that he trusted Philadelphia's observance would have greater dignity and pertinence than a world's fair.[53] It is to be hoped that Roy Nichols, historian, teacher, and erstwhile expert in anniversaries of all kinds, would have approved of being made a party to this set of essays, reflecting the intellectual perspectives of the University of Pennsylvania, generated by the atmosphere surrounding the American Bicentennial.

Times and Places

Yet to walk with Mozart, Agassiz and Linnaeus
'neath overhanging air, under sun-beat
Here take they mind's space.

Ezra Pound, Class of 1906
Canto CXIII

[overleaf]

Main Reading Room, Furness Library, circa 1890
The lofty reading room, four stories high and deriving its inspiration from Viollet-le-Duc, was at the heart of Frank Furness' design to house the University Library. The open space, later divided up by obtrusive additions, was well lighted from above and around the upper walls. In a novel arrangement for the time, the book stacks were set apart in a separate unit.

16

A Campus Evolves

In his analysis of the relation between biography and history, Roy F. Nichols emphasized the importance of understanding the physical surroundings both as a backdrop and as an active element which molds the individual personality. It is in the setting of the University that these portraits of scholars and leaders from the last two hundred years have been presented, and their lives and endeavors thus provide a commentary on the various stages of its changing history. In addition, the personality of the University itself is expressed in its physical character while continuously reflecting the evolution of its programs and aspirations. It is as impossible to do justice to each building or plan which has contributed to the changing surroundings as it is to comprehend an entire era or even one branch of academic life through reference to a few of the persons of stature who have graced the intellectual community at various times in the course of our history. Nonetheless, further light is thrown on these individuals, as well as on the changing nature of the University— which, in turn, reflects the development of education in America—by a profile of the physical campus. In no way complete, this last portrait aims at projecting, through a series of "stills," the form of an institution as it has evolved in over two hundred years.

University City, as it is called, on the west bank of the Schuylkill River and adjacent to Philadelphia's center city, has changed both with the times and as a result of the transformation of the objectives at the University and nearby institutions in the course of a century. Anyone who graduated from the University of Pennsylvania as recently as the mid-sixties cannot fail to be struck by how much its physical facilities have been altered since that time. But this alteration is in keeping with the process of continuous development since the University settled in West Philadelphia shortly before the American Centennial. By that time, it had already occupied two principal locations in the city in the course of a previous century and a quarter.

Starting with the large but simple Georgian brick meetinghouse in which the combined Academy and Charity School classes began in 1751 in the colonial port on the Delaware, the University has been housed in the Academy, and the University were all confined to the limits of the old college and dormitory buildings on Fourth Street while the classes of the buildings designed in the Federal, Adam, Classical Revival, Gothic Revival, and Victorian Romanesque styles on into modern times, with its latest buildings by contemporary architects including Eero Saarinen and Louis Kahn. The "New Building," a rectangular, brick tabernacle measuring one hundred feet by seventy feet, had been erected in 1740–42 by followers of the dynamic English preacher George Whitefield for use both as a place of public worship and as a school. It was the largest structure in colonial Philadelphia, exceeding in size the State House itself, as Independence Hall was then called. The facade was symmetrical: the fan-lighted doorway, surmounted by a balcony and Palladian window, interrupted two rows of six arch-headed windows and was framed by columns rising two stories to a triangular pediment. The steeple which, in 1755, housed the school bell appears in a contemporary print beside the spires of Christ Church and the State House.[1] Since the great hall of the Academy was used by the Continental Congress, the University's first home also served temporarily as the national capitol.

Philadelphia's foremost architect, Robert Smith, received the commission to adapt the great hall for its academic purposes by dividing it into two floors. Of the four large classrooms on the main floor, one was designated in 1762 as a "Library and Apparatus Room" for the electrical instruments loaned for lectures by Ebenezer Kinnersley, the professor of English. The instruments for "Experimental Philosophy" purchased by Franklin in London and, later on, the telescope and micrometer presented to Provost Smith by Thomas Penn, as also the Rittenhouse orrery, were added to the scientific equipment. The meeting hall now occupied the upper floor. It housed the organ played at commencement by Francis Hopkinson, member of the first graduating class and later trustee of the College, who published the first book of songs in the colonies.

Among the first students attending the Academy were the Mohawk brothers Jonathan and Philip Gayienquitioga. A number of Jewish students were sent to the Academy in the sixties, and Moses Levy who went on to graduate from the College in 1772 served as a trustee from 1802 to 1826. Accommodation for students coming from the other American colonies and the West Indies was provided by the addition to the academic enclave of a rectangular, three-story brick dormitory in 1762. Shortly before the Revolution, the College grounds were enclosed by a brick wall with an iron gate opening on Fourth Street. At the same time, a commodious residence was built at the corner of Fourth and Arch Streets for the first provost, William Smith.

The College of Philadelphia and the University of the State of Pennsylvania were united in 1791, and the University's lease of Philosophical Hall was terminated in 1794. For a time the Charity School, medical department met in "Surgeons Hall" on Fifth Street below Philosophical Hall. In 1800 the crowded conditions induced the trustees to seek a new location. They went to public auction for the first and only time and purchased a property on the west side of Ninth Street. Extending a full city block from Market to Chestnut, the site which they acquired included the "President's House," the most spectacular mansion in the city, originally intended as the residence for presidents of the United States. It was not completed, however, until after John Adams' election. The second President declined to live in it and, when during his administration the capital moved to Washington, the state legislature, which still held bills of over $110,000 for its construction, was only too happy to find a purchaser.

The President's House, whose grand rooms were altered by architect Benjamin Henry Latrobe in accordance with its new functions, was a superb example of the "new classicism" popularized in England by Robert Adam. The massive, three-story structure of brick, stone, and ornamental marble was crowned by a hipped roof surmounted by a glass dome and cupola. The facade, with its twin Palladian windows, and eight Corinthian pilasters rising to a balustrade-crowned cornice, was similar to those of Library Hall on Fifth Street and the centerpiece of the Pennsylvania Hospital. The dome lighted a columned circular hall in the center, fifty feet in diameter, from which a flight of double steps led to the gallery above. There were niches in the hall containing urns, and an abundance of Italianate festoons and allegorical figures in plaster enriched the public parlors below and the state suite above. Today, but two souvenirs remain of the University's beautiful second home. One is the marble cornerstone "laid May 10, 1792 when Pennsylvania was happily out of Debt" and saved from destruction by Albert Monroe Wilson, the notable black steward, "known to fifty classes of Pennsylvania men as 'Pomp.' "[2] The other, a paneled double door, is displayed as a backdrop to the furniture of George Washington at the Historical Society of Pennsylvania although the general never put his hand to its knob.

Much of the vitality of the University in the first two decades of the new century lay in its medical department. To accommodate its enrollment, a semidetached building was added to the south side of the President's House in 1807. The new medical school, in the form of an octagon with a low Roman domed roof lit by a lantern, was designed by Benjamin Latrobe. Its severe lines echoed the style of Sir John Soane and was a notable example of the classical revival. In 1817, the medical building was enlarged by William Strickland, Latrobe's brilliant former apprentice who also restored the steeple of Independence Hall. Twelve years later, he was commissioned by the trustees to replace the President's House and its additions with two new buildings to house the collegiate department and the faculty of medicine. Responding to the Emperor Augustus' claim that

The University on Ninth Street, above Chestnut
Wood engraving by C. H. Reed, mid-nineteenth century
From 1829 until the move to West Philadelphia in 1872, the collegiate department and the faculty of medicine occupied twin marble-trimmed brick buildings designed in the Georgian style by Philadelphia's foremost architect, William Strickland. At the beginning of the 1830s, the total student body numbered 535, with 410 medical students. By the end of the 1860s, the total number was 736.

College Hall in 1874
Rising from meadowland, the new College Hall, with its twin clock-towers, presented an imposing sight to centennial Philadelphia. Part of the first University hospital can be seen on the left, and Medical Hall (now Logan Hall) stands on the right. All three of the earliest buildings on the West Philadelphia campus were designed by University professor and architect Thomas W. Richards in green serpentine stone.

he found Rome a city of brick and left it a city of marble, the Philadelphia architect, known as the master of the Greek Revival, observed that there was less brick and more marble in Philadelphia than in Rome.[3] Strickland built almost exclusively in marble, which he used for the construction of the Second Bank of the United States, the first public building in America to be modeled after the Parthenon. At Ninth Street, however, Strickland seems to have been influenced by the structure which had been demolished: the two new University buildings were also late Georgian in style, their facades adorned with four pilasters and Palladian windows at each end. There was no accommodation for students and staff, who now lived privately in the attractive tree-lined streets nearby.

The genteel life in the residential quarter of the city just west of Washington Square—one of William Penn's original squares—began to change in the years prior to the Civil War. Householders who could afford to do so were moving to fashionable new terraces going up to the west between Broad Street and Rittenhouse Square, leaving their houses to become rundown boardinghouses of the type which often served as student lodgings. Provost Stillé, who took office in 1868, found the iron-fenced campus in Ninth Street in a "vile neighborhood, growing viler every day."[4] When an alumnus suggested that the University should move to a new location by acquiring from the city part of the large tract on the other side of the Schuylkill attached to the Blockley Almshouse, Stillé saw a chance for the institution to begin a new life. Ten acres of the Almshouse farm were bought in 1870 for $80,000.[5] Within four years, four neo-

Gothic buildings rose to house the University and to provide its medical school with a hospital. All were built of the curious green serpentine stone found in nearby Chester County. They were designed by Thomas W. Richards who subsequently became the first professor of architecture at the University.

The centerpiece of Richards' scheme, College Hall, was erected in 1871–72. Collegiate Gothic in design, but with a French mansard roof, it originally had slender clock towers at each end. These were removed in 1914 and 1929. With a basement floor and three stories above ground, the building dominated the open plain ascending gradually from the Schuylkill on the east and south and the brick row houses and Italianate villas of the streets to the west and north. The central pavilion, housing the chapel, library, and assembly rooms, was flanked by the department of science—soon to become the Towne Scientific School—which occupied the east wing, and the department of liberal arts, in the west range. Each faculty member had a communicating classroom and office. Most of the third floor was occupied by the lecture hall of the law school, which had formerly held its classes in College Hall on Ninth Street. "Even by modern standards College Hall has much to recommend it," wrote an architectural historian in 1961, "and when it was built it must have represented one of the most advanced academic plants in the country."[6]

Economy, as much a consideration then as now, dictated a simple interior for College Hall. Only in the arch-headed windows, in a few similar doors, and in the quatrefoil-decorated ironwork of the stairway was there much evidence of the Victorian richness suggested by the buttressed exterior walls and commanding towers. A photograph of the faculty room, today the office of the provost, reveals its furnishings: hanging gas chandeliers, a floral carpet, a long heavy wooden center table and caned armchairs. A round institutional clock resembling a parliament clock grown into a tall case, made by Isaiah Lukens, has been returned to its original position in the same room. In the year 1873, the University had a student body of 759 of whom 486 were in medicine.

The medical faculty, like the academic departments, exchanged their old hall on Ninth Street for a similar hybrid "Franco-Norman" structure in West Philadelphia. Known as Medical Hall on its completion in 1874, it was renamed in 1904 after a prominent colonial trustee, James Logan. It successively housed departments of the school of medicine and the Wharton School. The American Academy of Political and Social Science also had quarters in Logan for many years. In spite of warnings by the professor of mineralogy, the material used for construction was the same serpentine stone of which College Hall was built. It proved as vulnerable to disintegration from the atmosphere and the weather as predicted, and on numerous occasions in the present century large infusions of concrete have been required to keep Richards' greenish-hued structures standing and safe.

**"The Faculty Room,"
College Hall, Nineteenth Century**
The one-time University Faculty Room, 102 College Hall, now serves as the office of the provost. Several of the caned armchairs, as well as the Isaiah Lukens tall case clock seen in this photograph are back in the office today. At the time the University moved to West Philadelphia, there were 36 faculty members (1871); two years later there were 60, and the number has been increasing ever since. A large auditorium is necessary for a meeting of the present faculty of arts and sciences alone.

The third Gothic essay in serpentine stone by Richards was the
Robert Hare Laboratory of Chemistry, built in 1877–78 and named for the
famous University professor of chemistry. The architect's work for the
University also included the building which he had put up several years
earlier to house the first hospital in the United States owned and operated
by a university. Originally so like its neighbors as to be almost indistin-
guishable from them, its small remaining core has since been effectively
concealed by the great hospital pavilions which front Thirty-fourth and
Spruce Streets today. No building in the University complex has been so
consistently altered and added to as the hospital, starting in 1883 and
continuing right up to the present time. In 1976, construction began on the
Silverstein Pavilion and an entirely new medical education building
between the hospital and the old school of medicine.

The neo-Gothic halls of Thomas Richards were described in a
contemporary account as "a modest quartette, substantial, but far from
beautiful, and with only fifteen acres they could call their own."[7] Within
twenty years the new campus quadrupled in size, and these staid buildings
provided a foil for the totally unpredictable red brick and terra-cotta
University Library commissioned from the imaginative and vigorous
Frank Furness, now recognized as one of America's great designers. This
architect, whose work was the subject of an exhibition at the Philadelphia
Museum of Art in 1973, was a principal force behind Philadelphia's new
silhouette, which reflected the city's attainment of a new urban maturity
in the last two decades of the nineteenth century. Erected in 1888–1891,
the Library was the architect's largest and most important commission and
represented a staggering variety of materials and textures. With its great
iron and glass profile, the Library featured Romanesque arches and
columns, Mozarabic massing, and ornamentation ranging from stone
gargoyles and tracery of Venetian-Gothic inspiration, to terra cotta plant
decorations—a favorite of Furness—and embryonic Art Nouveau windows
of leaded glass. All combined to give the building tremendous richness
and vitality.

This dominant structure rose from the fields to the east of College
Hall with all of the drama of the pyramids above the sands of Egypt.

University Library,
Perspective From Northwest
Ink drawing, 1888
The design for the University Library by
Frank Furness, the foremost Philadelphia
architect of his day, appears in a drawing
by Joseph Hutton of the firm Furness,
Evans and Co. Plans for an extended
book stack to the right were modified in
construction. Otherwise the building,
completed in 1890, adhered to the
architect's basic design.

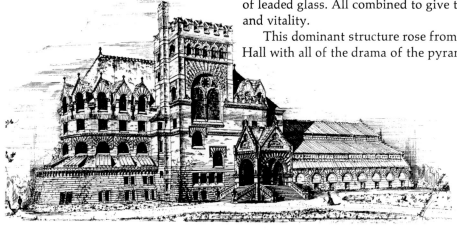

Appropriately enough, when the cornerstone was laid in October of 1888, the ceremony was performed with full Masonic rites by the Grand Master and officers of the Right Worshipful Grand Lodge of Free and Accepted Masons of Pennsylvania.[8] During the next half century, however, tastes changed so that the Library came to be described in the official history of the University of 1940 as "in doubtful taste and of questionable adaptation of its uses."[9] This was ten years after Robert Rhodes McGoodwin made drawings which would have converted the Library into a neo-Gothic structure with a tower reminiscent of Magdalen College, Oxford. Even without such a transformation, Furness's conception came to be masked over the years by three separate additions, and the interior spaces were obstructed by an intrusive second floor put up in the twenties. But despite the additions and tamperings, the monumental effect of this magnificent building is in no way diminished. Moreover, it is now appreciated that the original design embodied the most advanced library planning of its day. Storage and service functions were separated from the central reading room, around which were clustered classrooms and book and periodical processing areas. The main building was fireproof as was the book stack which had a capacity of ten times the size of the original collection because an ingenious device for expansion permitted the rear wall of the stack to be moved outward on a series of jacks.

One of Furness' main concerns had been to utilize natural light. For this reason, large windows illuminated the main reading room while the stacks themselves were described in a contemporary account as "a glass palace . . . wherever one looks, the ceiling, the flooring . . . one sees nothing but glass."[10] At the close of the nineteenth century the essayist Agnes Repplier expressed her disdain for Philadelphia's civic architecture with a comment on "the tireless ingenuity with which an architect will go far out of his way to illustrate the meretricious." She had nothing but praise, however, for Furness's work: there are two pictures of the Library in a book of hers on Philadelphia, and she comments favorably on recent developments at the University. In her opinion, the most admirable of its new possessions were "a library [and] . . . museum under the same roof containing valuable collections of Egyptian, Babylonian, and American antiquities."[11]

The idea that it could be considered a serious function of a university to establish a permanent archaeological collection was new at the time. William Pepper had the precedent of the British Museum in mind when he approved the plan for a library building which would combine books and artifacts under the same roof. It soon became apparent, however, that a separate museum would be needed to house the expanding collection, and the first problem was to acquire land close to the University. A grant for a site owned by the city was eventually obtained, and the year of his retirement as provost found Pepper touting the virtues of a piece of real

The Visit of President William McKinley
Cover, *Harper's Weekly*, March 5, 1898
The First City Troop escorted the President of the United States, William McKinley, to the Library, now known as the Furness Building, where he delivered the University Day address in 1898. In 1975, Gerald R. Ford became the fourteenth President to visit the University of Pennsylvania when he received an honorary LL.D. at commencement ceremonies commemorating the attendance, two hundred years earlier, of George Washington and the members of the Continental Congress.

The University of Pennsylvania Museum
Set in a courtyard with a water-lily pool,
the University Museum suggests the
twelfth century arcaded buildings of
northern Italy. The dome of the rotunda,
formed by concentric circles of over-
lapping tiles without any supporting
members, resembles that of San Stefano
in Bologna. The architects Wilson Eyre,
Jr., Cope & Stewardson, and Frank Miles
Day and Brother who designed the
Museum in 1896 were all connected with
the University's school of architecture.

estate which had long been used as a dump near the railway tracks. The
scene in which he enthusiastically sought—and gained—the support of one
of Philadelphia's philanthropic citizens is worth an aside, particularly in
view of the handsome building that eventually occupied the site:

> One gray March day in 1894, Dr. Pepper and Mrs. Stevenson,
> with Mr. Justus C. Strawbridge, whom they were anxious to
> interest in the project, and to whom they wished to show the
> new land, met by appointment at the end of South Street bridge.
> A strong east wind blew from the river, and the whole outlook
> was hopelessly dismal. Mr. Strawbridge stood looking over the
> dreary waste, whilst Dr. Pepper enthusiastically explained the
> glorious possibilities offered to his view by the wretched stretch
> of land before them. With each passing train a dense black
> smoke rolled up in sooty masses, enveloping railroad tracks,
> goats, and refuse in a black mist, whilst blasts of coal gas
> smothered the lungs of the visitors. Mr. Strawbridge gravely
> listened to Dr. Pepper's vivid description. He even nodded in
> courteous approval as the complete plan, at an estimated cost of
> over two millions of dollars, was explained to him; but his face
> wore a perplexed expression. As Dr. Pepper turned away for a
> moment to call the attention of a passing policeman to
> trespassers, Mr. Strawbridge whispered to his companion: "I
> cannot bear to throw cold water on Dr. Pepper's enthusiasm;
> but what an extraordinary site for a great museum! Of course, I
> would like to help him; but what a site!"[12]

Originally, the Museum was planned as a gigantic building on twelve
acres at Thirty-third and South Streets. As finally constructed, the building
combined the different designs of no less than four architects. Among these,

Wilson Eyre is credited with the notion of long arcaded galleries fronting rotundas derived from the lanterns of Romanesque churches, while the partners Cope & Stewardson were probably responsible for the landscaped courts and reflecting pools which contrast forcefully with the massed buildings of dark-colored brick. When the first section was opened in 1899, all that was completed of the original tripartite design was the west court. The plans had called for an identical wing on the eastern side of an even larger central section with a great dome and arched portico, but the structure held its own as built, particularly after the rotunda was added in 1912.[13] Accumulation of funds permitted only the addition of the Coxe and Sharp wings by the firm of alumnus Frank Miles Day in 1924–26. The courtyard provided perfect surroundings for displaying the sculptures of A. Stirling Calder, father of the creator of the mobile.

A further addition was begun in the late 1960s, when a nineteenth century Eskimo snow shovel from the Museum's collection was used for the ground-breaking ceremonies. The new academic wing on the eastern side of the building was designed by the Philadelphia firm headed by Ehrman Mitchell and Romaldo Giurgola who had been on the architectural faculty. The gold medal–winning structure is a splendid example of the way a new building can be made to harmonize with the old. In the new wing, "brick, tile, and roof pitch are carried over in a genteel, self-effacing gesture to the old building," while the modern addition has "its own presence *within*."[14]

If the inspiration for the University Museum came from the Lombard Renaissance architecture of southern Europe, the influence of the English Jacobean is apparent in the Quadrangle buildings at Thirty-seventh and Spruce Streets. The University's first residence halls were begun in 1895 by Cope & Stewardson. Elsewhere on campus, the Lewis building designed for the law school by this firm is reminiscent of the Georgian revival and

Original Plan for the Residence Halls
by Cope & Stewardson, 1895
Looking rather like a transplanted college from Oxford or Cambridge, the architects' design for the dormitories originally included an elaborate Gothic chapel and matching dining hall. The execution of the plan was rather different with modifications to the gates and the towers. The southern range of the complex facing the medical school was not completed until 1954.

The Quadrangles from Memorial Tower Archway, 1919
The statue of the Reverend George Whitefield, dedicated at the first commencement festivities after World War I, appears in this vista of the "Triangle" of the Quadrangle. It is framed by the archway of Memorial Tower, dedicated in 1901 in memory of the students and graduates of the University of Pennsylvania who had served in the Spanish-American War.

derives specifically from the work of Sir Christopher Wren at Hampton Court.[15] When the law school was finally able to move into this building in 1900, it was a cause for two days of celebrations with dinners and endless speeches. The same firm of architects also designed Bennett Hall. For the thirty-one interlocking residence houses surrounding five interior courts they chose the eclectic mix of Gothic and classical elements characteristic of the Jacobean style. The material employed—hard Flemish bond brick set off with white Indiana limestone trim, rather than cold gray stone—was directly inspired by St. John's College, Cambridge. During a visit to England, John Stewardson had cabled his office to stop work on the design until the substitution could be made.[16] The brick, with its white stone accents, enhanced the richness and detail of a design, replete with pilasters and balustrades and decorated dormer and oriel windows.

Each of the houses was on a separate staircase, and the outer doors opened into the five courtyards known as the Little Quad, the Triangle, the Big Quad, East Quad, and South Quad. Entrance to two of the Quadrangles was by way of the Memorial Tower, the main gateway from the street which commemorated sons of the University who served in the Spanish-American War; access to the other three was through the archway of the Provosts' Tower on Thirty-sixth Street. Distinctive corner tourelles topped by onion-shaped roofs finished in copper were used for both entrances.

The dormitory scheme was as grand in its way as that of the Museum. South of the Provost's Tower along the east side of East Quad was the Graduate House with a club room and accommodations for twenty-nine students of the Graduate School. Mask and Wig, which has long provided theatrical humor at the University, contributed to another building in the same courtyard. "By varying the shapes and levels of the courts," writes George B. Tatum, "Cope & Stewardson created at Pennsylvania a series of architectural adventures of which even the most callow undergraduate cannot be wholly unaware. At one moment confined and intimate, the next spacious and formal, the five courts provide a setting for almost any mood."[17] The same firm of architects built St. Anthony Hall at a time when fraternity houses were beginning to offer alternative residential accommodation on campus. Another fraternity, Phi Delta Theta, was designed in the style of the residence halls in 1900. Earliest among the twenty-nine fraternities that maintain their houses in a rich variety of styles on or near campus is Psi Upsilon's centrally located Gothic "castle."

The Museum, the dormitories, and the Law School Building were completed as part of the building program of Provost Charles C. Harrison. "Just as thirteen new departments had been established in the same number of years of Provost Pepper's administration," notes the University's historian in 1940, "so thirteen buildings to house or re-house them and some new departments were provided in the sixteen years of Provost Harrison's."[18] As the influential chairman of the trustees' Ways and Means Committee, Harrison had demonstrated his devotion to the University for many years. When ill health led to Pepper's resignation in 1894, his former classmate who had, by then, retired from business appeared the obvious choice to succeed him.

The building program, initiated during Pepper's administration, gathered momentum under Harrison who worked tirelessly to obtain the necessary funds as well as contributing generously himself. The Birthday House in the residential complex was given as a sixty-fourth birthday present to her husband as well as to the University by the provost's wife, who also undertook the landscaping and beautification of the campus at her own expense. In addition, she contributed to the Robert Morris House in memory of her own great-grandfather, a trustee and financier of the Revolution. In this way, names reminiscent of the University's early history and, in some cases, that of the nation— Franklin, Hopkinson, Morgan, McKean, and Morris—mingled with others which recognized contemporary generosity: Bodine, Fitler, and Foerderer.

With their attention to ornament, the plans drawn up for the residence halls provided an opportunity to restore the tradition whereby, from medieval times, academic institutions had been known for their patronage of fine ironwork. In 1772, the trustees had commissioned a brick wall "with an Iron Gate in the Centre" similar to the one leading into neighboring Christ Church Burial Ground. A fence of the simple "picket" design had also enhanced the twin buildings of 1829 along the entire Ninth Street front. Because of the haste with which the first buildings in West Philadelphia were erected, the only ironwork initially included was a fence of arrow-headed picket sections between granite piers along Woodland Avenue fronting College Hall. With the construction of new buildings, three gates were designed for strategic sites in the Quadrangle plan and another was placed next to Houston Hall. Two more followed, one providing access to Franklin Field while yet another, somewhat dominated by the elaborate brick arcade which encases it, framed the entrance to the University Museum.

The Class of 1872 Memorial Gate, between the Hospital and the Quadrangles, the Class of 1894 Memorial Gate under Memorial Tower in the Quadrangles, and the gateway between Houston Hall and the Williams Humanities and Language Hall designed by E. P. Bissell and W. C. Hays as the gift of their Class of 1893, were all attractive Georgian designs of cartouches and scrolls set between stone and brick posts. Each of the three gives much needed definition to academic precincts although the 1872 Gate has, for the time, been placed in storage because of its vulnerable position at the motor entrance to the Hospital. The same is true of the Class of 1873

A Fraternity House
Among the fraternities and sororities that maintain houses on or adjacent to the campus, the grey Gothic "Castle" at Thirty-sixth Street and Locust Walk, designed by Victorian architect William D. Hewitt, was the first structure built for a Greek letter fraternity, Psi Upsilon (1894). Phi Delta Theta's house was designed in the style of the residence halls (1900), and University architects Cope & Stewardson built St. Anthony Hall for Delta Psi (1909).

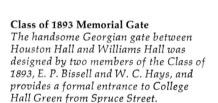
Class of 1893 Memorial Gate
The handsome Georgian gate between Houston Hall and Williams Hall was designed by two members of the Class of 1893, E. P. Bissell and W. C. Hays, and provides a formal entrance to College Hall Green from Spruce Street.

Gateway, designed and erected in 1899 by Cope & Stewardson associate Frederick M. Mann. It was intended to close the vista at the far end of the stately avenue of Lombardy poplars, planted the entire 1,100 feet of Hamilton Walk. Remarkable for beautiful workmanship of "late English Renaissance" inspiration, twenty feet in width, the gate was originally set between two great posts of alternating bands of brick and limestone.

The residence hall complex provided an excellent opportunity for the display of other forms of art work. The exterior walls of the houses bear an array of armorials and University insignia, and there are more than three hundred Gothic grotesques of men and beasts, many of which overlook the Quadrangles—like the Museum courts, a natural site for outdoor sculpture. In 1900, Provost Harrison suggested to the Class of 1892 that a suitable memorial gift would be a drinking fountain to provide chilled, filtered drinking water to the residence hall. In a niche in the arcade leading to East Quad, is the bronze sculpture and fountain commissioned from A. Stirling Calder. Soon afterwards, a sundial was added in Little Quad, and, after World War I, the lively life-size statue of the Reverend George Whitefield by R. Tait McKenzie was placed in the Quad. Much of the work of this sculptor and doctor who was director of physical culture at the University for many years is now in the Lloyd P. Jones gallery of the Gimbel Gymnasium. "Young Franklin," "Whitefield," and the statue of Provost Edgar Fahs Smith on the walk named after him remain to enhance the outdoor environment. A likeness of another provost—Charles C. Harrison, by Lynn Jenkins—was a fitting addition to the residential complex, one of the most notable contributions to campus facilities and architecture of his administration.

The University's empiricism, like that of Philadelphia, had kept it from grand overall plans, such as Jefferson's University of Virginia or for the type spawned by the 1893 World's Fair in Chicago and exemplified by McKim, Mead and White's scheme for Columbia. The great burst of building activity during Harrison's administration did, however, lead to serious concern for comprehensive planning. Throughout the history of the College and University, academic considerations had gone hand in hand with regard for expanding facilities. In two cases, the trustees had made the decision to move the University when conditions became overcrowded and the neighborhood in which the institution was located fell into decay. After it crossed the Schuylkill, "the University entered a semi-rural region traversed by quiet streets and country roads, reached by two car lines of slow-moving horsecars and ideally situated for a community requiring academic quiet and comparative isolation."[19] But, by the time Paul Philippe Cret and his colleagues, Warren Powers Laird and the Olmsted brothers, were called upon to draw up a report on future development of buildings and grounds and the conservation of the surrounding territory, the area of the city had changed as radically as had the Ninth Street campus which the institution had left less than fifty years before. "Noise, dust and smoke resulting from these conditions," they wrote in 1913, "have become a serious nuisance and street traffic an obstruction to University life." The University, while finding itself in a position of "the greatest strategic importance to its function as an instrument of public service," was nonetheless threatened by these unforeseen developments.[20]

The report commissioned from Cret while Harrison was still provost confronted present conditions and faced up to the importance of planning for the future. The administration was "determined that, with adequate foresight, planning, and concern, Pennsylvania and the surrounding communities should not be obliged to repeat the Ninth Street experience of the previous century."[21] One of the most disruptive factors on the campus as it had developed by the time of the 1913 report was the busy thoroughfare, Woodland Avenue, which ran in a diagonal direction immediately in front of College Hall and bisected much of the existing University. According to the Cret report "the surface cars and other vehicles even now threaten to create a wall of separation between the parts that lie on either side of it" in addition to being a major cause of the noise and dust. Cret had been a strong advocate of the City of Philadelphia's plan to put its public transit system underground.[22] He did not anticipate the closing of Woodland Avenue between Market and Thirty-eighth Streets—a development which came about in 1957. When

Drinking Fountain by A. Stirling Calder
Photograph by Mike Rosenman
The second in three generations of sculptors, A. Stirling Calder was commissioned by the Class of 1892 to design a drinking fountain for the residence halls (1900). The bronze which portrays a student in academic dress and a football player was installed in the arcade leading to East Quad where, with modifications, it remains in use today. Among other works by Calder, a lion's head basin adorns the south side of the Museum lily pond.

the streetcars were put underground from center city to Fortieth Street, a marvelous new space was gained which did as much for the campus as any scheme for a central architectural feature which had figured in previous plans. Shaded by mature trees which had for years lined the city street it replaced, College Hall Green instantly provided a quiet park in the heart of the University.

Little immediate action resulted from the 1913 plan, partly because of the recent period of expansion unprecedented in the University's history. It remains, however, the projection to which all future planners refer. In the period from the beginning of the first to the end of the second World Wars when Sydney E. Martin, chairman of the trustees' committee for physical development of the University, presented a new report, its spirit was retained and extended.[23] Even so, the conditions to which the Landscape Development Plan of 1977 addresses itself have arisen in large part because Cret's principle of creating open spaces enclosed by buildings was ignored. Instead "these buildings sit in isolation as on a chessboard" with little attempt at "renewing the landscape between them."[24]

If the development of facilities often proceeds as the University takes advantage of fortuitous circumstances as much as acting in accordance with a plan for the future, the reverse is also true. Because of the discrepancy between a university's needs at any given moment and its economic position, actual construction often lags behind the developments proposed. By the time action can be taken, the original set of circumstances has, on occasion, been transformed. This was true of the plans for a women's campus, put forward for the first time in 1948, since in Cret's day there

Hill Hall, 1961
A women's hall of residence was designed by the internationally famous architect Eero Saarinen in 1960. Four adjoining houses forming a quadrangle around a roofed court overlook the dining terrace surrounding a fountain on the ground level. The fortress-like exterior belies the light and grace of the interior spaces. It is now a coeducational college house in which some faculty as well as students share a varied cultural as well as residential life.

Van Pelt Library
Photograph by Frank Ross
The Charles Patterson Van Pelt University Library (1962) and its extension, the Dietrich Graduate Library (1967), designed by Harbeson, Hough, Livingston and Larson, successors to Paul Philippe Cret, make up east and west wings of the University Library Center. The buildings house the main collection. the Rare Book collection, Furness Library (Shakespeare), Lea Library (medieval and renaissance), the Lippincott Library (management), and the W. Norman Brown Library (South Asia studies).

were no female undergraduates. Not implemented at the time, the plans were readily available some years later when a site which had been cleared for an apartment building at Thirty-fourth and Walnut Streets suddenly become available for purchase. Since a plan had been drawn up for "a completely integrated Women's College with provisions for the accommodation of some 500 girls in residence and 700 day scholars" further to the west, the University was able to take advantage of the circumstances.[25] The women's dormitory, Hill Hall, was designed by Eero Saarinen and Associates and dedicated in 1961. The largest college house on campus, it is now coeducational like most other University residences.

In drawing up his plans for the campus, Cret envisaged the development of a strong north-south axis which would originate at the steps of College Hall and introduce "an open vista more than a thousand feet long" with new University buildings on either side.[26] The streetcars only bifurcated a part of it, but they still passed conveniently close to College Hall for arriving professors to be set down practically on the front steps. When the trustees appointed a committee on the physical development of the University in 1948, the axis proposed this time ran east-west along Locust Walk—right through the library designed by Furness. Indeed, the report closed with the remark: "While it may become desirable eventually to replace some of the old buildings, it is only necessary to demolish the present Library building to make a start towards accomplishing our objectives."[27]

Between the report of 1948 and the beginning of a new wave of construction and development in the sixties under the stimulus of President Gaylord P. Harnwell, a major change in emphasis had come about. The Cret report had included the word "conservation" as well as "development" in its title—although the term was there applied to surroundings rather than to buildings. In the plans which were effected over the next years, new buildings were added while those already existing were gradually recognized for what they were: a direct and continuing link with the University's past, in some cases superb examples not only of bygone taste but of superior architectural design. The trustees' committee of 1948 foresaw the possibility that "future generations might decide that College Hall had outlived its usefulness" and a tower building in which they proposed to house the administration at a focal point on campus was advocated as making it "possible to demolish Logan Hall and the Hare Laboratory and acquire another splendid area for academic expansion."[28]

By 1962, the changing attitude towards the existing campus is apparent in a plan which specifically calls for reference, in all future construction, to such heterogeneous elements from the past as "Irvine Steeple, Franklin Field, the Medical-Biological Research Towers, the University Library and the University Museum." The Locust axis, no longer necessitating the destruction of Furness and now described as "the main unifying east-west spine," has become a "Walk," in line with a new concern for pedestrians.[29] In the seventies, this concern with open space and landscaping led to the Landscape Development Plan for the overall improvement of the campus, which was commissioned in 1976 and prepared by a group of faculty members of the graduate school of fine arts under the direction of Dean Peter Shepheard. Since buildings necessarily continue to arise in isolation and as a function of the availability of funds, the problem is one of how best to incorporate structures of diversified provenance, designed for a wide variety of purposes, into the most satisfactory surroundings for a major, urban university.

This situation is inherent in all university and institutional development. As they surveyed the campus of their day, including what are now regarded as some of the best buildings on campus, the Cret commission remarked that "at the University of Pennsylvania, as in practically every other institution of its time, growth has preceded without plan and through mere accretion, advancing step by step through marginal enlargements, into an ever-increasing confusion . . . without organic arrangement."[30] But because no master plan was implemented at that time or later, many fine buildings have been successfully preserved from destruction. Any plan for the future must cherish the unique quality of different buildings and recognize that the diversity of the setting reflects the nature of the growth of the academic institution.

The developments of the sixties were facilitated by the federal urban renewal program and the certification by the Philadelphia Planning Commission of the University's redevelopment area. President Gaylord P. Harnwell created the executive planning committee on physical plant on which he himself sat along with Provosts Loren Eiseley, Jonathan E. Rhoads, who succeeded him, and then David R. Goddard, as well as Dean G. Holmes Perkins of the graduate school of fine arts.[31] Buildings were soon afterwards commissioned from such architects as Saarinen and Kahn, and contemporary structures arose to house the expanding University. In 1962, the new Charles Patterson Van Pelt Library was dedicated with the ringing of the Academy bell in "College Hall Quadrangle" for which it provided the boundary on the northern side. With the closing of Woodland Avenue, more space became available for landscaping beyond College Hall Green, and a wooded, urban garden was designed between Thirty-sixth and Thirty-seventh Streets. The University Mall created there by Ian L. McHarg, professor of landscape architecture and regional planning, comprises four walled courts along the strong diagonal between College Hall Green and Spruce Street. For the pedestrian walkway, cobblestones were salvaged from the old street, and rhododendrons, mountain laurels, and azaleas were planted as well as a stand of magnolia trees in a plaza which was the gift of the Class of 1933.

A different kind of space jealously preserved into the present is the

The Richards Building
Photograph by Lawrence S. Williams, Inc.
Beyond the lily pond and flowering trees of the University Botanical Garden rise the towers of the Alfred Newton Richards Medical Research Building, designed by professor of architecture Louis I. Kahn, and dedicated (1961) to the internationally famed biochemist. The subject of an exhibition at the Museum of Modern Art in New York, the Richards Building is considered one of the most important constructions in postwar America.

Botanical Garden. Back in the Ninth Street days, a garden had been supported by William P. C. Barton, professor of botany, on a forty-two-acre tract on the northern edge of the city. The limited use by both faculty and students of this remote site caused the trustees to part with the land, and a smaller garden with a greenhouse kept by the College steward, was provided adjacent to the President's House. The Botanical Garden on the present campus, originally four acres in extent, was established behind the residence halls in 1894 and included three greenhouses. Unpretentious rectangular and oval beds were bordered by gravel walks with Lombardy poplars, conifers, and bamboo plantings.

When Louis Kahn's medical research complex was erected on part of this site, new greenhouses were built south of the Leidy Laboratory of Biology to continue the propagation of plants used in botanical research. The original lily pond at the center of the garden laid out in 1894 continues to provide an enchanting spot on campus. It is regularly supplied with frogs and turtles from the neighboring laboratories and is surrounded by azaleas and perennials. Among its woodland trees are a huge gingko, a bald cypress, a sequoia, and other conifers. The Botanical Garden has a faithful band of bird watchers, and, over the years, more than 150 species of birds have been sighted. Although the bird life drawn to the old trees and water cannot be compared with what can be seen at the University's large Morris Arboretum in Chestnut Hill, it is a cause for pride that a university a mile from its city's downtown can continue to provide greenery enough to attract migrating birds.

Space of a totally different kind was procured and preserved with the decision to provide student residential accommodation in high-rise buildings. This was in marked contrast to the living accommodation supplied at Stouffer Triangle which, completed in 1972 and adjacent to the Quadrangle residence halls, continues the tradition for low-rise structures. Designed by the firm of Geddes, Brecher, Qualls and Cunningham, two of whose principals are a former and a present member of the faculty, Stouffer combines residential living for a hundred and fifty students with dining facilities for several times that number and includes stores on the street side. The Graduate Towers, for which Richard and Dion Neutra and Associates were design consultants, make it possible for a far greater number—one and a half thousand—of students to live at a conveniently central location on campus. The tallest building was named Nichols House and dedicated to "Roy F. and Jeannette P. Nichols, Distinguished Historians, Faithful Counselors, Devoted Companions."

Three more high-rise residential buildings in the area west of Locust Walk Bridge are combined with wide spaces and footpaths in another aspect of campus development: the vehicle-free superblock. A tradition of the older campus has been continued, reinforced by the provision that one percent of the construction cost of buildings on ground purchased from

A New Skyline: Graduate Towers
Photograph by Frank Ross
With the "high-rise" residence program represented in this photograph by Nichols House, one of the four Graduate Towers, the University departed from its tradition of medium height construction. Richard and Dion Neutra and Associates, and Bellante, Clauss, Miller and Nolan were the collaborating architects for these award-winning residences. Three undergraduate high-rise residence halls form the nucleus of the second "Superblock," designed by Eshbach, Pullinger, Stevens, and Bruder in conjunction with Perkins and Romanach (1970).

"Covenant" on Hey Day
Photograph by Eugene H. Mopsik
*Standing as another gateway to the
western campus beyond the Class of
1949 Bridge over Thirty-eighth Street,
the sculpture by Alexander Liberman is
hardly dwarfed by the high-rise student
residences. "Covenant," here forming a
canopy for the 1976 Hey Day procession,
is one of the works of art on the campus
specially commissioned by the University
of Pennsylvania.*

the City Redevelopment Authority be invested in works of art. For each high-rise building, the University commissioned a sculpture. A work by faculty sculptor, Robert M. Engman, "After Iyengar," commissioned by the department of chemistry, was installed in the chemistry building in 1977. A sculpture by Tony Smith, who held his first individual exhibition at the University's Institute of Contemporary Art in 1966, was installed on College Hall Green in 1975. Another work, "Covenant," the towering red sculpture by Alexander Liberman, stands like a modified Japanese torii at the entrance to the residential complex composed of high- and low-rise buildings. The atmosphere is very different from that of the older campus with its heterogeneous structures, but even there the sequences of greenswards and gardens are being extended on roads already closed to traffic.

The residential high-rise towers have also added a new silhouette to the University's skyline. In the early sixties, the towers of the Richards Building helped frame one part of the campus. Another landmark, impossible to overlook and often mentioned as another frame, is the Irvine Auditorium.[32] This extraordinary building which rises skyward to the south of the Furness Library at Thirty-fourth and Spruce Streets was designed by architect Horace Trumbauer and alumnus Julian F. Abele in fulfillment of a bequest from William B. Irvine, a onetime city treasurer, to provide the University with an auditorium in the spirit of the cathedrals of mediaeval France. A long nave was out of the question, given the small square plot available, and limited funds precluded the use of stone. Nevertheless, the sloping roof of Irvine soars over 200 feet, its brick walls—rather alien to Rheims—rendered in a random assortment of spires and turrets, arches and gargoyles, while the interior is decorated in brightly colored mediaeval designs. Drawing the ear as well as the eye, the building houses one of the world's largest organs, built for the Sesqui-centennial Exposition of 1926 and given to the University by the late Cyrus H. K. Curtis.

Most of the buildings constructed recently to accommodate the expanding needs of different departments of the University are of medium height, including the Williams Humanities and Languages Hall, designed by Nolen, Swinburne and Associates, and award-winning Vance Hall built to house the Wharton Graduate School by Bower and Fradley. Continuing a pattern which was largely serendipitous at its outset, new buildings have reinforced the presence of different disciplines and professions at distinct quadrants on campus: around the law school building to the north and the school of medicine to the south, with the social sciences on either side of Locust Walk between Thirty-seventh and Thirty-eighth Streets. The physical sciences are grouped to the east where two acclaimed additions to the Moore School of Electrical Engineering complement the structure acquired by the University in 1909 from a musical instruments manufacturer. An early contribution by Geddes *et al.*, the Pender Laboratory, has been praised for its solution to the problem of expanding on earlier eclectic buildings. No attempt was made in this modern structure of 1958 at conforming to "the Jacobean style of the Towne School on the left or to the thoroughly commonplace character of the Moore School, a former factory, on the right."[33] Instead, regard was shown for scale and height, and the use of the same materials or those producing a similar effect as the earlier buildings provides for an interesting blend of the new with the old. The same architects were commissioned to design the Graduate Research Building on the western side of the Moore School.

Along with concern that open spaces should accompany new

Irvine Auditorium
by Horace Trumbauer, 1926
Appearing French Gothic in this drawing from the office of architect Horace Trumbauer presented to the University by the Irvine family, the building is eclectic in style. The contribution to Philadelphia architecture of the firm's chief designer, Julian Francis Abele, a black graduate of the school of architecture (1920), has recently come to be appreciated.

Franklin Field Rebuilt
Photograph by Lawrence S. Williams, Inc.
*Aerial view, taken before the extension
of Thirty-fourth Street, showing the west
end of the Museum on the right, Cret's
chemistry building in the foreground on
the left, and the Philadelphia skyline
surmounting a crowded stadium. With
its track, field house, tennis courts, and
cricket crease, the original stadium,
which opened with the first Penn Relays
in 1895, was "the most complete athletic
facility in the country." It was not large
enough for the great era of collegiate
football, and the complex was enlarged
in 1922 in time for the Penn-Navy game
attended by President Harding. In 1925,
the double decking of the stands provided
additional seating for up to 60,000
spectators.*

The Class of 1923 Ice Skating Rink
Photograph by Frank Ross
*Dedicated in 1970, the rink designed by
Robert S. McMillan Associates was
presented by the Class of 1923 as its
forty-fifth reunion gift. It is excellent as
a hockey arena and for recreational and
figure skating, and seats 2,800 spectators.*

construction goes a recognition that buildings and areas must be designed
not only for study and scholarship but for other aspects of student life as
well. Franklin Field was opened in 1895, and the Weightman Hall and
Gymnasium were completed early in this century in Gothic style by
architect Frank Miles Day. With the construction by Martin, Stewart,
Noble, Class and Partners of the Gimbel Gymnasium in the mid-sixties,
recreational and athletic facilities were further expanded. The new
building includes courts for basketball, badminton, and squash, and an
Olympic-size college pool. When it opened in 1970, the Class of 1923
Ice Rink designed by McMillan Associates provided a spectacular new
recreational building which makes ingenious use of space between the
University's sports facilities below and the Walnut Street Bridge above.

A new dimension was added to University life with the dedication in
1971 of the Annenberg Center of Communication Arts and Sciences made
possible by a gift from the School of Communications founded by
alumnus and trustee Walter H. Annenberg. Designed by Vincent G.
Kling and Partners, the center includes the 900-seat Zellerbach Theatre and
the flexible 200-seat Harold Prince Laboratory Theatre. The Studio Theatre
is designed for films and smaller productions. Since it opened, the
Annenberg Center has been used both by undergraduates and professionals
for plays from the classical repertoire as well as for experimental theater.

Apart from the multiplicity of activities which go on at the University's
urban campus, various of its functions are carried out elsewhere. The
Gutman Center for Fine Arts near New Hope and the astronomical
observatory in Sugartown, designed by alumnus Alfred Bendiner, and,
even more, the farm at the school of veterinary medicine's New Bolton

center, also in Chester County, are in a direct line of descent from the land owned by the University since Colonial days. As early as 1758, Governor Thomas Penn endowed the College of Philadelphia with 2,500 acres of farmland forming one quarter of the Proprietary Manor of Perkasie in Bucks County. In the post-Revolutionary period, provision was made by the legislature for the trustees of the University of the State of Pennsylvania to acquire estates confiscated from Loyalists in all the counties surrounding Philadelphia.

Although these holdings were eventually sold, such farms were regarded during the eighteenth and nineteenth century as investment properties for the support of education. The possibility that they might be used for some form of educational activity was not considered until early this century when the "dust and grime of the city" once again began to threaten the University's campus.[34] In 1920, Senator George Wharton Pepper suggested that the University choose between "a routine college on the present campus or an academic home elsewhere."[35] The proposal to move part of the University gained substance in 1929 when, after three years' consideration, the University accepted a conditional gift from the president of the General Alumni Society, Henry N. Woolman, of the 175-acre estate Cressbrook Farm, close to the historic Valley Forge Park. The principal house on the property dated from 1740, the year to which the University traces its own foundation, and had served as the headquarters of the French General du Portail during the Valley Forge encampment.

For eight years the proposal to move part of the University twenty-two miles westward continued to be discussed, during which time, the alumni ranged themselves on both sides of the debate. In 1937, a proposal was

The Annenberg Center and School
Photograph by Lawrence S. Williams, Inc. *The Annenberg Center for Communication Arts and Sciences, designed by Vincent G. Kling and Associates (1971), houses the Zellerbach Theatre, the Harold Prince Theatre, and a Studio Theatre. The Annenberg School of Communications to the right provides classrooms, a library, and an auditorium. Completed in 1962, the school was designed by Alfred Easton Poor.*

The Willoughby Gateway of The Wharton Sinkler Center
Photograph by Suzanne Leahy
"Guildford" is one of the University's facilities in the Chestnut Hill area. The main house, constructed in the 1920s of architectural elements from historic houses in England, is entered through the sixteenth-century Willoughby gateway. Believed to have been a tomb canopy in pre-Reformation times, the stonework bearing the Willoughby arms came from the garden of Parham Old Hall in England. Named for the town in Surrey from which the gardener's cottage was moved to Philadelphia, "Guildford" stands among 30 acres of gardens. It was presented to the University for use as a conference center by Louise Elkins Sinkler in the name of her husband, a member of the class of 1906.

drawn up creating both a Freshman College and a recreation program "for the benefit of the male students of the whole University" at Cressbrook Farm. The project was intended to provide the cornerstone of the development program for the University's bicentennial in 1940. The year preceding the University celebration, the farm adjacent to Cressbrook together with the house occupied by Lafayette in 1777–78 was willed to the University. But 1939 also brought the outbreak of World War II: the Bicentennial Convocation, at which President Franklin Delano Roosevelt was the principal guest, was conducted under its menacing shadow, and the University of Pennsylvania soon became a wartime campus. The "Valley Forge Plan," viewed by many alumni as a means of recovering the advantages of undergraduate education in a small social unit, was set aside for the time.

"The problem of the University of Pennsylvania is Philadelphia's problem," said a trustee in 1928, and, even while the thought of setting up a liberal arts college in bucolic surroundings was at its brightest, the committee reporting to the trustees pointed out that, with proper development, the current urban location nonetheless offered the University "a unique opportunity . . . to improve the physical situation in West Philadelphia." By taking positive steps to improve existing conditions, the report stated, "we can reasonably look forward to a site and a campus which will compare favorably with those of other great American universities."[36] After the war the Valley Forge possibility continued to provide a tempting alternative, particularly by the fifties when it became clear that, if the University were to remain in the city, it would have to expand. Government approval at all levels was required for the acquisition by eminent domain of properties in the immediate area of the campus, and negotiations were conducted successfully with the city. As a result, the decision was made to remain an urban campus.

Although Pennsylvania freshmen never acquired their *lieu champêtre* in Chester County, the New Bolton Center, 32 miles southwest of the metropolitan campus, is the direct descendant of a smaller farm by that name which, when it was bequeathed to the University by the heirs of Effingham B. Morris, included a herd of Guernseys. A yet more rural home was needed for the programs of the veterinary school which, when it moved to South Brook Farm, on an initial tract of 650 acres near the village of London Grove in Chester County, was renamed the New Bolton Center. Surrounding the old fieldstone house there is now a complex of about 55 diagnostic, rehabilitation and treatment, classroom, and library buildings.

If this building—Allam House—is the earliest structure on a far-flung campus, parts of another are even older, having been imported from England. Among the University's three properties in Chestnut Hill is the beautiful house built in the 1920s by alumnus Robert R. McGoodwin on the model of Sutton Place near Guildford, in Surrey, until recently owned by J. Paul Getty. For the construction of "Guildford," more commonly known as the Sinkler House after its donor, Mrs. Wharton Sinkler, ancient tiling, flooring, windowglass, and paneling, and even bricks and terra-cotta mullions were imported for reassembly by the builders. Gateways, doors, a staircase, stone fireplaces, paneled rooms—one of them called "Pope's Parlour" because of a legend associating it with the poet—were brought from historic structures all over Britain. The gardener's cottage on the grounds, a sixteenth century house, was transported *in toto* from the town of Guildford. However one may view the collecting propensities of Americans abroad a generation or two ago, it is impossible not to admire the quality of the craftsmanship which has incorporated so much that is beautiful into a satisfying whole in a great house surrounded by walled gardens, terraces, lawns, and ancient trees.

If the Sinkler House, a conference center, is a remarkable transplant—a monument to painstaking architectural synthesis—the design of its neighbor, Paley House, is entirely the product of the imagination of its architect. "High Hollow," as the house George Howe designed for himself was originally called, bears evidence of the highly picturesque "minor European domestic" bias of his early career. Professor and architect Paul Cret praised its proportion and its simplicity. "High Hollow," he wrote, was "a logical continuation of the best traditions. It is as free from archaeological imitation as it is devoid of a pretentious striving for originality."[37] If it is a less directly derivative dwelling than "Guildford," "High Hollow" is nonetheless inspired by the past. The architect's strong feeling for site—for having his buildings relate naturally to the earth on which they sit, a characteristic of his entire career—is also in evidence at "High Hollow" on its enclosed wooded hillside bordering Fairmount Park and the Wissahickon. It became known as the Paley House after the alumni family who last owned it. It too is now used as a conference center in conjunction with the Sinkler house.

Howe discovered European modernism in architecture in the late twenties, some years before he departed to head the department of architecture at Yale. In 1930, together with William Lescaze, he designed the Philadelphia Savings Fund Society building, the forerunner of the contemporary skyscraper. If one considers the nature of the building which has passed into the University's hands, it is intriguing to realize that George Howe, whose protégé and partner in the forties was Louis Kahn, sold "High Hollow" in 1928 because of the mid-career change in his thought as an architect.

The house "Compton" at the Morris Arboretum, third of the University's sub-campuses in the Chestnut Hill neighborhood, was pulled down in accordance with the wishes of the family. The comfortable, four-storied, grey stone and shingled Victorian house on the property was

Paley House: George Howe's "High Hollow"
Early in a distinguished career, George Howe, who was later chairman of the department of architecture at Yale and a great exponent of the International Style, designed this weathered stone house for himself. "High Hollow" relates perfectly to its hillside site above the Wissahickon Creek in Chestnut Hill. It was renamed after it was given to the University in 1964 by the Samuel Paley Foundation.

Mask and Wig Club Program
by Maxfield Parrish, 1896
The Quince Street Club House occupied in 1894 by Mask and Wig, the University's oldest dramatic organization (founded 1889), was remodeled by architect Wilson Eyre, Jr., and decorated with murals by the young artist Maxfield Parrish who also created program cover designs for the Club's popular annual musical comedies and operettas. Through the years, Mask and Wig has played in over 30 cities and performed for the President of the United States. The club has made many benefactions to the University.

acquired as a result of the amalgamation with the Arboretum of the adjacent estate "Overlea." The Arboretum consists of a landscaped garden of 175 acres bordering the Wissahickon Creek with panoramic views of the Whitemarsh Valley. Because the planting was begun so long ago, the Arboretum contains one of the most remarkable collections of mature exotic trees in the nation, with notable specimens from the Orient. The "museum of trees" was begun in the last century by John T. Morris and his sister, Miss Lydia T. Morris, at whose death, in 1932, it came to the University.

The development of the campus reflects the growth of the University in the course of its history not merely in its physical proportions but in less tangible dimensions as well. After the move from the Ninth Street location had been completed, the decision to build the first halls of residence and to model them on the collegiate layouts of Oxford and Cambridge signaled a distinct change in an important aspect of the University's view of itself, this time related to nonacademic activities. On Ninth Street, while the medical students had enjoyed a somewhat Bohemian existence, the remainder of the student body had been kept quarantined from any possible influence outside the classroom: "For the rest, the students of the University came decorously every morning from their parents' homes on Walnut Street or from far-off Germantown, and were safely home by candlelight. And if, now and then, a man came from the interior of the State or from some southern State, it was only because he had friends in Philadelphia, with whom he could find a safe and real home."[38] At this time, no advantage—in fact quite the opposite—was seen in encouraging young people from a variety of differing backgrounds to associate with one another far removed from their families' watchful attention to morals and social connections.

When "beyond the Schuylkill a noble domain was secured," a new era began, attested to by "spacious new buildings equipped with all the appliances needed for the ever-widening scope of education today."[39] The construction of the Library and the Museum to supplement the "modest quartette" of collegiate Gothic buildings, was viewed by the Philadelphia essayist Agnes Repplier as concrete evidence of the way the University in the "spirit of strenuous, insatiable progress moved forward with over-mastering zeal."[40] In the study he made of the major universities in the country in the early twentieth century, Edwin E. Slosson expressed admiration for the physical plant of the University of Pennsylvania where, as a body, the "handsome new buildings" impressed him as unmatched anywhere else in the United States. Individually, the residence halls, the law school, or the engineering buildings might find their equals at Princeton, Harvard, and the University of California; but nowhere else did he note so many structures, not only favorably impressive to look at, but admirably adapted to the functions they served.[41]

Along with this evidence of academic expansion—"the outward symbols of an intense activity and earnestness, of professional devotion and consecrated munificence"—the construction of Houston Hall the first student union in the United States, shortly before the Quadrangles were put up, evinced a new awareness that much of importance in university life took place outside the classroom. "Houston Hall is to the University of Pennsylvania," remarked Slosson, "what the Forum was to Rome."[42] The student union, constructed in 1895 under the supervision of Frank Miles Day, was based on winning designs submitted by two students, William C. Hays ('93) and Milton B. Medary ('94). One of the things Slosson admired about this focal point on the urban campus, where students from all over the University met to exchange ideas and spend free time together, was the democratic and cosmopolitan atmosphere associated with life at the University.[43]

The present-day campus bears testimony to these social developments as well as to shifts in the philosophy of high education. At the same time, since its growth is predicated on changes in its historic role and priorities, and its extended possessions often result more from beneficent bequests than design, much that has evolved on the modern campus bears unself-conscious witness to the past. This slow growth also permits constant reevaluation of individual buildings from that past to take place. Thus, after all the controversy, the Furness Library has come to be regarded not only as a familiar and delightful feature of campus architecture, but as one of the University's architectural treasures. In the same way, it is only quite recently that the merits of the Quadrangles designed by Cope & Stewardson were recognized to the full, with the result that designs for their rehabilitation were made by alumni Davis and Brody in order to convert them to college houses offering a varied cultural as well as residential life. Although the trustees of 1948 were convinced that Thomas Richards' quartet of buildings had outlived their purposes, only the Hare Building was actually pulled down. In 1976, College Hall—inspiration to alumnus Charles Addams, as to many generations of students who remember its protean succession of uses—was once more renovated for the latest round of demands made upon it after receipt of a gift for the purpose. The University's stance as it looks to the future without forgetting its debt and obligation to the past is once again epitomized in the refurbishing of this, the oldest building on the most recent campus.

"College Hall"
by Charles Addams
Cover, *Pennsylvania Gazette*, March 1973
Many buildings on campus have been recognizable from time to time in the cartoons of alumnus Charles Addams (class of 1934). Among these, College Hall has appeared on several occasions clearly identified by the artist. In this picture, Gomez, Morticia, and other members of the "Addams Family" have left the pages of the New Yorker *to pose in front of the inspirational building.*

Epilogue

I shall deal with the communion of love and need, avocation and vocation. I shall argue that the liberal learning ought to be bonded with a sense of the instrumental, the utilitarian, the professional. The vocation of which I shall speak, however, is vocation more as summons or moral call rather than job alone. Of course, the case for the liberal learning, whether modified or not, has not been won. The voices—and I count mine among them—for an education which exposes students to the humanistic and scientific achievements of man's past and present, and to the various methods through which truth is sought, are relatively few. But the rhetoric of our case appears tainted to a new generation of students who often speak scornfully of learning for its own sake. . . . Yet, in this and in other ways, our students have been our conscience. My answer . . . is to urge that in the years ahead, we unite the profession, the calling, with the liberal learning. If we do not, we shall have failed the rightful aspirations of many of the young.

Martin Meyerson,
"Play for Mortal Stakes: Vocation
and the Liberal Learning,"
Liberal Education, Vol. LV,
March 1969

Epilogue

It is never an easy matter to appraise a situation while it is in progress. This is as true of a university in its development as it is of all institutions which must constantly evolve in order to satisfy changing requirements. For the university, the difficulty is compounded because, although it stands at the forefront of change, it is more firmly anchored than most institutions in an inherited past. The forces of both the past and the future impinge upon its present—forces which the university ignores at its peril and which make that present a mix of conflicting tensions which are difficult to deal with or even to interpret or define.

Understanding the state of higher education at a given period and devising ways to renew the university are nonetheless constant necessities. Cardinal Newman's *Idea of a University*, written midway through the nineteenth century, was one such brilliant evaluation for British universities. Some years before, Wilhelm von Humboldt had fulfilled a similar function for secondary education in Germany and helped found the University of Berlin. In our own century, an appraisal by Abraham Flexner, who had deeply affected the development of America's medical schools and universities some years earlier, proved less fortunate since events shattered the validity of his prognostications. In 1928, while he was still looking to Germany for his model, not only scholarship but academic and civil freedom were on the verge of collapse in that country. As Clark Kerr commented in the 1960s, Flexner's proposals were, in fact, "a valedictory to a university form which was already passing."

At that very time, despite Flexner's scorn of the state of higher education in the United States, the American university—that remarkable achievement of the "American century"—was evolving as a blend of the components of its inheritance. Grafting the especially American form of utilitarian education on to a combination of the English undergraduate college and the German research university produced a set of institutions in the United States with the greatest national and international significance. Over the next thirty-five years, developments which Flexner saw as a threat to the American university (developments such as professionalism) led instead to premier influence on the world's higher education.

Among the centers of learning which attained or consolidated a position of eminence in the United States after Abraham Flexner had predicted their "eclipse" was the University of Pennsylvania, whose evolution we have attempted to evoke in the preceding chapters. In the last quarter of the twentieth century, as often in their past, the significant institutions of learning in the world find themselves faced by uncertainties which seem perennially to beset higher education. None of the current problems—certainly not financial constraint—is new at the University of Pennsylvania. The problems do differ in size and quantity, however, because society and its expectations have changed. Yet issues of governance, curriculum, scholarship, quality, and financing have always confronted the University, and their resolution has contributed to its continuous adaptation since colonial times. Change and conservation have been constant and coexistent themes throughout the development of this and every other major university, all of which share the challenge of preserving the continuities of civilization while venturing into the unknown whether in the natural or social sciences, the humanities, or the problem-solving professions. The ways the University surmounted previous difficulties provide precedents and serve as encouragement for it to build upon and transcend its traditional strengths.

Among the themes which have constantly recurred throughout our existence, none is more marked than the way divergent tensions and tendencies have repeatedly been brought into balance. Two centuries after the birth of American independence, the University of Pennsylvania continues to strive for a subtle balance among its objectives. While the aims of any complex institution, particularly of a distinguished university, are to a considerable extent the aims of its parts and of the individuals who compose it, there is necessarily a tension between such objectives and the imperative for certain central directions as well. Furthermore, current goals need to be tempered by a vision for the future. Our efforts at achieving balance are continually in process at the University between the theoretical and the applied, the graduate and the undergraduate, the broadly intellectual and the concentrated. This was at the root of the theme of "one university" which was the charge to the University's Development Commission in 1972 and, in turn, the conclusion in its 1973 report. That theme is facilitated by having a campus which, unlike many others, consolidates all its faculties on 250 acres virtually adjacent to the downtown of a great metropolis.

One consequence of the present striving for balance and one which permits us to anticipate that a new unity may be achieved is that now, more than at any time in our recent past, the boundaries among individual disciplines and professions at the University are fluid. A willingness to engage in new ventures has resulted in programs which combine medicine and economics, law and public policy, engineering and dentistry,

Vance Hall
Photograph by Eugene H. Mopsik
Vance Hall, designed by the firm of Bower and Fradley and completed in the fall of 1972, is the home of the Wharton graduate division and related academic and research units. On the Spruce Street side, the construction is predominantly brick, while the campus facade is a spectacular essay in glass.

psychology and the arts, archaeology and metallurgy. Students have benefited from opportunities offered by joint programs which draw on the liberal arts and sciences, on the one hand, and professional fields such as those in management, technology, and health, on the other. Unlike some comparable institutions, the University has not been afraid to maintain undergraduate professional programs so long as their content is balanced by the inclusion of the humanizing character of the arts and sciences. In the seventies, the balance between the theoretical and the applied we seek at the University of Pennsylvania includes the aim of imbuing professional fields with the methods and rigorous analysis employed in more theoretical areas, while, at the same time, seeking to impart to some of the disciplines the sense of purpose traditionally the hallmark of the professions.

This concern with the applied along with the theoretical appeared early in the development of the University of Pennsylvania. In general, the weight given to each in the modern world is the reverse of what it was in colonial days. Franklin's call for instruction in utilitarian subjects challenged the notion of learning as a finite body of knowledge and one which must be preserved and handed down in perpetuity from generation to generation. If his proposals constitute an early example of curricular reform, Franklin also helped initiate a debate which continues to occupy a prominent place in all discussions of the needed balance between general education and training in specific skills.

The danger today, however, is rather that education may become—or has become—too narrow and too applied, with the arts and sciences relegated to the periphery as insufficiently productive of the tangible results demanded by a modern world. It is to achieve a more tempered balance at the University of Pennsylvania, that a central focus for these disciplines was brought about by the creation of the Faculty of Arts and Sciences in 1974. This core division of the University gathers together what were formerly the College, College for Women, Graduate School of Arts and Sciences, as well as the social science departments of the Wharton School. We do well to remember that, in his enthusiasm for utilitarian skills, Franklin at no time rejected the existing classical tradition. What he envisioned was an expansion in learning, a program which would supplement, not replace, the more conventional classical curriculum of his day.

A variety of other current undergraduate and advanced programs are connected with our continuing aims of achieving appropriate balances between the theoretical and the applied and between general education and concentration. One of these has the object of wedding undergraduate instruction with the research conducted at the University. Through the University Scholars program started in 1974, talented undergraduates are able to combine breadth with specialized graduate or professional studies. In addition, the Benjamin Franklin Scholars program, open to a nationally selected group, offers opportunities for research with faculty who are leaders in their fields. While these programs involve a select group of students, every attempt is made to encourage as many students as would benefit to work out individualized majors and to pursue goals of their own selection. The intent of such efforts is to enable our undergraduates to draw upon the scholarly atmosphere and the research of professors and advanced students which comprise that indispensable function at the University of Pennsylvania of creating new knowledge and testing new ideas.

The great resources of the University have been fruitfully tapped for beginning students through the establishment in 1972 of freshman seminars in traditional as well as less common areas. Students in small groups study with a variety of scholars, including faculty from divisions of the University which ordinarily do not teach undergraduates. Immediately on entering the University, freshmen are thus given an insight into the specialized kinds of research on which we especially pride ourselves. At the same time, we are attempting to create a better balance between the breadth of a general education, which in recent times at the University of Pennsylvania and elsewhere has been neglected, and the concentration so ably supplied by the disciplines and the professions. The ideal of a "university college" experience which we envision for students includes an understanding of this and other cultures, of times past and present, of the methods and achievements of humanistic, scientific and technological, and other practical learning, as well as providing for concentrations in a particular field which takes place here in an environment infused with scholarly research and advanced professional programs.

Other measures have been devised to link the curricular with the extracurricular. For example, freshman seminars are made available to the residents of Hill Hall, one of the new college houses. Part of a "living-learning" program set up in 1971, college houses are a response to the question of how best to achieve the requisite balance between the impersonality of a large institution and the advantages of preserving some of the intimacy of earlier days when the University was still small in size. As the University grew, the problem of avoiding anonymity and impersonality was not always centrally recognized, and in that era the fraternities and sororities played an important role. In addition to providing housing, the college houses and related programs of the 1970s contribute further to cultural and educational experiences. For example, the focus of Ware College House, the first result of renovating the Quadrangle, is a program on health and society. Some programs are grouped around specialized themes with the aim of encouraging students who wish to pursue a particular interest, including modern languages, the arts, black culture, international studies, and Japanese culture. They are housed in high-rise as well as low-rise buildings.

The Trustees of The University of Pennsylvania
Photograph by Frank Ross
Former chairman of the trustees William L. Day (B.S. 1931, LL.D. 1971) appears on the steps of the Furness Building with his fellow trustees and a few other University officials after attending his last meeting of the full board of trustees, in October 1973. A chair was established in memory of this leader of the University, who headed the largest bank in Philadelphia, and of his father Charles, a former trustee.

In a setting in which old divisions and isolations are being questioned, the University attempts to serve undergraduates and advanced and research students by offering them wide choices. While many students, along with some of the staff and faculty, wish to live in low-rise buildings and college houses (including the Quadrangle, modeled on some of the features of Oxbridge colleges), others prefer a home more closely resembling the apartment dwellings of the city, a fitting part of our urban campus.

In this respect, the University harks back to its origins as a small colonial college which was nonetheless an integral part of a great city. Its location has been a source of problems and enrichment from the time when Philadelphia was the metropolis of the colonies. To judge by the University's decision to change its location on two occasions before the turn of the present century, the problems faced by the cities in recent years are hardly new. And if the University's tendency to move at intervals of between sixty and seventy years was not repeated as the third such epoch elapsed, this reflects in part a change in attitude towards the community of which it is a part.

There are continuing advantages to a situation in the center of the fourth largest metropolis of the nation, within easy reach of its social and cultural offerings and only an hour or two away from the rest of that region from New York to Washington which combines the world's greatest concentration of educational resources. In the dense, cosmopolitan setting of Philadelphia, the University has developed as a sprawling campus whose architecture and landscape are evidence of a delightfully haphazard growth. Not only does it have the great advantage of housing all its major educational parts on a single campus: Pennsylvania students are also free to study at neighboring institutions as part of a cooperative program with Bryn Mawr, Haverford, and Swarthmore Colleges. Close ties have been developed with institutions overseas, and students and faculty are able to pursue their studies in Paris, Seville, and Munich as well as in Japan or Egypt or Israel or Iran. Recently, an exchange, in the truest sense of the word, has been set up with the University of Edinburgh, and for many years the fund sponsored by Sir John Thouron and Esther du Pont Thouron has enabled Pennsylvania students to study for an extensive period in the United Kingdom and has brought to our campus a select group of graduates from British universities.

The large and impersonal, the small and custom-formed, the local and the cozy, the distant and the strange—all these elements contribute to the intricate fabric of the University of Pennsylvania. As has been suggested, our aim is to balance the intimate with the cosmopolitan in such a way as to maintain something of the atmosphere of neighborhood enclaves in the heart of an academic metropolis.

From the time when the University began to grow rapidly late in the last century—it had 1,600 full-time students in 1890, 16,000 in 1976—its

President Ford and the Academic Guests of 1975
Photograph by Frank Ross
In commemoration of the 200th anniversary of the commencement of the College of Philadelphia in 1775, which was attended by the Continental Congress (including delegate George Washington), the University Commencement of May 1975 brought together the leaders of the English-speaking universities which were in existence prior to the American Revolution. The honored guests, the heads of Oxford, Cambridge, St. Andrews, Aberdeen, Edinburgh, Glasgow, and Trinity College, Dublin—and the President of the United States—are here shown with President Martin Meyerson and Provost Eliot Stellar. The degree-granting universities and colleges of the colonial period —eight in addition to the University of Pennsylvania—were honored as well that day.

student population has contributed to this rich variety. In his study of the great American universities in 1910, Edwin E. Slosson commented on the exceptionally diversified student body he found at the University of Pennsylvania.[1] Although American universities were often exclusive in their choice of students and our own history is uneven in this respect, once more a compensating balance and reconciliation occurred, focused between meritocracy and democracy, excellence and equity. The University opened its doors to the poor, to ethnic groups, to women and to blacks, with less fanfare, occasionally begrudgingly, but often earlier than comparable institutions.

In the course of its development, the College of Philadelphia had its share of trauma resulting from questions of political control and support. Nowadays, the University of Pennsylvania continues as an independent institution with a privately rather than governmentally controlled board relying largely for support on its students and their families, its alumni, and foundations and friends, both corporate and individual, as well as on endowments. But it is also a public institution. Through its education and research, it serves its state and its nation. Its hospitals and clinics, libraries and museum, recreational and other facilities, and to a considerable extent the talents of its faculty and students, are widely used by the community. In recognition of such public roles, the University receives financial support for educational programs from the Commonwealth and much of its research support from the federal government.

This mixed economy, balancing support from private and public sources, is a pattern which has existed throughout most of the University's existence. The private funds procured by Franklin for the colonial College were supplemented by moneys furnished after the Revolution by the Commonwealth, which thus affirmed its support for the newly reorganized University. Today, it is the special role of the University within the Commonwealth that most distinguishes our mixed economy. This relationship has been continuous since late in the last century. The Commonwealth provides substantial support to student aid, to the museum, to the University's health schools, and to its general operations. Although this amounts to a relatively small proportion of our total revenues, it nonetheless constitutes an essential component. Unique as a system of mixed public and private support, this relationship is being examined as a model for other independent universities and their states.

Our efforts in seeking and spending resources, both private and public, are guided by the aim of excellence. Professors and students alike require for their intellectual development a shared exposure to provocative points of view in a setting supportive of speculation and experiment as well as of tested knowledge. A primary objective must be to preserve and enhance our distinguished faculty—a faculty which matches devotion to students with achievement in research and scholarship and in creative accomplish-

"Medal of Honor Rag"
Photograph by Jack Hoffman
José Ferrer is the psychiatrist and Clifton Davis his patient, a recipient of the Medal of Honor, in Tom Cole's play. From the Western Savings Bank—Annenberg Center Theatre Series (1976).

ment in artistic and applied fields. The professoriate requires a sustained standard of living comparable to that in other professions. At a time when this was far from being achieved, President Eliot of Harvard found solace in the thought that virtue brought its own reward. At his inaugural in 1869, he declared: "The poverty of scholars is of inestimable worth in this money-getting nation. It maintains the true standards of virtue and honor. . . . Luxury and learning," he concluded, "are ill bedfellows."[2] A century later, the situation he sought to justify no longer existed; nonetheless, by the mid 1970s, discrepancies were growing between the incomes of professors and other professionals.

Entrance to the Museum Rotunda, circa 1950
Flanked by two stone lions, since replaced by others of cloisonné, the objects on display include eighth century guardian statues from T'ien Lung Shan, fourteenth century wall paintings from Moonhill Monastery (Honan), and, in the center of the arch, the Maitreya Buddha. A great favorite with visitors of all ages is the crystal sphere of the empress dowager dating from the nineteenth century which stands under the beautiful rotunda. It is the second largest example known.

At the same time as it seeks to maintain diversity and choice, the University must aim to apply its resources selectively. The need to reinforce those programs most vital to the academic and intellectual fabric must, in some cases, lead to substitution, however painful this may be. The pursuit of excellence is subject to obvious financial constraints. The challenge of avoiding shortsighted financial policies was never more clearly elucidated than by Edmund Burke in a letter he addressed to the Duke of Bedford towards the end of the eighteenth century:

> It may be new to his Grace, but I beg leave to tell him that mere parsimony is not economy. It is separable in theory from it, and in fact it may, or it may not, be a *part* of economy, according to circumstances. Expense, and great expense, may be an essential part in true economy. If parsimony were to be considered as one of the kinds of that virtue, there is, however, another and a higher economy. Economy is a distributive virtue, and consists, not in saving, but in selection. Parsimony requires no providence, no sagacity, no powers of combination, no comparison, no judgment. Mere instinct, and that not an instinct of the noblest kind, may produce this false economy in perfection. The other economy has larger views. It demands a discriminating judgment, and a firm, sagacious mind. It shuts one door to impudent importunity, only to open another, and a wider, to unpresuming merit.[3]

Nothing could do the University more credit than to have our efforts succeed in guiding the allocation of resources by these principles.

The heritage of the University of Pennsylvania is long and complex. Unique in some ways, and never more so than in the balance it sets out to achieve among so many contrasting forces, its destiny is nonetheless shared by other institutions that draw upon different and varied experiences and backgrounds. Our past and present attributes are such that we at the University of Pennsylvania may properly continue to build on them, recognizing that difficult periods have often been ones in which truth and sage judgment have triumphed.

As in earlier times, our work for the future continues to be facilitated by involvement and assistance from many quarters: a faculty both distinguished and devoted; students, undergraduate and advanced, whose complaints are as many here as anywhere but who gradually acquire an affectionate attachment before they leave; a board of unsurpassed trustees; and alumni, both sentimental and watchful, many of whom remember a campus and an educational process which were very different, not so many years ago.

In recent times, the University of Pennsylvania has become much larger and more stimulating than the modest center where our cast of characters performed their diverse roles. Almost inevitably, the greatest of our teachers and leaders have heard themselves compared, on some formal

Ben Franklin and Abbie Dinglebender (Mask & Wig Style)
Wide World Photo
From the opening performance in 1889 at the Chestnut Street Opera House, the operettas, musical comedies, and reviews of the Mask & Wig club have been enjoyed by campus and Philadelphia audiences and, on tour, in over thirty American cities. These two Mask and Wiggers, since become illustrious in other ways, spoofed the University founder in "High as a Kite," the production in 1940 in honor of the University's bicentennial.

occasion, to Benjamin Franklin—considered as heirs to that particular mantle of Elijah of which his city and his university like to boast. The true heirs of Franklin, however, are not only the faculty who uphold his enthusiasm for research and education, or the trustees who continue in an office he founded, but all those who go out into the larger world from the University of Pennsylvania. For our students, graduate and undergraduate, are the special beneficiaries of Franklin's vision, the latest links in the chain which connects us with him and with our past, and our best hopes for the future.

Chronologies

Chief Executives of the University of Pennsylvania

Benjamin Franklin	Founder
The Reverend William Smith	Provost 1755–1779
The Reverend John Ewing	Provost 1779–1802
John McDowell	Provost 1806–1810
The Reverend John Andrews	Provost 1810–1813
The Reverend Frederic Beasley	Provost 1813–1828
The Reverend William Heathcote DeLancey	Provost 1828–1834
The Reverend John Ludlow	Provost 1834–1853
Henry Vethake	Provost 1854–1859
The Reverend Daniel Raynes Goodwin	Provost 1860–1868
Charles Janeway Stillé	Provost 1868–1880
William Pepper	Provost 1880/1–1894
Charles Custis Harrison	Provost 1894–1910
Edgar Fahs Smith	Provost 1910–1920
General Leonard Wood	President-elect 1921–1922; did not serve
Josiah Harmar Penniman	Provost (Executive) 1921–1930; Provost (non-Executive) 1930–1939; President 1923–1926
Thomas Sovereign Gates	President 1930–1944; Chairman of the University 1944–1945
George William McClelland	President 1944–1948; Chairman of the University 1948–1951
Harold Edward Stassen	President 1948–1953
Gaylord Probasco Harnwell	President 1953–1970
Martin Meyerson	President 1970–

Heads of the Trustees

College of Philadelphia

Benjamin Franklin	President of the Board of Trustees 1749–1755 (Academy), 1755–1756, 1789–1790 (College), Trustee 1779–1790 (University)
Reverend Richard Peters	President 1756–1764
James Hamilton	President 1764–1764
John Penn	President 1764–1771
James Hamilton	President 1771–1773
Richard Penn	President 1773–1774
John Penn	President 1774–1779
Benjamin Franklin	President 1789–1790
Right Reverend William White	President 1790–1791

University of the State of Pennsylvania

Joseph Reed	President 1779–1781
William Moore	President 1781–1782
John Dickinson	President 1782–1785
Thomas McKean	President 1788–1791

University of Pennsylvania

His Excellency the Governor of the Commonwealth	President *ex officio* 1971–present*
William Pepper	President *pro tempore* in the absence of the Governor 1880–1894
Charles Custis Harrison	President *pro tempore* 1894–1911 Chairman 1911–1926
Josiah Harmar Penniman	Chairman 1926–1928
Thomas Sovereign Gates	Chairman, Executive Board 1928–1948 Chairman of Trustees 1945–1948
Robert Thompson McCracken	Chairman 1948–1956
Alfred Hector Williams	Chairman 1956–1961
Wilfred Donnell Gillen	Chairman 1961–1968
William Lang Day	Chairman 1968–1973
Robert Galbraith Dunlop	Chairman 1974–1974
Donald Thomas Regan	Chairman 1974–

* From 1791 to 1880 there was no elected Chairman. Meetings of the Trustees were chaired by one of those present.

Milestones

1740	Trust to establish the Charity School granted
1742	Building at Fourth and Arch Streets completed
1749	Trustees for the Academy named, with Benjamin Franklin as president
1750	Transfer made of the Charity School Building and its trust to the Academy trustees
1751	Academy opened (January) Free Charity School opened (September)
1755	College chartered; Reverend William Smith first provost; first non-sectarian college in Colonies; first scientific curriculum
1757	First College class graduated
1765	Medical School established (first in the Colonies)
1775	Continental Congress, including delegate George Washington, attends Commencement
1778	Continental Congress meets in College Hall
1779	College Charter reorganized by State Assembly; property vested in new body, University of the State of Pennsylvania; first application of the title "university" to an American institution
1780	Continental Congress attends Commencement; A.M. conferred on Thomas Paine
1783	LL.D. conferred on Washington
1784	Louis XVI donates books to University library
1787	LL.D. conferred on Lafayette
1789 (–1791)	Reactivation of College of Philadelphia
1789 (–1794)	University occupies hall of American Philosophical Society
1790	Law lectures by James Wilson, first professor of Law and one of the four original Associate Justices of the U.S. Supreme Court
1791	Act of Legislature unites University of the State of Pennsylvania and College of Philadelphia as University of Pennsylvania
1800	Purchase of "President's House," intended for U.S. President when Philadelphia was the capital

1802 (–1829) University (Arts and Medical) occupies President's House

1813 Philomathean Literary Society

1822 500 full-time students

1829 (–1872) Occupancy of two new buildings designed by William Strickland—one for Department of Arts, the other for Department of Medicine

1836 Alumni Society of the College

1849 Delta Phi, University's first Greek-letter fraternity

1850 Law School reorganized

1852 Professorship of Civil Engineering and Mining inaugurated

1863 Scientific "Lazzaroni" under Professor Alexander Dallas Bache bring about foundation of National Academy of Sciences

1870 Purchase of Almshonse farm in West Philadelphia as new site for University

1872 Classes begin in College Hall on new campus
Department of Science established (Towne Scientific School, 1875)

1873 Athletic Association

1874 Professorship of Architecture inaugurated
University Hospital (first teaching hospital owned by a university)

1875 *Daily Pennsylvanian* originates as *University Magazine*

1876 First Pennsylvania intercollegiate football game

1878 School of Dental Medicine

1879 1,000 full-time students
First Pennsylvania intercollegiate crew race

1880 First Pennsylvania degree conferred on a woman

1881 Wharton School of Finance and Commerce, first collegiate school of management

1882 Graduate School of Arts and Sciences

1884 School of Veterinary Medicine

1887 University Museum (Archaeology and Ethnology)

1889	First earned Ph.D. awarded Mask and Wig Club
1891	Degree course in Electrical Engineering
1892	Wistar Institute of Anatomy and Biology (and Museum)
1893	School of Chemical Engineering Graduate School of Education
1894	Forerunner of College of General Studies for adults
1895 (–1899)	Law School classes in Congress Hall (Independence Hall)
1896	Houston Hall, first Student Union in the United States Psychological Clinic (first in country)
1900	Association of American Universities established, University of Pennsylvania one of fourteen founding members
1909	5,000 full-time students School of Social Work (a separate school affiliated with the University in 1935)
1912	Thomas W. Evans Museum, School of Dental Medicine
1913	Paul Philippe Cret, Warren Powers Laird, and Olmsted Brothers plan for future development of buildings and grounds and conservation of surrounding territory
1919	10,000 full-time students
1920	School of Fine Arts
1921	Graduate Division of Wharton School
1924	Moore School of Electrical Engineering
1930	Thomas Sovereign Gates, first full-time president and chief executive
1932	Morris Arboretum
1933	College of Liberal Arts for Women
1935	School of Nursing (Hospital nurse's diploma began 1886)
1937	Fels Institute of State and Local Government
1946	ENIAC, first all-electronic digital computer dedicated
1947	South Asia Regional Studies
1950	School of Allied Medical Professions

1952   New Bolton Center (large-animal division of Veterinary
            School)
            Faculty Senate

1954   The Educational Survey inaugurated under the direction of
            Joseph H. Willets (completed 1959)
            Ivy group established as formal League by eight institutions
            including University of Pennsylvania

1959   Annenberg School of Communications

1960   Laboratory for Research on the Structure of Matter

1962   Development Program of the Sixties inaugurated (completed
            1969)

1963   Institute of Contemporary Art

1967   Leonard Davis Institute for Health Economics
            Leon Levy Center of Oral Health Research

1971   Annenberg Center for Communication Arts and Sciences
            First College House (Van Pelt)

1972   Freshman seminar program
            Affirmative Action program for women and minorities
            Three scientists with University of Pennsylvania ties receive
            Nobel Prizes

1973   Development Commission "One University" report
            Boards of Overseers instituted

1974   Faculty of Arts and Sciences combining College, College for
            Women, Graduate School of Arts and Sciences, and social
            science departments from Wharton School
            School of Public and Urban Policy

1975   Program for the Eighties, fund drive for $255 million,
            announced

1975–76   University celebrates the American Bicentennial by special
            convocations

1977   About 8,000 full-time undergraduates, 8,000 advanced
            degree students, other part-time students; 1,600 full-time
            faculty, almost as many part-time; 320 million dollar
            budget; facilities carry almost one billion dollars
            replacement value.

Notes

Chapter 1

1. *The Works of the Right Honorable Edmund Burke* (London, 1887), II, 125.
2. Ronald T. Reuther, "Animals, Philadelphia, and the American Bicentennial," *America's First Zoo*, XX, no. 4 (December, 1975), 46.
3. Charles Coleman Sellers, *Charles Willson Peale* (Philadelphia, 1947), II, 228.
4. James Hosmer Penniman, *Philadelphia in the Early Eighteen Hundreds* (Philadelphia, 1923), 22.
5. *Ibid.*, 8.
6. John S. Brubacher and Willis Rudy, *Higher Education in Transition: A History of American Colleges and Universities, 1636–1968* (rev. ed.; New York, 1968), 19.
7. Gilbert W. Mead, "William Smith—Father of Colleges," *Bulletin of the Association of American Colleges*, XXVII, no. 1 (March, 1941), 276–277.
8. Benjamin Franklin,*Proposals Relating to the Education of Youth in Pennsilvania* (Philadelphia, 1749).
9. Brubacher and Rudy, *op. cit.* 23, 4.
10. *Ibid.*, 7–8.
11. *Ibid.*, 23.
12. *Ibid.*, 23–24.
13. *Ibid.*, 51.
14. Francis Wayland, *Thoughts on the Present Collegiate System in the United States* (Boston, 1842), 15–17.
15. Brubacher and Rudy, *op. cit.*, 61.
16. U.S. Com. Ed. *Report*, 1889–90, quoted in Laurence R. Veysey, *The Emergence of the American University* (Chicago, 1965), 13–14.
17. Brooks Mather Kelly, *Yale: A History* (New Haven, 1974), 185.
18. A. Hunter Dupree, *Science in the Federal Government* (Cambridge, Mass., 1957), 14–15, 66.
19. University Archives, Archives General—1864, Trustees.
20. Martin Meyerson, "The American College Student," *Daedalus*, XC, no 3. (Summer, 1966), 715.
21. Henry James, *The American Scene* (New York, 1946), 274–278.
22. Walt Whitman, *Song of the Broad-Axe* (Philadelphia, 1924), sec. IV, 2.

Chapter 2

1. Photograph of original document in the University of Pennsylvania Archives. All original documents and biographical files are from the same source unless otherwise noted.
2. *Philadelphia Deed Book* E-5, 168.
3. Edward Potts Cheyney, *History of the University of Pennsylvania, 1740–1940* (Philadelphia, 1940), 26.
4. Lawrence A. Cremin, *American Education: The Colonial Experience, 1607–1783* (New York, 1970), 306.
5. Quoted by Rufus M. Jones, *The Quakers in the American Colonies* (London, 1911), 465.
6. Jones, *op. cit.*, xviii–xix.
7. Cremin, *op. cit.*, 304–305.
8. Quoted in "The Quakers in Pennsylvania," in Jones, *op. cit.*, 467.
9. The Abbé Ferdinando Galiani to Madame d'Epinay, May 18, 1776, quoted by Cremin, *op. cit.*, 267.
10. *The Autobiography of Benjamin Franklin*, ed. Leonard W. Labaree (New Haven, 1964), 194.
11. *Ibid.*, 192–193.
12. *The Papers of Benjamin Franklin*, ed. Leonard W. Labaree (New Haven, 1959–1976), III, 399–419.
13. Franklin, *Autobiography*, 60.
14. *Ibid.*, 60–61.
15. Franklin, *Papers*, III, 408.
16. *Ibid.*, 415.
17. *The Writings of Benjamin Franklin*, ed. Albert Henry Smith (New York, 1907), X, 29–31.
18. Franklin, *Papers*, III, 397.
19. Franklin, *Autobiography*, 195–196.
20. *Minutes of the College Trustees*, March 9, 1789.
21. Claude-Ann Lopez and Eugenia W. Herbert, *The Private Franklin* (New York, 1975), 283.

Chapter 3

1. *The Papers of Benjamin Franklin*, ed. Leonard W. Labaree (New Haven, 1959–1976), IV, 467–470.
2. William Smith, "A Poem on Visiting the Academy of Philadelphia, June 1753," (Philadelphia, 1753), 14–15. Rare Book Collection, University of Pennsylvania.
3. "A General Idea of the College of Mirania," in *Discourses on Public Occasions in America*, by William

Smith, D.D., 2d ed. (London, 1762).
4. No. 1442, August 12, 1756, reproduced by Lawrence Cremin, *American Education: The Colonial Experience, 1607–1783* (New York, 1970), 382–383.
5. *Ibid.*, 404.
6. Albert Frank Gegenheimer, *William Smith, Educator and Churchman, 1727–1803* (Philadelphia, 1943), 73.
7. *Minutes of the Trustees*, February 4, 1758.
8. Neda M. Westlake, "William Smith, First Provost of the University," *Library Chronicle of the Friends of the University of Pennsylvania Library*, XXVI (1960), 31.
9. Franklin, *Papers*, X, 234.
10. For complete lists, see "A Calendar of Events: The American Revolution and the University of Pennsylvania," compiled by Francis James Dallett, University Archivist (1974).
11. Edward Potts Cheyney, *History of the University of Pennsylvania, 1740–1940* (Philadelphia, 1940), 122–125.
12. Smith to William White, April 1792, in Gegenheimer, *op. cit.*, 91–92.

Chapter 4

1. The book, with John Morgan's name on the flyleaf, and a list of the first graduating class in a contemporary hand on p. 128, is in the Rare Book Collection of the University of Pennsylvania.
2. John Morgan, *A Discourse upon the Institution of Medical Schools in America* (Philadelphia, 1765), 32, 2.
3. Benjamin Franklin to John Morgan, February 5, 1772, Rare Book Collection, University of Pennsylvania.
4. William Hewson to Morgan, December 14, 1762, Carson scrapbooks, College of Physicians of Philadelphia.
5. Quoted by Francis C. Wood, "The College of Physicians," *Medical Affairs* (University of Pennsylvania, June 1967), 4.
6. Whitfield J. Bell, Jr., *John Morgan, Continental Doctor* (Philadelphia, 1965), 79, 94, 96.

7. George W. Corner, *Two Centuries of Medicine: A History of the School of Medicine, University of Pennsylvania* (Philadelphia, 1965), 19.

8. Francis C. Wood, "Medical Education in America before 1910," *Journal of Medical Education,* XXXVIII, no. 8 (August 1963), 631.

9. Morgan, *op. cit.,* 5; 11–13.

10. *Ibid.,* 15; 17–18.

11. Bell, *op. cit.,* 71.

12. Morgan, *op. cit.,* i–xxvi.

13. *Ibid.,* 18, 21, 24.

14. Rush to John Morgan, July 27, 1768, *Letters of Benjamin Rush,* ed. L. H. Butterfield (Princeton, 1951), I, 62.

15. Bell, *op. cit.,* 39.

16. *Ibid.,* 46; Corner, *op. cit.,* 8.

17. Morgan to Smith, November 16, 1764, quoted by Bell, *op. cit.,* 99.

18. Ticket of Jonathan Easton, 1771, University Archives; William Pepper, "An Early Set of Lecture Tickets," *General Magazine and Historical Chronicle,* XXXV, No. 2, (January, 1933), 158–163.

19. Benjamin Rush, "Travels through Life," in *The Autobiography of Benjamin Rush,* ed. George W. Corner (Princeton, 1948), 21–169.

20. Rush, "Travels," 50; Rush, *Letters,* I, 33–48.

21. Rush to Walter Minto, September 19, 1792, *Letters,* I, 622.

22. Rush, "Travels," 36–37.

23. *Ibid.,* 40, 76.

24. *Ibid.,* 58–59; *Boswell in Holland, 1763–64,* ed. F. A. Pottle (New York, 1953), 10n, where Morgan is described as *"un fat bonhomme."*

25. *The Autobiography of Benjamin Franklin,* ed. Leonard W. Labaree (New Haven, 1964), 177.

26. Rush, "Travels," 56–57.

27. Rush to Morgan, January 20, 1768, July 27, 1768, and November 16, 1766, *Letters,* I, 49–51, 61–62.

28. Quoted by Francis C. Wood, President's Address, *Transactions and Studies of the College of Physicians of Philadelphia,* 4 ser. XXXV, no. 4 (April 1968), 134.

29. Hazard to Samuel A. Otis, October 12, 1793, quoted by Butterfield in *Letters,* II, 702n.

30. Rush, "Travels," 101.

31. *Porcupine's Gazette* (New York), no. 779, January 13, 1800, 62.

32. Rush, "Travels," 81, 89.

33. *Ibid.,* 36.

34. Rush, *Letters,* I, 83–84.

35. Rush, "Travels," 113–114.

36. *Diaries of George Washington, 1748–1799,* ed. J. C. Fitzpatrick (Boston, 1925), II, 199.

37. Rush, "Travels," 112–113.

38. *Ibid.,* 124, 127.

39. Rush to Lady Jane Wishart Belsches, April 21, 1784, *Letters,* I, 327–329.

40. Rush, "Travels," 117–118.

41. Rush to Mrs. Rush, June 1, 1776, *Letters,* I, 101.

42. Rush, "Travels," 159; italics added.

43. Corner, *op. cit.,* 37; Nathan G. Goodman, *Benjamin Rush: Physician and Citizen* (Philadelphia, 1934), 321.

44. Rush, "Travels," 90.

45. Rush, *Medical Inquiries and Observations upon the Diseases of the Mind* (Philadelphia, 1812), 179; 17–18. See Goodman, *op. cit.,* 255–271.

46. Rush, "Travels," 108.

47. *Ibid.,* 148.

48. *Ibid.,* 85–86.

49. *Ibid.,* 84.

50. Goodman, *op. cit.,* 130–132.

51. "An Account of the Late Dr. John Morgan . . . ," *The American Museum* (November 1789), 353–355.

52. Rush, *Autobiography,* 180.

53. Jefferson to Adams, May 27, 1813, *The Writings of Thomas Jefferson,* Memorial Edition, ed. Andrew T. Lipscomb (Washington, 1904), XIII, 246.

54. E. Gerry to Richard Rush, April 8, 1814, Benjamin Rush Collection.

Chapter 5

1. *The Works of James Wilson,* ed. Robert Green McCloskey (Cambridge, 1967), I, 45. The first law professorship was established at William and Mary in 1779.

2. *Ibid.*

3. *Ibid.,* 7.

4. Quoted by Charles Page Smith, *James Wilson, Founding Father* (Chapel Hill, 1956), 211.

5. *Ibid.,* 4.

6. *Ibid.,* 18.

7. The Right Reverend William White was a trustee of the College of Philadelphia and the University of Pennsylvania, 1774–1836.

8. *The Autobiography of Benjamin Rush,* ed. George W. Corner (Princeton, 1948), 150.

9. Willard Hurst, "Treason in America," *Harvard Law Review,* LVIII (1944), 404n.

10. Sir James Steuart, *An Inquiry Into the Principles of Political Oeconomy* (London, 1767).

11. Smith, *op. cit.,* 146.

12. *Ibid.,* 382.

13. Rush, *Autobiography,* 237.

14. Wilson, *Works,* 403.

15. Smith, *op. cit.,* 231; Wilson, *Works,* 15–16.

16. Smith, *op. cit.,* 266.

17. *Minutes of the College Trustees,* September 25, 1779.

18. *Ibid.,* March 16, 1789, July 10, 1790, August 14, 1790, August 17, 1790. The trustees seem to have been superstitious about dating the meeting which fell on Friday 13 August in 1790.

19. *Ibid.,* August 14, 1790.

20. Wilson, *Works,* 72.

21. *Ibid.,* 37.

22. *Ibid.,* 402.

23. *Ibid.,* 59.

24. Quoted by Smith, *op. cit.,* 388.

25. In 1906, he was reinterred at Christ Church in Philadelphia.

26. Wilson, *Works,* 42.

27. In line with his customary fate, Wilson's portrait which originally hung in the main stairway was relegated to a lecture hall during recent renovations, from which position he viewed the Bicentennial.

Chapter 6

1. Frederick Rudolph, *The American College and University: A History* (New York, 1962), 32.

2. William Barton, *Memoirs of the Late David Rittenhouse, LL.D., F.R.S.* (Philadelphia, 1813), 97.

3. Benjamin Rush, *An Eulogium Intended To Perpetuate the Memory of David Rittenhouse, Late President of the American Philosophical Society,* delivered on December 17,

1796 (Philadelphia, n.d.), 23–24.

4. *Ibid.*, 19.

5. Jefferson to Rittenhouse, July 19, 1778, *The Writings of Thomas Jefferson, 1776–1781,* ed. Paul Leicester Ford, II (New York, 1893), 163–164.

6. Barton, *op. cit.,* 118.

7. *Ibid.*, 118–119.

8. Rush, *Eulogium,* 12.

9. Brooke Hindle, *David Rittenhouse* (Princeton, 1964), 68.

10. M. J. Babb, "The Relation of David Rittenhouse and His Orrery to the University," *The General Magazine and Historical Chronicle,* XXXIV, No. 2 (January, 1932), 221.

11. Barton, *op. cit.,* 196.

12. *Minutes of the American Philosophical Society 1786–96,* 6.

13. *Minutes of the Trustees,* December 23, 1782.

14. Smith to Thomas Barton, May 12, 1770, quoted by William Barton, *op. cit.,* 216n.

15. Rittenhouse to Charles Pettit, chairman of the trustees, December 26, 1793, quoted by Babb, *op. cit.,* 231–232.

16. Rush, *Eulogium,* 13.

17. Hindle, *op. cit.,* 309.

18. *Letters of Benjamin Rush,* ed. L. H. Butterfield (Princeton, 1951), II, 853n.

19. Rush, *Eulogium,* 21.

Chapter 7

1. *Science in Nineteenth-Century America: A Documentary History,* ed. Nathan Reingold (New York, 1964), 64; A. Hunter Dupree, *Science in the Federal Government* (Cambridge, 1957), 8.

2. Quoted from the *New York Evening Post* in Edward Potts Cheyney, *History of the University of Pennsylvania, 1740–1940* (Philadelphia, 1940), 191.

3. *Remarks on the Present Situation of Yale College for the Consideration of its Friends and Patrons* (January 1823), quoted in Stanley M. Guralnick, *Science and the Ante-Bellum American College* (Philadelphia, 1975), 21.

4. C. Seymour Thompson, "Reorganization of the University in 1828," *General Magazine and Historical Chronicle,* XXXIII, no. 2 (January 1931), 182.

5. Guralnick, *op. cit.,* 170–171.

6. In articles on the non-conducting power of ice and on rainfall published in vols. XII and XVII of the *Journal of the Franklin Institute.*

7. Varina Howell Davis, *Jefferson Davis: A Memoir by His Wife* (New York, 1890), I, 40, 260.

8. Joseph Henry, *Eulogy on Professor Alexander Dallas Bache* (Washington, 1872), 9n.

9. Benjamin Apthorpe Gould, "Address in Commemoration of Alexander Dallas Bache," *Proceedings of the American Association for the Advancement of Science,* XVII (1868), 3; Merle M. Odgers, *Alexander Dallas Bache: Scientist and Educator* (New York, 1943), 11.

10. Henry, *op. cit.,* 8.

11. *Report to the Committee of Controllers of the Public Schools on the Organization of a High School for Girls,* in Odgers, *op. cit.,* 82–83.

12. University of Pennsylvania pamphlets, 1818–32, University of Pennsylvania Library.

13. Quoted by Cheyney, *op. cit.,* 201.

14. *Minutes of the American Philosophical Society,* November 15, 1839.

15. Quoted by Odgers, *op. cit.,* 123.

16. Edgar Fahs Smith, *Chemistry in America* (New York, 1914), 230.

17. Gould, *op. cit.,* 22; Henry, *op. cit.,* 7–8.

18. Odgers, *op. cit.,* 23.

19. Henry, *op. cit.,* 8.

20. Quoted by Odgers, *op. cit.,* 85.

21. From Bache's personal journals in the Library of Congress, quoted by Odgers, *op. cit.,* 61, 70.

22. Henry to Bache, August 9, 1838, in Reingold, *op. cit.,* 83–85.

23. Odgers, *op. cit.,* 131.

24. Henry, *op. cit.,* 10.

25. Varina Howell Davis, *op. cit.,* 582.

26. Lillian B. Miller, *The Lazzaroni: Science and Scientists in Mid-Nineteenth Century America* (Washington, 1972), 16.

27. *Proceedings of the American Association for the Advancement of Science,* VI (1851), xli–lx, in Miller, *op. cit.,* 4.

28. Peirce to Bache, May 8, 1855, in Edward A. Lurie *Louis Agassiz: A Life in Science* (Chicago, 1960), 182–183.

29. Peirce to Bache, October 26, 1863, in Dupree, *op. cit.,* 144.

30. Quoted by Lurie, *op. cit.,* 182.

31. Miller, *op. cit.,* 11.

32. March 6, 1863, in Reingold, *op. cit.,* 203.

Chapter 8

1. Bache to Frazer, March 12, 1863, in *Science in Nineteenth-Century America: A Documentary History,* ed. Nathan Reingold (New York, 1964), 206.

2. Quoted in Henry Fairfield Osborn, "Biographical Memoir of Joseph Leidy, 1823–1891," *National Academy of Sciences Biographical Memoirs,* VII (February 1913), 367.

3. Leidy to Hayden, April 28 and June 7, 1863, in Reingold, *op. cit.,* 209, 212.

4. Leidy to Meek and Hayden, 1859, quoted in Osborn, *op. cit.,* 349.

5. *Philadelphia Inquirer,* ca. 1930. All newspaper articles referred to are from clippings in the individual biographical folders in the University Archives.

6. William Hunt, M.D, "In Memoriam: Dr. Joseph Leidy," in *Two Addresses upon Joseph Leidy, M.D., LL.D.* (Philadelphia, 1892), 53.

7. "Address of the President of the Association of American Physicians," *University Medical Magazine* (October 1891), 29.

8. W. S. W. Ruschenberger, M.D., *A Sketch of the Life of Joseph Leidy, M.D., LL.D.* (Philadelphia, 1892), 40.

9. Quoted by Osborn, *op. cit.,* 357.

10. *Ibid.*, 369.

11. William S. Middleton, "Joseph Leidy, Scientist" (unpublished manuscript), 25, Leidy biographical folder, University Archives.

12. Henry C. Chapman, M.D., "Memoir of Joseph Leidy, M.D., LL.D."

Proceedings of the Academy of Natural Sciences (Philadelphia, 1891), 14.

13. Ruschenberger, *op. cit.*, 23.
14. William Pepper, *A System of Practical Medicine* (Philadelphia, 1885), II, 962.
15. Leidy to Baird, in Osborn, *op. cit.*, 346.
16. Darwin to Leidy, March 4, 1860, Academy of Natural Sciences of Philadelphia.
17. Leidy to Darwin, December 10, 1859, in Middleton, *op. cit.*, 20.
18. Joseph Leidy, "A Flora and Fauna within Living Animals," *Smithsonian Contributions to Knowledge*, V (1853), 9–11.
19. Reingold, *op. cit.*, 236–250.
20. Cope to Marsh, January 30, 1873, *ibid.*, 243.
21. Henry Fairfield Osborn, *Cope: Master Naturalist* (Princeton, 1931), 20.
22. Hunt, *op. cit.*, 27–29.
23. Quoted by Middleton, *op. cit.*, 28.
24. Hunt, *op. cit.*, 31–35.
25. *A Fairy Tale, Written for and first read to Allie, Joseph, Jr., and Clarence Leidy at a dinner given to Professor Joseph Leidy, M.D. September 9th, 1882* (n.p., n.d. c. 1883), 9, 15–16.
26. Hunt, *op. cit.*, 42.

Chapter 9

1. Laurence R. Veysey, *The Emergence of the American University* (Chicago, 1965), 1–7.
2. John L. Stewart, "A Historical Sketch of the University of Pennsylvania," in *Benjamin Franklin and the University of Pennsylvania*, ed. F. N. Thorpe (Washington, 1893), 230.
3. Vethake to William M. Meredith, November 27, 1852, University of Pennsylvania Miscellaneous Pamphlets, 3–5, University of Pennsylvania Library.
4. Professor Allen's Remarks on the Letter and By-Law Reported November 3, 1852. University of Pennsylvania Library.
5. Richard J. Storr, *The Beginnings of Graduate Education in America* (New York, 1969), 81.
6. William Osler, "William Pepper," in *An Alabama Student and Other Biographical Essays* (New York, 1909), 211, 227.
7. Charles Janeway Stillé, *Reminiscences of a Provost* (privately printed, n.d.), 52, 53.
8. *Ibid.*, 5, 6–7.
9. *Ibid.*, 29n.
10. *Ibid.*, 23, 30.
11. Edward Potts Cheyney, *History of the University of Pennsylvania, 1740–1940* (Philadelphia, 1940), 280, 281; Stillé, *op. cit.*, 45.
12. Stewart, *op. cit.*, 229.
13. Stillé, *op. cit.*, 40.
14. Cheyney, *op. cit.*, 280.
15. Stillé, *op. cit.*, 40.
16. Howard H. Furness, *Commencement Address* (Philadelphia, 1894), 5.
17. Charles Franklin Thwing, "William Pepper," in *Friends of Men* (New York, 1933), 368–369.
18. George W. Corner, *Two Centuries of Medicine: A History of the School of Medicine, University of Pennsylvania* (Philadelphia, 1965), 244.
19. Furness, *op. cit.*, 4.
20. Quoted by Francis Newton Thorpe, *William Pepper, M.D., LL.D.* (Philadelphia, 1904), 249–250.
21. *Ibid.*, 459.
22. *Ibid.*, 43.
23. *Ibid.*, 56.
24. *Ibid.*, 46–47, 59.
25. Pepper to John S. Billings, December 3, 1895, in Thorpe, *ibid.*, 136.
26. As enumerated on the invitation sent out on the occasion, these were: the University of Pennsylvania, the American Philosophical Society, the Historical Society of Pennsylvania, the College of Physicians, the Franklin Institute, the Academy of Natural Sciences, the Pennsylvania Academy of the Fine Arts, the Law Academy. See Thorpe, *op. cit.*, 236.
27. Hampton L. Carson, *History of the Celebration of the One Hundredth Anniversary of the Promulgation of the Constitution of the United States* (Philadelphia, 1889), II, 362.
28. Thorpe, *op. cit.*, 103–107.
29. Osler, *op. cit.*, 229.
30. Thorpe, *op. cit.*, 113, quotation p. 119.
31. Joseph Wharton to the trustees, (March 1, 1881), *Agreement, Joseph Wharton and the Trustees of the University of Pennsylvania* (1923), 10.
32. Cheyney, *op. cit.*, 354.
33. Edwin E. Slosson, *The Great American Universities* (New York, 1910), 487.
34. Cheyney, *op. cit.*, 317–319.
35. Gordon Hendricks, *Eadweard Muybridge: The Father of the Motion Picture* (New York, 1975), 206–207.
36. *Annual Report of the Provost of the University of Pennsylvania . . . for the Year Ending October 1, 1887* (Philadelphia, 1888), 15–16, 14.
37. William Pepper, "Higher Medical Education," *Two Addresses Delivered before the Medical Department of the University of Pennsylvania on October 1, 1877, and October 2, 1893* (Philadelphia, 1894), 14–15.
38. Quoted by Thorpe, *op. cit.*, 227.
39. *Ibid.*, 203.
40. *Ibid.*, 229–230.
41. "The Ideal University," address to the alumni of Columbia University, 1890, *ibid.*, 286.
42. Furness, *op. cit.*, 3–4.
43. William Pepper, "The Medical Department," in *Benjamin Franklin and the University of Pennsylvania*, ed. F. N. Thorpe (Washington, 1893), 277.
44. Diary, June 13, 1886, quoted by Thorpe, *op. cit.*, 213.
45. "Addresses made at the Meeting Held in Memory of William Pepper, M.D., LL.D.," University of Pennsylvania, November 29, 1898, *American Philosophical Society Memorial Volume* (Philadelphia, 1899), 37.
46. Thorpe, *op. cit.*, 525.

Chapter 10

1. "Remarks on the Higher Education of Women, delivered at Ogontz, June 1888," in Francis Newton Thorpe, *William Pepper, M.D., LL.D.* (Philadelphia, 1904), 265.
2. William Pepper, "The Scope of the University," in *Benjamin Franklin and the University of Pennsylvania*, ed. F. N. Thorpe (Washington, 1893), 212.
3. University Catalogue, 1875–1876, 18.
4. Edward Potts Cheyney, *History of the University of Pennsylvania, 1740–1940* (Philadelphia, 1940), 303.
5. *Public Ledger*, April 22, 1917.
6. Speech to the Alumni, 13 February 1888, in Thorpe, *op. cit.*, 250.
7. Sara Yorke Stevenson, *The Free Museum of Science and Art, Department of Archaeology and Paleontology of the University of Pennsylvania*, pamphlet (November 18, 1895), 2.
8. "On the Remains of the Foreigners Discovered in Egypt by Mr. W. M. Flinders-Petrie, 1895, now in the Museum of the University of Pennsylvania," *Proceedings of the American Philosophical Society*, XXXV, 1896.
9. *Maximilian in Mexico: A Woman's Reminiscences of the French Intervention 1862–1867* (New York, 1899).
10. Owen Wister, "Address," January 23, 1922, in *Sara Yorke Stevenson, A Tribute From the Civic Club of Philadelphia* (Philadelphia, 1922), 62.
11. *Ibid.*, 10, 9.
12. Thorpe, *op. cit.*, 125.
13. Ruth B. Molloy, "The Emperor of Brazil Was a Great Help," *Philadelphia Inquirer Magazine*, February 17, 1957.
14. *Minutes of the Trustees*, September 4, 1877.
15. Emily L. Gregory to Ella Weed, dean of Barnard College, May 6, 1893, "in answer to a question how I obtained a fellowship in Penn. Univ. previous to the time when women were admitted there." Communication from Julie V. Marsteller and John W. Chambers, Barnard College, Columbia University.
16. *Notable American Women, 1607–1950* (1971), II, 329–330.
17. "The Address of Carrie Burnham Kilgore before the Legislature of Pennsylvania," pamphlet (1881), 25.
18. "The Address by William Pepper, M.D.," in *Addresses at the Inauguration of William Pepper, M.D., as the Provost of the University, February 22, 1881* (Philadelphia, 1881), 55–56.
19. *Minutes of the Trustees*, September 11, 1764.
20. Pepper, "Address," 57, 56.
21. Recollection of M. Carey Thomas, president emeritus of Bryn Mawr, NBC address, April 16, 1935.
22. "Ogontz address," in Thorpe, *op. cit.*, 261–266.
23. *Tribute*, 12.
24. *Ibid.*
25. Address of 1902, quoted in *Tribute*, 36.
26. *Sara Yorke Stevenson, 1847–1921*, Memorial Meeting in the University Museum, April 29, 1922, 10.
27. *Tribute*, 13.
28. *Ibid.*, 47.

Chapter 11

1. George W. Corner, *Two Centuries of American Medicine: A History of the School of Medicine, University of Pennsylvania* (Philadelphia, 1965), 174–175.
2. William Hunt, *Two Addresses upon Joseph Leidy, M.D., LL.D.* (Philadelphia, 1892), 13.
3. Corner, *op. cit.*, 222.
4. Annual Report of the Provost to the Board of Trustees, 1899–1900 (Philadelphia, 1900), 23.
5. Corner, *op. cit.*, 208.
6. Howard A. Kelly, "Osler as I Knew Him in Philadelphia and in the Hopkins," *Sir William Osler, Bart.* (Baltimore, 1920), 107.
7. Harvey Cushing, *The Life of Sir William Osler* (Oxford, 1925), I, 222.
8. *Ibid.*, 235, 252.
9. Corner, *op. cit.*, 205–206.
10. *Ibid.*, 229–231.
11. George W. Pierson, *The Education of American Leaders: Comparative Contributions of U.S. Colleges and Institutions* (New York, 1969), 54.
12. Carl F. Schmidt, "Alfred Newton Richards, 1876–1966," *Annals of Internal Medicine*, Supplement 8, "Alfred Newton Richards: Scientist and Man," LXXI (November 1969), 19.
13. Quoted by Corner, *op. cit.*, 234.
14. November 8, 1957. A copy of the address is in the Medical School Library, University of Pennsylvania.
15. Isaac Starr, "A Memorial Written for the Medical Faculty of the University of Pennsylvania," in *Annals*, 88.
16. Corner, *op. cit.*, 285.
17. Joseph Stokes, Jr., "Presentation to Dr. Isaac Starr of the Kober Medal," *Transactions of the Association of American Physicians*, LXXX (1967), 32–33.
18. Isaac Starr in *Annals*, 8.
19. Quoted by Joseph T. Wearn, "Alfred Newton Richards, 1876–1966," *Transactions of the Association of American Physicians*, LXXIX (1966), 68.
20. Quoted by Wearn in *Annals*, 45.
21. Schmidt in *Annals*, 19.
22. Schmidt, "Alfred Newton Richards, 1876–1966," *Biographical Memoirs of Fellows of the Royal Society*, XIII (November 1967), 331.
23. Schmidt in *Annals*, 22.
24. Wearn in *Annals*, 45.
25. J. T. Wearn and A. N. Richards, "Observations on the composition of glomerular urine with particular reference to the problem of reabsorption in the renal tubules," *American Journal of Physiology*, LXXI (1924), 209.
26. Carl W. Gottchalk, "Dr. A. N. Richards and Kidney Micropuncture," in *Annals*, 30, 36.
27. Starr in *Annals*, 7.
28. *Annals*, 50.
29. Detlev W. Bronk, "Alfred Newton Richards, 1876–1966," *Perspectives in Biology and Medicine*, University of Chicago Press, in preparation.
30. *Ibid.*
31. Letter from President Roosevelt to Dr. A. N. Richards, Richards Memorial Room in the University of Pennsylvania School of Medicine.
32. Vannevar Bush, *Remarks Made at a Dinner in Honor of Alfred Newton*

Richards, *Given to a Group of His Friends by the Board of Directors of Merck & Co., Inc.*, May 25, 1959 at the Philadelphia Club, 3; Bronk, *op. cit.*

33. John T. Connor in *Remarks Made at a Dinner in Honor of Richards*, 7.
34. Displayed in the Richards Memorial Room.
35. Bush, *op. cit.*, 3.
36. *British Medical Journal*, August 5, 1944, 186.
37. Schmidt in *Annals*, 26.
38. A. N. Richards, "Production of Penicillin in the United States, 1941–1946," *Nature*, CCI (1964), 443.
39. Chester S. Keefer, "Dr. Richards as Chairman of the Committee on Medical Research," *Annals*, 66.
40. *British Medical Journal*, *op. cit.*, 79.
41. Schmidt, *Annals*, 26.
42. Corner, *op. cit.*, 299–300. The remarks were made by Surgeon-General Norman Kirk.
43. Connor in *Remarks*, 9.

Chapter 12

1. *The Economic Mind in American Civilization*, ed. Joseph Dorfman (New York, 1959), III (1865–1918), 161.
2. *The Wharton School: Its First Fifty Years, 1881–1931* (University of Pennsylvania, 1931), 16.
3. Henry R. Seager, "Tribute of the American Academy of Political and Social Science to the Memory of Dr. Simon N. Patten," *Annals of the American Academy of Political and Social Science*, Supplement, CVII, no. 196 (May 1923), 338.
4. *New York World*, August 27, 1922.
5. Samuel McCune Lindsay, "Tribute," 355, 357.
6. Rexford G. Tugwell, "Notes on the Life of Simon Nelson Patten," *Journal of Political Economy*, XXXI, no. 2 (April 1923), 165–166.
7. Daniel M. Fox, *The Discovery of Abundance: Simon N. Patten and the Transformation of Social Theory* (New York, 1967), 22.
8. *Ibid.*, 25.
9. Tugwell, *op. cit.*, 184.
10. Scott Nearing, "A Prince among Paupers," *Great Teachers Portrayed*

by Those Who Studied under Them, ed. Houston Peterson (New Brunswick, 1946), 158.
11. Tugwell, *op. cit.*, 180.
12. Fox, *op. cit.*, 43.
13. *Ibid.*
14. Simon N. Patten, "The Making of Economic Literature," *Publication of the American Economic Association* (1908), ser. III, vol. X, no. 1, 8.
15. *Ibid.*, 2–3, 5.
16. Patten, *The Development of English Thought* (New York, 1899), vi.
17. Tugwell, *op. cit.*, 185–186.
18. Patten, "The Educational Value of Political Economy," *Publication of the American Economic Association* (1890), ser. I, vol. V, no. 6, 25.
19. Patten, "A New Year's Resolution," *Survey*, XXXI (March–October 1913), 362.
20. Ely to Clark, May 2, 1902, quoted in Dorfman, *op. cit.*, III, 187.
21. Nearing, *op. cit.*, 161.
22. Samuel McCune Lindsay to Ernest Minor Patterson, May 7, 1955, James biographical folder, University Archives.
23. Nearing, *op. cit.*, 157, 155.
24. Nearing, *Educational Frontiers: A Book about Simon Nelson Patten and Other Teachers* (New York, 1925), xii, 48–49.
25. Tugwell, *op. cit.*, 191.
26. J. P. Lichtenberger, "Tribute," 342.
27. *Op. cit.*, 340–341.
28. *New York Herald Tribune*, March 27, 1910.
29. *Examiner*, Lancaster, Pa., April 11, 1904.
30. Philadelphia *Bulletin*, July 25, 1922.
31. Tugwell, *op. cit.*, 181.
32. Lindsay, "Tribute," 355.
33. Newspaper report, March 28, 1917, Patten biographical folder, University Archives.
34. *Public Ledger*, April 6, 1917.
35. Fox, *op. cit.*, 126–127.
36. Nearing, *Educational Frontiers*, 45.
37. Tugwell, *op. cit.*, 189.
38. Bernard Sternsher, *Rexford Tugwell and the New Deal* (Rutgers University Press, 1964), 15.
39. Nearing, *op. cit.*, 28.
40. Fox, *op. cit.*, 95–96.
41. Nearing, *op. cit.*, 27–28.
42. Patten, *The New Basis of Civiliza-*

tion (New York, 1907–1921).
43. Roswell C. McCrea, "Tribute," 353.
44. Fox, *op. cit.*, 12, 144.

Chapter 13

1. George Wharton Pepper, *Philadelphia Lawyer* (Philadelphia, 1944), 48.
2. Margaret Center Klingelsmith, "History of the Department of Law," *The Proceeding at the Dedication of the New Building of the Department of Law* (Philadelphia, 1901), 220.
3. Pepper, *op. cit.*, 47.
4. Edward Potts Cheyney, *History of the University of Pennsylvania, 1740–1940* (Philadelphia, 1940), 235.
5. *Legal Intelligencer*, September 20, 1850.
6. Klingelsmith, *op. cit.*, 221.
7. Klingelsmith, *Report of the Librarian on Her trip to England and the Continent, 1910*, Presented by the Staff of the Biddle Law Library to their Friends with Holiday Greetings, December 1964 (mimeo Biddle Law Library), 8, 9, 26.
8. Pepper, *op. cit.*, 48.
9. Owen J. Roberts, "The Components of a Cultural Curriculum: A Symposium," *The General Magazine and Historical Chronicle*, XXXII, no. 2 (January 1930), 172.
10. Undated newspaper clipping, Roberts biographical folder, University Archives.
11. George W. Wickersham ('80), U.S. attorney general, 1909–1913, Roberts biographical folder.
12. David Burner, "Owen J. Roberts," *The Justices of the United States Supreme Court, 1789–1969: Their Lives and Major Opinions*, ed. Leon Friedman and Fred L. Israel (New York, 1969), III, 2255.
13. *Philadelphia Record*, February 27, 1937; see also Drew Pearson and Robert S. Allen, *The Nine Old Men* (New York, 1936), 151.
14. Burner, *op. cit.*, 2255.
15. Report from the Inquirer Bureau, Washington, Roberts biographical folder, University Archives.
16. Erwin N. Griswold, "Owen Roberts as a Judge," Memorial Issue,

University of Pennsylvania Law Review, XIV, no. 3 (December 1955), 335–336.

17. *Ibid.*

18. *Old Colony Railroad Company* v. *Commissioner of Internal Revenue* 284 U.S. 552 (1932).

19. *Nebbia* v. *New York*, 291 U.S. 502 (1934).

20. *New York City Sun*, March 7, 1934.

21. Pepper, *op. cit.*, 348–349.

22. *University of Cincinnati Times Star*, April 30, 1940.

23. Newspaper reports of January 9, 1934, and March 11, 1934, Roberts biographical folder.

24. *Philadelphia Inquirer*, December 17, 1941.

25. *Morehead* v. *New York ex rel. Tipaldo*, 298 U.S. 587 (1936); *Adkins* v. *Children's Hospital*, 261 U.S. 525 (1923); and *West Coast Hotel Company* v. *Parrish*, 300 U.S. 379 (1937).

26. Burner, *op. cit.*, 2261.

27. Felix Frankfurter, "Mr. Justice Roberts," *University of Pennsylvania Law Review*, 311–317.

28. Burner, *op. cit.*, 2262.

29. Frankfurter, *op. cit.*, 313; Griswold, *op. cit.*, 340–344. For an opposing view, see John W. Chambers, "The Big Switch: Justice Roberts and the Minimum-Wage Cases," *Labor History*, X, no. 1 (Winter 1969), 44–73.

30. Pearson and Allen, *op. cit.*, 152.

31. Quoted in the *Philadelphia Inquirer*, May 18, 1955.

32. *New York Times*, December 12, 1948.

33. *Chicago Daily News*, October 29, 1945.

34. John J. McCloy, "Owen J. Roberts' Extra Curiam Activities," *University of Pennsylvania Law Review*, 351.

35. *Philadelphia Evening Bulletin*, August 10, 1948.

36. McCloy, *op. cit.*, 352.

37. *Korematsu* v. *United States*, 323 U.S. 225–226 (1944).

38. Frankfurter, *op. cit.*, 317.

39. Roberts biographical folder, 1946.

40. *Philadelphia Evening Bulletin*, May 24, 1947.

41. Quoted by Edwin R. Keedy, "Owen J. Roberts and the Law School," Memorial Issue, *University of Pennsylvania Law Review* (1955), 318–319.

42. *Philadelphia Evening Bulletin*, August 10, 1948.

43. George Wharton Pepper, "Roberts the Man," Memorial Issue, *University of Pennsylvania Law Review* (1955), 379.

44. McCloy, *op. cit.*, 353.

Chapter 14

1. Benjamin Franklin, *Proposals Relating to the Education of Youth in Pensilvania* (Philadelphia, 1749), II, 12n.

2. Edwin Bateman Morris ('04), in *Book of the School: Department of Architecture, University of Pennsylvania, 1874–1934* (Philadelphia, 1934), 12–13.

3. Apart from gaining first place on entering the Ecole des Beaux-Arts in 1896 and winning the Paris prize, he had won the Rougevin Prize and the Grande Médaille d'Emulation at the Ecole (1901).

4. *Public Ledger*, November 10, 1914.

5. Theo B. White, *Paul Philippe Cret: Architect and Teacher* (Philadelphia, 1973), 23.

6. *Philadelphia Evening Bulletin*, April 1, 1919.

7. "The Question of Education: Evolution or Revolution?" *Journal of the American Institute of Architects*, XII, no. 9 (September 1924), 409.

8. White, *op. cit.*, 24.

9. Quoted by White, *ibid.*, 27.

10. David Van Zanten, "Remarks on the Museum of Modern Art Exhibition: The Architecture of the Ecole des Beaux-Arts," *Los Angeles Institute of Contemporary Art Journal* no. 11 (May–June 1976), 32.

11. Kenneth Reid, "Paul Philippe Cret, Master of Design," *Pencil Points*, XIX, no. 10 (October 1938), 609.

12. Cret, "A Recent Aspect of an Old Conflict," *General Magazine and Historical Chronicle*, XL, no. 4 (July 1938), 414–415.

13. Paper read before the Philadelphia

Chapter, A.I.A., 1909, quoted in White, *op. cit.*, 50.

14. Thomas Hine, *Philadelphia Inquirer*, August 1, 1976.

15. *Pennsylvania Gazette*, XL, no. 4 (January 1942), 109.

16. See pp. 213–216.

17. Arthur Drexler, Preface to the Exhibition, "The Architecture of the Ecole des Beaux-Arts," Museum of Modern Art, New York (October 29, 1975–January 4, 1976), 3.

18. *Ibid.*, 4.

19. Van Zanten, *op. cit.*, 34.

20. White, *op. cit.*, 28.

21. *Ibid*; Morris, *op. cit.*, 15.

22. Francis S. Swales, "Draftsmanship and Architecture as Exemplified by the Work of Paul S. Cret," *Pencil Points*, IX, no. 11 (November 1928), 703.

23. Quoted by White, *op. cit.*, 25.

24. *University of Pennsylvania: School of Fine Arts: Architecture* (Philadelphia, n.d.), 32.

25. Vincent Scully, Jr., *Louis I. Kahn* (New Haven, 1962), 10.

26. Quoted by Robert Hughes, "Building with Spent Light," *Time*, January 15, 1973, 65.

27. Louis I. Kahn, "Order and Form," *Perspecta, The Yale Architectural Journal*, III (1955), 59.

28. Kahn, "Silence and Light," *Architecture and Urbanism*, III, no. 1 (1973), 9.

29. Kahn, "Form and Design," *Architectural Design*, XXXI (April 1961), 145–184.

30. Vincent Scully, Jr., *Modern Architecture: The Architecture of Democracy* (New York, 1961), 119, 45.

31. Jonas Salk, "Louis I. Kahn, 1901–1974," *Memorial Convocation*, at the University of Pennsylvania (mimeo), April 2, 1974.

32. Scully, *Kahn*, 27.

33. Romaldo Giurgola and Jaimini Mehta, *Louis I. Kahn, Architect* (Boulder, 1975), 200.

34. "Order in Architecture," *Perspecta*, IV (1957), 64.

35. Kahn, "Form and Design," 149.

36. Peter Shepheard, "Louis I. Kahn, 1901–1974," *Almanac*, XX, no. 27

(University of Pennsylvania, March 26, 1974), 1.

37. Hughes, *op. cit.*, 6.
38. Kahn, *Perspecta*, III, 59.
39. Auguste Komendant, *18 Years with Architect Louis I. Kahn* (Englewood, 1975), 23.
40. Kahn, *Perspecta*, IV, 59.
41. Kahn, "Silence and Light," 20.
42. "Comments on Architecture by Louis Kahn," *Light Is the Theme: Louis I. Kahn and the Kimbell Art Museum* (Fort Worth, 1975), 22, 43.
43. Kahn, "Form and Design," 148.
44. Scully, *Kahn*, 10.
45. Kahn, "Silence and Light," 22.
46. Wilder Green, "Medical Research Building—Louis Kahn," *Arts and Architecture*, LXXVIII (July 1961), 14. Reprint of text in *Museum of Modern Art Bulletin*, XXVII, no. 1, 1961.
47. Kahn, "Form and Design," 151.
48. Ada Louise Huxtable, *New York Times*, June 11, 1961.
49. Wilder, *op. cit.*, 28.
50. Kahn, "Form and Design," 149.
51. "Louis I. Kahn Talks with Students," *Architecture at Rice University*, XXVI (1969), 12–13.
52. Hughes, *op. cit.*, 60.
53. "Space and the Inspirations," address reproduced in *L'architecture d'aujourd'hui*, no. 142 (février–mars 1969), 16.

Chapter 15

1. David M. Potter, "Roy F. Nichols and the Rehabilitation of American Political History," *The Worlds of Roy Franklin Nichols*, ed. William G. Shade, *Pennsylvania History*, XXXVIII (1971), 3.
2. Roy F. Nichols, *A Historian's Progress* (New York, 1968), 63.
3. Jeannette P. Nichols, "Along the Way," *Worlds*, 53.
4. Ezra Pound to Roy F. Nichols, April 8, 1936, Rare Book Collection, University of Pennsylvania.
5. Unpublished autobiographical essay (1930), quoted in Emily Mitchell Wallace, "Penn's Poet Friends," *Pennsylvania Gazette* (February 1973), 33–34.

6. Ezra Pound to Roy F. Nichols, June 18, 1935, Rare Book Collection, University of Pennsylvania.
7. Nichols, *A Historian's Progress*, 68.
8. Potter, *op. cit.*, 6.
9. Nichols, *The Historical Study of Anglo-American Democracy* (Cambridge, 1949), 5.
10. *Ibid.*, 30.
11. Nichols, "Biography and the Teaching of History," *Proceedings of the Association of History Teachers of the Middle States and Maryland*, no. 25 (1927), 89.
12. *Ibid.*, 91.
13. Nichols, "The Genealogy of Historical Generalizations," in *Generalization and the Writing of History*, ed. Louis Gottschalk (Chicago, 1963), 130–144.
14. Orville J. Victor, *The History, Civil, Political and Military, of the Southern Rebellion*, quoted by Nichols in *Generalization*, 132.
15. Nichols, "Genealogy," 141.
16. Nichols, *A Historian's Progress*, 152, 159.
17. Potter, *op. cit.*, 20.
18. Nichols, "Postwar Reorientation of Historical Thinking," *American Historical Review*, LIV, no. 1 (October 1948), 82.
19. *Ibid.*
20. Philip S. Klein, "Laborer in Penn's Vineyard," in *Worlds*, 36.
21. Nichols, "A Great Party Which Might Have Been Born in Philadelphia," *Pennsylvania Magazine of History and Biography*, LVII, no. 228 (October 1933), 374.
22. Nichols, *The Pennsylvania Historical and Museum Commission: A History* (Harrisburg, 1967), 25–26.
23. Nichols, *A Historian's Progress*, 113.
24. "History Teaching in This Intellectual Crisis," in *Proceedings of the Middle States Association of History*, no. 31 (1933), 29.
25. Nichols, *A Historian's Progress*, 96.
26. *Ibid.*, 105.
27. Nichols, "History Teaching in This Intellectual Crisis," 36, 38–39.
28. "Postwar Reorientation in Historical Thinking," 84.
29. Nichols, "History Teaching," 41.
30. Potter, *op. cit.*, 8.

31. Nichols, *A Historian's Progress*, 116–117, 121.
32. Thomas C. Cochran, "Roy Franklin Nichols (1896–1973)," *Year Book of the American Philosophical Society* (1973), 135.
33. Nichols, "The Historian's Dilemma," in *Proceedings of the Middle States Association of History and Social Science Teachers*, XXXVIII, no. 1 (1940–1941), 1; "Postwar Reorientation," 80.
34. Nichols, "The Mission of the Liberal Arts," *Franklin and Marshall Papers*, I, no. 12 (December 1937), 59.
35. Nichols, "History Teaching," 40.
36. Nichols, "The Mission of the Liberal Arts," 57, 58–59.
37. Margaret F. and Harry M. Tinkcom, "Roy F. Nichols and the Goals of History," *Worlds*, 22.
38. "The Magic Square," *American Philosophical Society Proceedings*, CV, no. 3 (June 1961), 241.
39. "The Mind You Find May be Your Own," *General Magazine and Historical Chronicle*, LIX, no. 1 (Autumn 1956), 36, 39, 41.
40. "The Memorial Service for Roy F. Nichols" (mimeo), January 30, 1973, Nichols biographical folder, University Archives, 6.
41. Jeannette P. Nichols, *op. cit.*, 52.
42. Cochran, *op. cit.*, 139–140.
43. Nichols, "Address" to The Athenaeum of Philadelphia (May 1962), 5.
44. Potter, *op. cit.*, 8.
45. "A Hundred Years Later: Perspectives on the Civil War," *Journal of Southern History*, XXXIII, no. 2 (May 1967), 153.
46. Nichols, "Politics as Played when Philadelphia was the National Capital, 1790–1800." Address to The Athenaeum of Philadelphia (1956), 5.
47. Nichols, *A Historian's Progress*, 17.
48. Cochran, *op. cit.*, 136.
49. Nichols, "The Mission of the Liberal Arts," 56.
50. Nichols, *A Historian's Progress*, 12.
51. Nichols, "History and the Science of Society: The Problem of Synthesis," *The Social Sciences at*

Mid-Century, Essays in Honor of Guy Stanton Ford (Minneapolis, 1951); *Blueprints for Leviathan: American Style* (New York, 1963).

52. Nichols, "1461–1861: The American Civil War in Perspective," *Journal of Southern History*, XVI, no. 2 (May 1950), 143.

53. *Wichita Beacon*, April 9, 1966.

Chapter 16

1. "An East Prospect of the City of Philadelphia from the Jersey Shore," drawing by George Heap under the direction of Nicholas Scull, surveyor-general of Pennsylvania. London, 1754 (Historical Society of Pennsylvania).

2. Plaque dedicated to Albert Monroe Wilson in College Hall, where the cornerstone is also on display.

3. Agnes Addison Gilchrist, *William Strickland, Architect and Engineer, 1788–1894* (Philadelphia, 1950), 36–37.

4. Stillé to Frederick Fraley, Esq., chairman, Trustees Committee on Endowment, September 26, 1868. *Minutes of the Trustees*, October 6, 1868.

5. The terms of the sale were established by an ordinance of Select Council of the City of Philadelphia, approved by Daniel M. Fox, mayor, December 18, 1869.

6. George B. Tatum, *Penn's Great Town* (Philadelphia, 1961), 102.

7. Agnes Repplier, *Philadelphia: The Place and the People* (New York, 1898), 379.

8. Francis Newton Thorpe, *William Pepper, M.D., LL.D.* (Philadelphia, 1904), 271.

9. Edward Potts Cheyney, *History of the University of Pennsylvania, 1740–1940* (Philadelphia, 1940), 324.

10. Morris Jastrow, "The University Libraries," in *Benjamin Franklin and the University of Pennsylvania*, ed. F. N. Thorpe (Washington, 1893), 394.

11. Repplier, *op. cit.*, 373, 379.

12. Thorpe, *op. cit.*, 440.

13. Tatum, *op. cit.*, 121–122.

14. William Marvin, *Christian Science*

15. Tatum, *op. cit.*, 122.

16. *Ibid.*, 119.

17. *Ibid.*

18. Cheyney, *op. cit.*, 333–334.

19. Paul Philippe Cret et al., *Report to the Board of Trustees of the University of Pennsylvania upon the Future Development of Buildings and Grounds and the Conservation of Surrounding Territory* (Philadelphia, 1913), 6.

20. *Ibid.*, 7.

21. *A Brief History and Compilation of Trustees' Actions Concerned with the Planning and Development of the West Philadelphia Campus.* University of Pennsylvania: Department of Facilities Development (September 1976), 7.

22. *Philadelphia Evening Bulletin*, March 1, 1924.

23. *A Brief History*, 7.

24. Peter Shepheard, *Landscape Development Plan, University of Pennsylvania*, prepared by the Center for Environmental Design, Graduate School of Fine Arts, University of Pennsylvania and submitted to President Martin Meyerson, February 1977.

25. *A Brief History*, 38.

26. *Report to the Board of Trustees*, 13.

27. Report submitted to the president by the Trustees' Committee for the Physical Development of the University of Pennsylvania, October 25, 1948, reprinted in *A Brief History*, 40.

28. *Ibid.*, 38.

29. *University of Pennsylvania Development Plan* (March 1961), 35.

30. Cret et al., *Report to the Board of Trustees*, 7.

31. Other members of the committee were Henry Pemberton, followed by Harold Manley, vice-president for financial affairs, and EPC chairman John C. Hetherston, vice-president for coordinated planning.

32. *Development Plan*, 35.

33. Tatum, *op. cit.*, 136.

34. Statement quoted in *The Valley Forge Ideal and the University of Pennsylvania* (Philadelphia, n.d.), 5.

35. Quoted by E. Bigelow Thompson in

Monitor, Friday, June 2, 1972.

"Shall Old Penn, Founded by Franklin, move to Valley Forge?" *Boston Transcript*, November 10, 1928.

36. Newspaper report, February 28, 1928; report of the Valley Forge Committee, *Minutes of the Trustees*, April 10, 1929.

37. Paul P. Cret, "A Hillside House: the Property of George Howe, Esq., Chestnut Hill, Philadelphia, Mellor, Meigs & Howe, Architects," *Architectural Record*, XI (August 1920), 97.

38. University of Pennsylvania. The Dormitory System as designed by Cope & Stewardson, Architects (1895), 4–5.

39. *Ibid.*

40. Repplier, *op. cit.*, 379.

41. Edwin E. Slosson, *Great American Universities* (New York, 1910), 358–359.

42. *Ibid.*, 345.

43. *Ibid.*, 363.

Epilogue

1. Edwin E. Slosson, *Great American Universities* (New York, 1910), p. 362.

2. Charles William Eliot, *Educational Reform, Essays and Addresses* (New York, 1898), p. 21.

3. *The Works of the Right Honorable Edmund Burke* (7th ed., Boston, 1881), p. 21.

Index

The Authors

Martin Meyerson is president of the University of Pennsylvania and a university professor. Educated at Columbia and Harvard, he began teaching at the University of Chicago and subsequently joined the faculty of the University of Pennsylvania. Although he left Philadelphia to become Frank Backus Williams Professor of city planning and urban research at Harvard and the first director of the M.I.T.-Harvard Joint Center for Urban Studies, he could not resist returning to what he believes he was the first to describe as "America's most livable city" and "America's most balanced university." He was gone for a baker's dozen of years which he spent as teacher and administrator in Cambridge, Berkeley (dean and acting chancellor), and Buffalo (president), but he describes the most important events of his life, including his successful courtship of his wife to be, Margy, as taking place in Philadelphia. Author of books and articles, lecturer, and consultant here, abroad, and to the United Nations, he belongs to the American Philosophical Society and the American Academy of Arts and Sciences (he chaired its Assembly on University Goals and Governance and serves on the Editorial Board of its journal *Daedalus*). His directorships have ranged from the International Association of Universities, the Philadelphia Museum of Art, and the National Urban Coalition, to various scientific, professional, religious, industrial, and governmental agencies including the Center for Environmental Studies in Great Britain.

Dilys Pegler Winegrad is assistant to the president for special projects at the University of Pennsylvania. A graduate of Lady Margaret Hall, Oxford, a student of history and literature (particularly the work of Montaigne), she holds a Ph.D. in romance languages from the University of Pennsylvania and has taught at Bryn Mawr College and Haverford College. Now a U.S. citizen, she stoutly claims descent from a Welsh patriot slandered in one of Shakespeare's historical plays.

Mary Ann Meyers holds an A.M. and a Ph.D. in American civilization from the University of Pennsylvania, where she has been a member of the staff of the president.

Francis James Dallett, archivist of the University of Pennsylvania, was educated at Haverford College and the University of Pennsylvania, from which he received an A.M. in American civilization.